THE PRINCETON REVIEW

GRE Verbal workout

34, 28, 19, 89

1 11

THE PRINCETON REVIEW

GRE Verbal workout

By YUNG-YEE WU

Random House, Inc.
New York 1997
http://www.randomhouse.com

Princeton Review Publishing, L.L.C.
2315 Broadway
New York, NY 10024
e-mail: info@review.com

ISBN: 0-679-77890-X

Permission has been granted to reprint portions of the following:
"The Self-Reproducing Inflationary Universe," by Andrei Linde. *Scientific American*, Nov. 1994,pp. 48-49.
Compulsive Beauty, by Hal Foster. MIT Press, Cambridge, MA, c 1993 Massachusetts Institute of Technology, pp. xi-xiii.
Death Comes to the Maiden: Sex and Execution, 1731-1933, by Camille Naish. Routledge, a division of Routledge, Chapman and Hall Inc., NY c 1991, pp. 5-6.
Free Soil, Free Labor, Free Men: The Ideology of the Republican Party Before the Civil War, by Eric Foner. Oxford University Press, NY, c 1970, pp. 2-4.
The Perils of Humanism, by Frederick C. Crews, Princeton University Press, Princeton, NJ, 1962, pp. 3-6.
Gender Differences at Work: Women and Men in Nontraditional Occupations, by Christine L. Williams, University of California Press, Berkeley and Los Angeles, c 1989, pp. 3-6.
"Cerebral Meningitis Epidemics," by Patrick S. Moore and Claire V. Broome. *Scientific American*, Nov. 1994, pp. 44-45.
City of Women: Sex and Class in New York, 1789-1860, by Christine Stansell. University of Illinois Press, Chicago, IL, c 1982, pp . xi-xiii.
California Indian Shamonism, edited by Lowell John Bean, Ballena Press, Menlo Park, CA, pp. 15-16.

Editor: Amy Zavatto
Production Editor: Rich Klin
Designer: Meher Khambata
Production Coordinator: Matthew Reilly

9 8 7 6 5 4 3 2 1

First Edition

ACKNOWLEDGMENTS

The acknowledgments page isn't for anyone but the author really, so I'll keep it as short as possible.

My first thank you's must go to the people at The Princeton Review who helped me put together this tome. Thank you, Jeannie Yoon, for helping me and for always listening. Thank you, Amy Zavatto, for providing me with critical feedback and for actually reading every word. And thank you, Meher Khambata, for taking this book through the pagemaking process.

Finally, three personal thank you's: Thank you, Fritz Faerber, for feeding me while I wrote. Thank you, thank you, thank you Lin, Shi-yu, Yung-Hsing, and Mie-Mie (a.k.a. my family) for keeping me sane. And last, but not least, thank you Woobie (a.k.a. Huckleberry, a.k.a. Muffin Man, a.k.a. Budgie) for being you.

TABLE OF CONTENTS

Introduction 1

Chapter 1: Paper or Computer? 9

Chapter 2: Strategies for the Paper Test 13

Chapter 3: Strategies for the Computer Test 23

Chapter 4: Sentence Completions 33

Chapter 5: Analogies 71

Chapter 6: Reading Comprehension 123

Chapter 7: Antonyms 181

Chapter 8: Vocabulary 229

INTRODUCTION

READ THIS STUFF FIRST

So you've finally decided what to do with your post-college life. You're not going to pursue the vaunted M.D., nor are you going to chase the lucrative J.D. Rather, the initials you desire to follow your name are M.A., M.S., or Ph.D. In short, you want to go to graduate school.

Unfortunately, before you can attend graduate school, you must first tackle the admissions process, and that means you have to take the Graduate Record Examination, otherwise known as the GRE. As you probably know, the GRE is a multiple-choice, standardized test. It is written and administered by Educational Testing Service (ETS), the same company that brought you the infamous college entrance exam the SAT.

WHAT DOES THE GRE MEASURE?

According to ETS, the GRE measures "certain developed verbal, quantitative, and analytical abilities that are important for academic achievement." You might interpret this statement in several ways. For example, you might think the GRE predicts how well you will perform in graduate school. Or, you might think the GRE is an accurate gauge of your intelligence. Well, guess what? Neither is true. There is absolutely no correlation between GRE scores and grades in graduate school. Nor is there a correlation between GRE scores and aptitude.

So what does the GRE measure? Well, the best way to look at it is the following: All the GRE measures is how well you do on the GRE. In other words, the GRE is about test-taking skills.

If the GRE doesn't do anything except evaluate test-taking ability, then why do graduate schools require it? The answer: convenience. Graduate schools need to have something that allows them to compare applicants from different backgrounds. An "A" at the small liberal arts college X may not be the same thing as an "A" at the big public university Y; however, a 500 earned on the GRE is a 500 earned on the GRE.

HOW IMPORTANT IS THE GRE?

How important the GRE is varies from school to school. Some schools place a great deal of weight on the test; others couldn't care less about it. Schools that tend to emphasize the GRE are usually those that have large applicant pools. These schools use GRE scores, along with college GPAs, to cut down the number of applications they have to look at. Other schools, however, don't consider GRE scores to be quite as important and use them primarily to determine financial awards.

The bottom line is: you want to do well on the GRE because you can be sure graduate schools will look at your scores. However, *how* well you need to do depends on the schools to which you're applying. Also, keep in mind the following:

1. Don't just look at a school's average GRE scores and say that you can't apply because your scores are too low. Remember, the school is reporting *average* scores. In other words, some people accepted to the school score higher than the average, and some people accepted to the school score lower.

2. Think about the type of program to which you're applying. If you're applying to an English literature program, then how important is your math score? If you're applying to an engineering program, then how important is your verbal score? Note that many programs, whether liberal arts or science, don't consider the analytical score. Find out whether the programs in which you're interested do or don't.

3. Don't forget there are other factors besides the GRE that can have an impact on your application. College GPA, work experience, extracurricular activities, academic honors, and letters of recommendation all affect your chances of admission.

PAPER VS. COMPUTER

There are two formats in which you can take the GRE: paper or computer. ETS intends to phase out the paper test in the next few years, but for now you have the option of taking one or the other (or even both, though this is something we would not recommend).

Which format should you take? There is no hard-and-fast answer. In chapter 1, we discuss the pros and cons of each format. For now, just know this: although you see the same subjects and the same question types on the two formats, the paper and the computer tests are *not* the same, and, therefore, you *cannot* approach them in the same way.

STRUCTURE OF THE GRE

One of the most obvious differences between the paper test and the computer test involves structure.

- On the paper test, there are always six scored sections and one unscored experimental section.

- On the computer test, there are always three scored sections and either one or two unscored experimental sections.

The charts below outline the structural differences between the two formats in more detail.

PAPER TEST			
SECTION TYPE	NUMBER OF SECTIONS	NUMBER OF QUESTIONS PER SECTION	NUMBER OF MINUTES PER SECTION
VERBAL	2	38	30
MATH	2	30	30
ANALYTICAL	2	25	30

COMPUTER TEST			
SECTION TYPE	NUMBER OF SECTIONS	NUMBER OF QUESTIONS PER SECTION	NUMBER OF MINUTES PER SECTION
VERBAL	1	30	30
MATH	1	28	45
ANALYTICAL	1	35	60

THE VERBAL GRE

As shown in the above charts, the paper test contains two verbal sections while the computer test contains only one.

- On the paper test, each verbal section lasts for 30 minutes and consists of 38 questions.

- On the computer test, the verbal section lasts for 30 minutes and consists of 30 questions.

In spite of these differences, the two formats share the same question types:

- Sentence completions

- Analogies

- Reading comprehension

- Antonyms

However, the *number* of each question type differs ...

Paper Test (per section)	Computer Test (per section)
7 sentence completions	5–7 sentence completions
9 analogies	6–8 analogies
11 reading comprehension questions (2 passages)	6–10 reading comprehension questions (2–4 passages)
11 antonyms	8–10 antonyms

... as does the *order* in which the question types appear.

Paper Test (per section)	Computer Test (per section)
#1–7 sentence completions #8–16 analogies #17-27 reading comprehension questions #28–38 antonyms	Any order

(There is no way to anticipate question-type order on the computer test, so don't even try. It's a waste of time.)

HOW IS THE VERBAL GRE SCORED?

The verbal GRE, whether paper or computer, is scored on a scale from 200 to 800. For the paper test, each correct answer is worth one raw score point. Incorrect answers, as well as questions left blank, are worth zero raw score points. Since there is a total of 76 questions on the two verbal sections, the highest raw score possible is 76. ETS takes the raw score and then converts it to the 200 to 800 scaled score. Clearly, a 76 raw score would translate to an 800.

For the computer test, you begin with an approximate scaled score of 500. Each correct answer raises your score, and each incorrect answer lowers your score. How much your score is raised or lowered depends on where you are on the verbal section. What about questions left blank? Well, it's impossible to leave a question blank on the computer test because the computer never gives you another question unless you've answered the question that's on the screen. That means you can *never* skip a question on the entire test. It also means you're forced to guess whenever you don't know the answer to a question.

WHAT'S A GOOD SCORE?

A good score on the verbal GRE varies from person to person. Why? It all goes back to how important the GRE is to a school. Remember, some schools care about the GRE; others don't. It's your job to find out into which category the schools of your choice fall.

HOW TO SCORE HIGHER

To get a higher score, there's one thing you have to do: work hard. It's as simple as that. You have to put in the time as well as the effort.

However, don't take this statement the wrong way. Working hard *doesn't* mean doing lots and lots of practice questions. In fact, that's one of the big mistakes people make when preparing for the GRE. Working hard means doing an hour or two of work every day and, most importantly, reviewing the work you do to analyze your strengths and weaknesses. Just doing lots and lots of practice questions, without looking at *why* you got questions right or wrong, merely enforces the bad habits you have. In short, your score isn't going to improve.

HOW TO SCORE HIGHER ON VERBAL

To improve your verbal score, there are several things you can do.

1. Read. This means read, read, read. Read every day, and read every night. Magazines, newspapers, books — read whatever you can get your hands on. The more you read, the stronger your verbal skills.

2. Master our techniques. The great thing about our techniques is that they're very consistent and very methodical. They teach you how to think like ETS, which shows you, in turn, how to get rid of wrong answer choices. Be careful, though: learning a technique isn't the same thing as mastering a technique.

Mastery comes *after* you've learned a technique and then applied it consistently on practice questions. Also, be aware that, at first, techniques slow you down. *You must expect this*. It's natural for techniques to slow you down initially because you're unfamiliar with them. So don't worry about speed at the beginning. It'll come with practice.

3. Improve your vocabulary. Ultimately, the fastest way to improve your verbal score is to learn new words. Why? Because three of the four question types test your vocabulary. Analogies, sentence completions, and antonyms—if you have a good vocabulary, these question types are much easier to tackle. Chapter 9 discusses vocabulary in more detail, particularly what's the best way to learn new words. It also provides you with The Princeton Review's Hit Parade, a list of the most frequently tested words on the GRE.

HOW TO USE THIS BOOK

It's hoped that you've read everything up to this point in the introduction. If not, go back and read what you skipped. Everything in this book is essential.

Okay—now that you've read everything up to this point, here's how to use this book. This book's goal is to improve your verbal score. And it can do just that. However, it is our suggestion that you also obtain practice materials other than this book. Specifically, we recommend that you get your hands on real GREs written by ETS.

Currently, ETS publishes two books that contain real practice tests: *Practicing to Take the GRE: The Big Book* and *Practicing to Take the GRE: Book 9*. ETS also produces software called PowerPrep that is especially helpful for those people taking the computer test. (You can actually take a practice computer test on this software.) Ultimately, which product you buy doesn't matter. You just want to have real tests so that you can practice our techniques on real questions.

That being said, be aware that while we recommend ETS materials, we do *not* recommend following ETS's advice. In fact, we wholeheartedly disagree with most of what ETS says. Furthermore, anytime ETS provides an explanation for doing a certain question, skip that explanation. You bought this book to learn our techniques. Reading ETS's explanations will send you mixed messages and, therefore, only confuse you.

CHAPTER 1

Paper or Computer?

THE BIG QUESTION

So which should you take: the paper GRE or the computer GRE? As we said in the introduction, it really depends on your specific needs.

Perhaps the most important thing to consider is the level at which you're currently scoring. (If you don't know what level you're at, take a practice test.) It's our recommendation that you take the paper test if you're scoring either less than 400 or more than 650. If you're somewhere in between (that is, between 400 and 650), it doesn't matter which format you take.

> Take this recommendation to heart: Neither format is any easier than the other *unless* you're scoring in a certain range.

THINGS TO CONSIDER

That being said, let's discuss some other considerations that might help you choose which format is better for you.

Registration Fee

- The paper test costs $64.

- The computer test costs $96.

What this means to you: If money is an issue—because applying to graduate schools can become very expensive—then take the paper test.

Number of Test Administrations

- The paper test has a limited number of test administrations each year. In the 1996-97 school year, ETS offered a total of three administrations: October, December, and April.

- The computer test can be taken just about any day in the year. In the 1996-97 school year, ETS offered the computer test for the first three weeks of every month (except for Sundays).

What this means to you: If you have a very busy schedule, then it's probably more convenient to take the computer test.

Registration Deadlines

- To take the paper test, you must register with ETS four to six weeks before the test date.

- To take the computer test, you can register with ETS on any day before the test. In fact, you can even register the day before (if you want), as long as space is available.

What this means to you: If your application deadlines are coming up in the very near future, then take the computer test.

Number of Times You Can Take the Test

- You can take the paper test as many times as you want.

- You can only take the computer test once every 60 days.

What this means to you: Not a whole lot, unless you intend to take the GRE more than once. If you want to take the GRE more than once, get a copy of the registration bulletin and see which dates each format is offered. You can obtain a copy of the bulletin by calling ETS at (609) 921-9000.

Test Booklet

- The paper test is given in a booklet that you can use to mark on and cross out wrong answer choices.

- The computer test has no test booklet because all questions are presented on-screen. Instead, you are given scratch paper on which to do your work.

What this means to you: If you hate staring at a computer screen for three or more hours, or if you don't want to copy questions from a computer screen on to scratch paper, then take the paper test.

Skipping Around

- On the paper test, you can answer the questions in a given section in any order that you want. You don't have to answer a question if you don't want to, and you can return to a question at any time.

- On the computer test, you don't have these options. You must answer the questions in the order presented, and you can never leave a question blank or you never see another question on the test. Furthermore, you can never return to a question once you've answered it.

What this means to you: If you like to skip around, then take the paper test.

Environment

- The paper test is usually given in a large room with dozens of other test takers.

- The computer test is usually administered in a small room with approximately 5 to 10 other test takers.

What this means to you: If you don't like crowds, then take the computer test.

A THING NOT TO CONSIDER

These are the major factors you should consider before choosing a format in which to take the GRE. However, the one thing you should *not* consider is length. While it's true that there are fewer scored questions on the computer test (83) than there are on the paper test (186), length is, quite simply, not very important. Just because the computer test is shorter doesn't mean it's any easier.

FINAL THOUGHTS

Before you start plowing through the rest of this book, take the time to figure out which format is better for you. There is no right or wrong answer as to which format is easier or more fun or whatever. What's important is that you don't rush into a decision.

What's also important is that you *make* a decision. Don't waffle! Pick a format and then prep for that format. And again, make this decision before you read any further. It's pointless for you to read the remaining pages if you haven't decided in which format you want to take the GRE. Though some of our techniques are usable for both the paper and the computer tests, certain strategies are very, very different. In fact, the overall approach to each test—which is how you gain the most points—is incredibly different. So don't get yourself more confused by trying to learn strategies for both formats.

Enough preaching: If you're going to take the paper test, go on to chapter 2 and skip chapter 3. If you're going to take the computer test, skip chapter 2 and go on to chapter 3.

CHAPTER 2

Strategies for the Paper Test

AN IMPORTANT REMINDER

This chapter is all about the paper test. Do *not* apply these strategies to the computer test because they won't work. If you haven't picked a format yet, go back and reread chapter 1. You should *not* read this chapter unless you know without question that you intend to take the paper test.

LESS IS MORE

Most people approach the GRE with one goal in mind: to finish. In other words, "I must work on each and every question on this test because if I don't, I lose potential points." Well, guess what? This thinking is why most people do poorly on the GRE.

The first thing you have to realize is that you are in the land of ETS, and you can't operate in the land of ETS as you do in the real world. In the real world, the more you do, the better. But in the land of ETS, the more you do, the worse.

If you read through this book and learn only one thing about the paper test, it should be: The best way to improve your score is *not* to finish. Rather, it is to work on fewer questions and make sure you get those questions right. Less is actually more.

ORDER OF DIFFICULTY

How? How can doing less actually get you more? It doesn't make a lot of sense until you understand how ETS constructs the GRE.

Basically, there are three types of questions on the GRE: Easy questions, medium questions, and hard questions. What makes an easy question easy? An easy answer. What makes a hard question hard? A hard answer. In short, by definition, easy questions have easy answers, and hard questions have hard answers.

So easy questions have easy answers, and hard questions have hard answers. Well, how do you know which questions are easy and which questions are hard? It's incredibly simple. ETS follows a rigid order of difficulty on the GRE. On the verbal sections, the first third of the group of any question type is easy, the next third is medium, and the last third is hard. In other words:

Easy sentence completions	#1-2
Medium sentence completions	#3-5
Hard sentence completions	#6-7

Easy analogies	#8-10
Medium analogies	#11-13
Hard analogies	#14-16
Easy antonyms	#28-30
Medium antonyms	#31-34
Hard antonyms	#35-38

Notice that the one question type not mentioned above is reading comprehension. For reading comprehension, there is no order of difficulty. It's the only question type that doesn't fit the mold.

ACCURACY, NOT SPEED

Let's use this knowledge about order of difficulty to find out why less is more.

Here's how a typical test taker approaches a given section—we'll call this typical test taker "Joe Bloggs." Joe starts the section with the easy questions. How does he do? (Keep in mind that Joe's primary goal is to finish.) Joe gets most of the easy questions right. He gets most of them right because, after all, they're easy. However, he also misses some because he's rushing to finish the section—and that causes Joe to make careless mistakes.

Joe gets to the medium questions. How does he do here? (Again, keep in mind that Joe's desire is to finish.) So-so. Joe's not stupid, so he gets about half of the questions right. Why does Joe miss the other half? Because the questions are getting harder and, more important, because he's still rushing, which causes him to make careless mistakes.

Joe moves on to the hard questions. On a typical hard question, only 15 percent of the people answering the question get it right. So how do you think Joe does? He tanks; he bombs. Joe spends the majority of his time trying to answer the hard questions, and he gets them all wrong.

To review: Joe misses easy questions, he misses medium questions, and he misses hard questions. What's wrong with this picture?

Does Joe get more points for answering hard questions than he does for answering easy questions? No. Remember, every correct answer is worth one raw score point. Then why should Joe spend all of his time on the hard questions when he's going to miss them anyway? Why should *you* spend all of your time on the hard questions when you're going to miss them anyway?

Joe and you need to focus on what he and you *can* do, not what he and you can't. By slowing down and concentrating on the easy and medium questions, your score is going to improve. Ignore the hard questions. Don't even look at them. Beating the GRE is all about pacing yourself correctly. Accuracy is more important than speed.

In a nutshell: Unless you're scoring a 650 or above, you should not be answering every question on the verbal sections.

MORE ON LESS IS MORE

One more time: The way to get a higher verbal score is to do fewer questions. The chart below outlines specifically how many questions you need to answer *correctly* on each verbal section to achieve a certain score.

VERBAL	400	450	500	550	600	650	700	750	800
Sentence completions (7)	4	5	5	6	6	6	7	7	7
Analogies (9)	5	5	6	6	7	8	8	9	9
Reading comprehension (11)	3	4	5	6	6	7	8	9	10
Antonyms (11)	5	6	7	7	8	9	9	10	11
TOTAL	17	20	23	25	27	30	32	35	37

Let's say that you're currently scoring a 500. You want to pick a target score that's about 50 points higher—in other, words, a 550. Now, a 550 may not be your final goal. Don't worry. You want to set, at first, a small goal that you can reach. Once you reach this small goal, set another small goal (e.g., 600), and continue to do so until you reach your final goal. So your target score for now is 550. You can get a score of 550 by answering *correctly* six sentence completions, six analogies, six reading comprehension questions, and seven antonyms. That's a total of 25 questions you need to get right out of a total of 38. In other words, you can afford to ignore *13 questions* on each verbal section.

Unfortunately, that's assuming you don't miss any questions at all. Since you probably want to give yourself some room for error (and the chart above doesn't do that), here's another chart. This chart takes into account that you're going to make some mistakes, so use this one to determine how many questions you need to work on to get the score you want.

VERBAL	400	450	500	550	600	650	700	750	800
Sentence completions (7)	All	All	All	All	All	All	All	All	All
Analogies (9)	6	6	All	All	All	All	All	All	All
Reading comprehension (11)	1/2 the long passage	The entire long passage	The entire long passage	The entire long passage and 1/2 the short passage	Both passages	Both passages	Both passages	Both passages	Both passages
Antonyms (11)	All	All	All	All	All	All	All	All	All
TOTAL	28	31	34	36	38	38	38	38	38

HARD QUESTIONS AND DISTRACTORS

Before we move on, let's go back for a second and talk a little more about Joe Bloggs. We said earlier that Joe is the typical test taker, and that means he gets easy questions mostly right, medium questions half right, and hard questions all wrong. Well, why does Joe miss the hard questions?

Joe misses the hard questions because they're hard. Again, on a typical hard question, only 15 percent of the people answering the question get it right.

This statistic is incredibly important. Why? Let's say that when you take the GRE, you guess randomly on every question. There are five answer choices for every verbal question, so that means, on any given question, you have a one-in-five—or 20 percent—chance of getting that question right.

But only *15 percent* of the people get a hard question right. Why this discrepancy? Why do people do worse on hard questions than if they guessed randomly?

REMEMBER ... HARD QUESTIONS HAVE HARD ANSWERS

Why do only 15 percent of the people get a hard question right? Why does Joe always miss a hard question? Because of distractors. A distractor is an answer choice that is obvious, an answer choice that screams, "Pick me! I'm right!" In other words, a distractor is an *easy* answer. But on a hard question, can an easy answer be right?

No! By definition, a hard question must have a hard answer. A hard question is hard *because* it has a hard answer.

BE JOE BLOGGS

At this point, you should be slightly annoyed with ETS for creating distractors on hard questions. But use this knowledge of distractors to your advantage. Anytime you work on a hard question, pretend that you're Joe Bloggs, the typical test taker. What answer choice jumps out at you as the right answer? That answer—the obvious answer, the easy answer, the Joe Bloggs answer—must be wrong. Cross it out.

Take advantage of Joe's answer on hard questions. He'll help you out time and again. But in order to use Joe Bloggs, you have to know where you are on the test. You have to know what type of question you're working on—easy, medium, or hard. That means the first thing you should do before starting to work on any question is check out what number it is. A number 16 is *always* going to be a hard analogy. A number 28 is *always* going to be an easy antonym.

POE

Pacing is all about recognizing that less is actually more. Joe Bloggs is all about knowing where you are on the test and understanding that easy questions have easy answers and hard questions have hard answers. Along with pacing and Joe Bloggs, we have one more major technique that applies to the entire test. We call it POE.

What's POE? It's short for process of elimination, and though it's not a very flashy technique, it's very, very important.

Anytime you can eliminate an answer choice, you're improving your chance of getting a question right. Remember, if you were to guess randomly on a question, you would have a one-in-five (20 percent) chance of getting the question right. Well, if you could eliminate just one answer choice, you would now have a one-in-four (25 percent) chance. Eliminating two answer choices would give you a one-in-three ($33\frac{1}{3}$ percent) chance, and eliminating three answer choices would give you a one-in-two (50 percent) chance.

What does this mean for you? Take advantage of the test booklet. If you know that an answer choice is wrong, physically cross it out. POE never hurts; it can only help.

WHAT ABOUT GUESSING?

And last—but certainly not least—when should you guess? The answer is *always*. On the paper test, there is no penalty for an incorrect answer, so if you can only eliminate one answer choice, or even if you can't eliminate any, guess, guess, guess.

Now, a word about guessing. On every question that you have no idea how to do (i.e., you can't eliminate any of the answer choices), guess the *same* answer choice. We call this technique "Letter of the Day."

Why should you use a Letter of the Day? Why not just guess randomly? Well, let's pretend you're taking the GRE and the questions you're going to guess on are numbers 6, 15, 16, 20, 36, and 38. The right answers to these questions are:

6.	A
15.	C
16.	C
20.	B
36.	D
38.	B

If you were to guess randomly, you might pick:

	Right answer	Your answer
6.	A	B
15.	C	D
16.	C	E
20.	B	A
36.	D	B
38.	B	A

In other words, you could miss every question, and you would gain zero points. But what happens if you pick one letter and use that same letter for every question? Let's say that you pick C.

	Right answer	Letter of the Day
6.	A	C
15.	C	C
16.	C	C
20.	B	C
36.	D	C
38.	B	C

You got numbers 15 and 16 right, simply by using Letter of the Day, and therefore picked up two raw score points. The bottom line for guessing is twofold.

1. Never leave blanks. That means even if your pacing tells you to do only one passage for reading comprehension, don't forget to bubble in answers for the other passage.

2. Don't guess randomly. Use Letter of the Day instead.

QUESTION-TYPE ORDER

As a final note, let's talk about question-type order. As we discussed earlier, there are four question types on each verbal section. ETS presents these question types in the following order:

- Sentence completions
- Analogies
- Reading comprehension
- Antonyms

Is this the order you're going to follow? Nope. Your approach to the verbal sections will follow this order:

- Analogies
- Sentence completions
- Antonyms
- Reading comprehension

Always do analogies first because (as you'll see in chapter 6) these questions are the most technique-able. Do sentence completions next because these questions are quite do-able, too. Do antonyms after that because, even though there aren't a lot of techniques to use for these questions, it doesn't take a lot of time to answer them. Save reading comprehension for last because it's boring, tedious, and (most of all) time-consuming.

Is it okay to work on the verbal sections in this order? Sure. ETS doesn't care if you start with question 38 and work backward to question 1. It only cares that you work on the right section—not the order in which you do the section.

IN SUMMARY ...

Please make sure that you understand what you've read in this chapter. If you're taking the paper test, this is the most important chapter for you to absorb. This is the foundation to cracking the paper GRE.

1. Slow down and pace yourself. Use the charts to determine how many questions you need to answer correctly and how many questions you should actually work on. Remember, hard questions aren't worth more than easy questions, so focus on what you can do, not what you can't. Accuracy is more important than speed, and less is actually more.

2. Remember that easy questions have easy answers and hard questions have hard answers. This is always, always true. A hard question is hard because it has a hard answer.

3. On hard questions, use Joe Bloggs. ETS tricks you on hard questions by using distractors. But an easy answer can never be right on a hard question.

4. Never leave a question blank—always guess. If you can't eliminate any answer choices, then use your Letter of the Day.

5. Don't follow ETS's question-type order. You want to do analogies first, then sentence completions and antonyms. Always save reading comprehension for last.

NOTE ON PROBLEM SETS

Finally, a note on the problem sets in this book. Do all of your work in the book itself. We want you to do this because you need to get used to the space you'll have available on the day of the real test. Also, remember that on the day of the real test, question number will reflect level of difficulty.

3

Strategies for the Computer Test

AN IMPORTANT REMINDER

This chapter contains strategies that apply only to the computer test. Don't use these strategies on the paper test because they just won't work. If you haven't picked a format yet, go back and reread chapter 1. You should *not* read this chapter unless you know without question that you intend to take the computer test.

THE COMPUTER ADAPTS TO YOU

To start off, let's talk some more about how the computer test is scored. If you recall, at the beginning of a given section, you have a scaled score of 500. If you get a question right, your score increases, and if you get a question wrong, your score decreases. The computer readjusts your score after each and every question. This constant score readjustment is, in large part, what makes the computer test special—or, at the very least, different. The computer test is *adaptive*. In other words, the computer responds to what you do.

The computer, however, isn't just adaptive in terms of scoring. It is also adaptive in terms of level of difficulty. At the beginning of each section, the computer starts you off with a question that is of a medium level of difficulty. (Basically, there are three question types on the GRE: easy, medium, and hard.) If you answer the question correctly, you get a harder question. If you answer the question incorrectly, you get an easier question.

How much does your score increase for a correct answer and how much does your score decrease for an incorrect answer? Well, it depends. Where are you on the section?

Let's pretend you're taking the computer test and you get the first question right. The computer readjusts your score to a 550, and it gives you a harder question. You get the second question right, so your score is now 600, and the computer gives you a harder question. You get the third question right, and your new score is 640. Your get the fourth question right, and your score is increased to 680.

Let's pose a different scenario. Let's say you get the first question wrong. The computer takes you down to a 450 and gives you an easier question. The second question you also get wrong, and your score is now at a 400. The computer gives you an easier question. After you answer the third question incorrectly, you have a 360, and after you answer the fourth question incorrectly, you have a 320.

As you've probably divined by now, for each of the first four questions, you have either gained or lost 40 to 50 points. Is this what happens at the end of a section? Do you still stand to lose 40 to 50 points? Nope. By the end of a section, instead of gaining or losing 40 to 50 points for each question, you only gain or lose 10 to 20 points.

Why is this the case? Why do you stand to gain or lose more at the beginning than you do at the end? The answer: The computer's goal is to determine what score level you're at. However, at the beginning of a section, the computer knows nothing about you. You and the computer are perfect strangers, so the computer has no information on which to base your score.

However, after you answer a few questions, the computer knows a little something about you, and by the end of a section, the computer knows you fairly well. The more information the computer has on you, the better it is able to place you. This is why, as the computer learns more about you, the number of points it gives or takes gets smaller and smaller.

Let's get a little more specific. At the beginning of a section, we said the computer starts you out at a score of 500. Well, that's not entirely true. It's more accurate to say that the computer places you in a score range: anywhere between 200 and 800. As you continue to answer questions, the score range gets narrower and narrower until the computer has zeroed in on your score.

#1	Correct	+50 points	550	200-800
#2	Correct	+50 points	600	200-800
#3	Correct	+50 points	650	210-800
#4	Correct	+40 points	690	210-800
#5	Incorrect	–40 points	650	210-790
...				
...				
...				
#28	Incorrect	–10 points	570	550-590
#29	Correct	+10 points	580	560-600
#30	Correct	+10 points	590	580-600

All this is somewhat heady stuff. All you really need to know is the following: Don't believe ETS when it says you get more credit for answering a hard question correctly than you do for answering an easy question correctly. It's not exactly true. Rather, you should think of scoring in these terms: You get more credit for answering a question at the beginning of a section correctly than you do for answering a question at the end correctly. By the end of a section, the computer is only fine-tuning your score.

THE IMPORTANT QUESTIONS

So which questions are the most important to you? The questions at the beginning or the questions at the end? The ones at the beginning, of course. These are worth 40 to 50 points each, whereas the ones at the end are worth only 10 to 20 each. Because of this, you have to approach the computer test in a special way.

Probably the biggest mistake people make on standardized testing is to try and finish the test. Why is this the biggest mistake? Because people who try to finish rush.

On the computer test, speed is your enemy, particularly at the beginning. Remember, if you miss the first four questions, your score is going to be in the low 300s. But if you get the first four questions right, your score is somewhere in the high 600s. That's a huge difference, and it's a difference that is incredibly hard to recover. Don't dig yourself in a hole by missing the questions early on in a section.

So here's your basic approach: Slow down. Don't rush. Take your time to get a question right, *especially* if it's in the first half of the section. A string of correct answers is what you want to achieve; a string of incorrect answers is what you want to avoid.

PACING

One more note on scoring...When ETS first introduced the computer test with adaptive scoring, it had a requirement that you had to complete a minimum number of questions per section in order to get a score. If you didn't reach the minimum number, then the computer gave you a "No Score" for that section.

For the 1997-98 school year, ETS decided that it would take out the minimum- number requirement. Now, ETS has instituted a new rule. Your score is based not only on your record of getting questions right or wrong, but also on *how many* questions you answer. In other words, a "penalty" will be applied if you don't answer every question in a given section. In ETS's words:

"Your score on the CAT [computer adaptive test] will now be dependent on how well you do on the questions presented as well as on the number of questions you answer. Therefore, it is to your advantage to answer every question even if you have to guess to complete the test."

So do we agree with ETS? Sort of. We do want you to *answer* every question on the test, but we don't think you should actually *work* on every question.

What do we mean by that? Well, first, remember that speed is bad. All it ever does is produce careless mistakes. On the computer test, you just can't afford to make careless mistakes, particularly at the beginning of a section.

Therefore, your goal is not to do every question on a given section. Rather, it is to work carefully and conscientiously on 80 percent of the questions.

> For the verbal section, that means you want to answer 24 out of 30 questions.

Now, you might be thinking 24 out of 30 questions is still a lot of questions. But this is a big deal. You're not going to do six questions—that means you're not even going to look at them. As a result, you have more time to do the questions at the beginning of the section. Remember, it's the first half of the section that really determines your score. So who cares about the last six questions?

To boil it down: It is your goal to work on 24 questions during the 30 minutes allotted on the verbal section. You want to put in the time and effort to get those 24 questions right as best you can. When you answer number 24, you want (ideally) to have one or two minutes left. Use that remaining time to guess to the end of the section. Guessing, at this point, doesn't hurt your score because it's only 10 to 20 points. It's better that you work slowly at the beginning of the section and then guess at the end. After all, it's accuracy at the beginning of a section that gets you points.

So—never leave any blanks on the test. Always put down an answer for every question. However, don't actually put *work* into each and every question. Your focus is going to be on the first 10 to 12 questions, and your goal is actually to work on 24 questions. At the end, if you're running out of time, just guess to the last question.

POE AND SCRATCH PAPER

Up to now, everything we've talked about has centered on pacing—that is, on focusing on the questions at the beginning rather than those at the end. While pacing is the most important strategy for you to understand, it's not the only one that you need to beat the GRE. Perhaps the second most important strategy is what we call POE.

What's POE? It's short for process of elimination, and it's one of the most underrated techniques around. You have to remember: Anytime you can eliminate an answer choice, you improve your chances of getting a question right.

How? On every verbal question on the test, you have five answer choices. Therefore, if you were to guess randomly on a question, you would have a one-in-five (20 percent) chance of getting the question right. Well, if you could eliminate just one answer choice, you would now have a one-in-four (25 percent) chance of getting the question right. Eliminating two answer choices would give you a one-in-three ($33\frac{1}{3}$ percent) chance, and eliminating three answer choices would give you a one-in-two (50 percent) chance.

So guess what? POE is a very powerful tool. However, POE on the computer test isn't as easy as POE on the paper test.

One of the negative sides to the computer test is your lack of a test booklet. (It's true that you have scratch paper, but it's not exactly the same as having a test booklet.) What's nice about a test booklet is the rows of (A) through (E) that you get for every question. You get to physically cross out an answer choice if you think it's wrong.

However, you can't physically cross out answer choices on the computer test since the test is on a screen. What should you do? Our solution is to take advantage of two things: the tutorial and your scratch paper.

What's the tutorial? At the beginning of the test, ETS offers you the chance to take a tutorial. Basically, the tutorial shows you how to use the mouse, how to click on the answer choices, how to scroll on reading comprehension passages, how to get to the next question, and so on. In short, the tutorial makes sure you know how to maneuver about the computer test.

The nice thing is that you get an unlimited amount of time to go through the tutorial. Technically, you could work on the tutorial for a solid hour and there would be no penalty. So use this time to your advantage. Since you don't have a test booklet with rows of (A) through (E), take your scratch paper and make rows of (A) through (E) on it. You should make enough rows for every question on the test. And again, take as long as you want to do this because the time during the tutorial is unlimited.

Don't consider using your scratch paper in this manner a waste of time. It isn't. It keeps you organized, and it helps you keep track of which answer choices are wrong.

(Note that ETS only provides you with two pieces of scratch paper. It is your right as a test taker to have more than just two pieces. Before you start the test, go ahead and ask for more paper. If the proctor says, "I just gave you some," then reply, "I just want to make sure I have enough." The last thing you want is to run out of paper and have to waste time by going up to the proctor in the middle of a section.)

GUESSING

And last, but not least, what about guessing? We mentioned guessing before in chapter 1, but let's go over it one more time because it's important.

On the computer test, you have to answer the questions in the order presented. If you don't answer the question that's on-screen, then you never see another question on the test. Also, once you answer the question, you can never return to it. All this means you're forced to guess if you don't know the answer to a question, because if you don't, you never get to the rest of the test.

Now, a word about guessing. On every question that you have no idea how to do (i.e., you can't eliminate any of the answer choices), guess the *same* answer choice. We call this technique "Letter of the Day."

Why should you do this? Why not guess randomly? Think of it this way. Let's say the questions you're going to guess on are numbers 6, 15, 16, 20, 29, and 30. The right answers to these questions are:

6.	A
15.	C
16.	C
20.	B
29.	D
30.	B

If you were to guess randomly, you might pick:

	Right answer	Your answer
6.	A	B
15.	C	D
16.	C	E
20.	B	A
29.	D	B
30.	B	A

In other words, you could miss every question, and you would gain zero points. But what happens if you pick one letter and use it for every question? Let's say that you pick C.

	Right answer	Letter of the Day
6.	A	C
15.	C	C
16.	C	C
20.	B	C
29.	D	C
30.	B	C

You got numbers 15 and 16 right, simply by using Letter of the Day.

So, anytime you come across a question that you just can't do, guess by using Letter of the Day.

JUDGMENT DAY: WHEN TO GUESS

Using Letter of the Day is all well and good, but there's a certain art to guessing. When should you guess? As we said just a second ago, when you have no idea what the question is talking about—then you definitely want to guess. But what about when you come across a question that's potentially do-able but also very hard or time-consuming?

Here's where you've got to exercise your judgment. If it's a question at the beginning of the section, take the time to get it right. If it's a question at the end of the section, be aggressive—do some POE, guess, and move on to the next question. If it's a question in the middle, ask yourself how you did on the questions preceding that question. Do you feel as if you got them right? If so, missing one question after you've answered three or four right in a row isn't going to hurt your score very much. Or do you think you missed the preceding questions? If so, missing another question is going to add another incorrect in a string of incorrect answers—something you want to avoid.

The important thing is always to ask yourself: *Where am I on the test?* If it's a question at the beginning, it's important to try to get it right, but if it's impossible, be aggressive and guess. If it's a question at the end, it's not too important, so be aggressive, do some POE, and then guess and move on.

NEVER EXIT, NEVER QUIT

A final note about the computer test: Never, never, never exit a section or quit the test. Don't ask why. Just don't do it. If you finish a section early and have time left over, just wait out the rest of the time. Think of it as a break.

(In case anyone's incredibly curious why you shouldn't exit or quit, here's the reason: The computer is a fallible thing and has been known to mess up on scoring. You can avoid this potential pitfall by never exiting and never quitting.)

IN SUMMARY...

Please make sure that you understand what you've read in this chapter. If you're taking the computer test, this is the most important chapter for you to grasp. This is the foundation to cracking the computer GRE.

1. Be familiar with how the computer adapts to your performance. If you get a question right, your score goes up and you get a harder question; if you get a question wrong, your score goes down and you get an easier question.

2. Slow down. Don't forget that accuracy is much more important than speed. Spend the time to get the first half of the questions right on the section. After all, the questions at the beginning are worth more than those at the end.

3. Remember to "bubble in" (or in computer terms, click on and confirm) an answer for *every* question. However, your goal is to actually work on 24 questions, not 30. Again, this goes back to the fact that questions at the beginning are more important than those at the end. If you're running out of time near the end, just guess (using Letter of the Day) up to number 30.

4. Take time during the tutorial to set up your scratch paper for POE. Those rows of (A) through (E) are indispensable.

5. When forced to guess (because you can't eliminate any answer choices), use Letter of the Day.

6. Never exit from a section, and never quit the test. Computers aren't perfect, so don't do something that might make it crash or mess up your score.

NOTE ON PROBLEM SETS

Finally, a note on the problem sets in this book. Do all of your work on scratch paper. We want you to do this because you need to get used to the space you'll have available on the day of the real test.

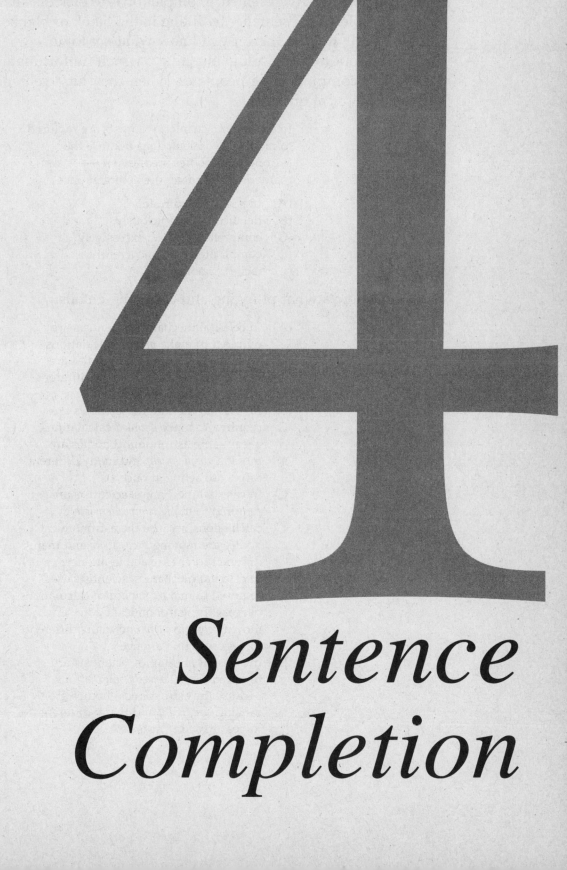

CHAPTER

4

Sentence
Completion

THE GOAL: FILL IN THE BLANK

Your job on any given sentence completion is to pick the answer choice that best completes the sentence by filling in the blank or blanks. Not too hard, right? Well, not too hard if you know what *not* to do.

What not to do is "plug and chug," which (unfortunately) is probably the most common thing people do when they hit a sentence completion. Here's a typical question:

> In celestial mechanics, scientists are required to make ------- calculations because the astronomical bodies are moving ------- and many different forces are acting at once.
>
> (A) precise . . . obdurately
> (B) detailed . . . auspiciously
> (C) comprehensible . . . excessively
> (D) complicated . . . concurrently
> (E) facile . . . nominally

And here's what plugging and chugging entails.

> (A) In celestial mechanics, scientists are required to make *precise* calculations because the astronomical bodies are moving *obdurately* and many different forces are acting at once.
>
> (B) In celestial mechanics, scientists are required to make *detailed* calculations because the astronomical bodies are moving *auspiciously* and many different forces are acting at once.
>
> (C) In celestial mechanics, scientists are required to make *comprehensible* calculations because the astronomical bodies are moving *excessively* and many different forces are acting at once.
>
> (D) In celestial mechanics, scientists are required to make *complicated* calculations because the astronomical bodies are moving *concurrently* and many different forces are acting at once.
>
> (E) In celestial mechanics, scientists are required to make *facile* calculations because the astronomical bodies are moving *nominally* and many different forces are acting at once.

In other words, when you plug and chug, you just take an answer choice and pop it back into the blank or blanks. How effective is this? Not very. People tend to plug and chug because they think it's the fastest way to answer a sentence completion, but guess what? It's not. In fact, it's the slowest way, because when you plug and chug, every answer choice *sounds* good. That is, every answer choice seems as if it could work.

IT'S YOUR WORD

Instead of plugging and chugging, the first thing you should do (and this goes for every single sentence completion) is cover up the answer choices. Cover up the answer choices so your mind is a complete blank as you start to read the sentence. The key to beating a sentence completion is not to get distracted by the answer choices. Rather, it's to focus on the sentence itself.

Let's take a look at an example. Remember, the first thing to do is cover up the answer choices.

> The actress, though portrayed by the media as
> an arrogant prima donna, was, in fact, both
> charming and -------.
>
> (A) improvident
> (B) gracious
> (C) enthusiastic
> (D) exceptional
> (E) lithesome

In reading the sentence, did you fill in your own word when you got to the blank? If so, you took control of the sentence. You should always do this: Cover up the answer choices, read the sentence, and come up with your own word(s).

What word might fit into the blank? *Nice, modest, delightful.* Anything in that vein. Now that you have your own word, go to the answer choices and pick the one that most closely matches your word. The best match doesn't have to be your word exactly—it doesn't even have to be a synonym of your word. It just needs to get across the same idea or feeling.

Before you do that, however, let's go over a very important point. On many questions, you may come across answer choices that contain words you don't know. What should you do? Well, you have to leave those answer choices in. You can't cross them out because they might be right. *Never* eliminate an answer choice if you don't know what a word means.

To go back to the above example: You want to find a word that matches *nice.* Don't cross out (A) if you don't know what *improvident* means. What about (B)? Does it work? Yes—*gracious* is a good match for *nice*. How about (C) and (D)? *Enthusiastic* and *exceptional* don't really match your word. And (E)? If you don't know what *lithesome* means, then you can't cross it out. So you're left with (A), (B), and (E). When you're down to a few answer choices and one works while the others contain words you just don't know, go with the answer choice that works. (B) is the best answer.

Note that in working through this example, we went through each and every answer choice. On any sentence completion—on any verbal question—you *have* to do this. You must. Why? Because verbal is about finding the *best* answer, not the right answer. That means you may come across an answer choice that seems to work, but another answer choice further down the road works even better. The lesson: Always, always look at every single answer choice. Let's try another sentence completion.

> Although perfumes were first created from the natural oils of plants, chemists have, since the early nineteenth century, produced thousands that contain ------- ingredients.
>
> (A) uncultivated
> (B) piquant
> (C) synthetic
> (D) aromatic
> (E) variable

Did you remember to cover up the answer choices? What word did you fill in for the blank? Probably something along the lines of *man-made*. (A) doesn't match your word, so eliminate it. (B) has a slightly hard word. If you don't know what *piquant* means, then you have to leave it in. (C) looks good—*synthetic* is a good match for *man-made*—still, don't forget to check out (D) and (E). *Aromatic* and *variable* aren't close to *man-made* at all. So you're left with (B) and (C). Which do you think is right? You know (C) is a good match and (B) contains a word you don't know. Pick the answer choice that works. The best answer is (C), *synthetic*.

QUIZ #1

In the following questions, come up with your own word for the blank.

1. The kidnapping of the son of Charles A. Lindbergh in 1932 so ------- the public that laws were soon adopted with severe penalties for the -------.

2. Though, in his lifetime, Mark Twain received much -------, today's critics esteem him to such a degree that they ------- him.

3. By mapping all of the genes on the human chromosomes, the Human Genome Project, established in 1990, hopes to gain ------- into human evolution and study the genetic similarities ------- by all species.

4. Even with the ------- of the battering ram and catapult, which reduced the effectiveness of large-scale fortifications, castles during the Middle Ages still remained -------.

5. Mosses, though limited to ------- habitats because they require water for fertilization and lack a vascular system for absorbing water, are considered ------- plants.

6. Wilson's reputation for being irresolute was ------- by her ability to make snap decisions whenever a crisis arose.

7. The judge did not wish to ------- the tensions between the feuding parties by seeming to favor one side over the other.

A CLUE, A CLUE, A CLUE

Let's take a look at a sentence completion that you'll never see on the real GRE.

ETS is ------- company.

(A) a nonprofit
(B) a wealthy
(C) a devious
(D) a cautious
(E) an enormous

How should you always approach a sentence completion? By covering up the answer choices and coming up with your own word for the blank. But if you do that for this particular question, guess what? Anything could go in the blank. (A) through (E) could all be right.

This particular question would never show up on the real GRE because there is no right answer—because any of the five answer choices could work. But what if we changed the question a little so that it looked like the following:

ETS, which earns over four million dollars each year, is ------- company.

(A) a nonprofit
(B) a wealthy
(C) a devious
(D) a cautious
(E) an enormous

What's the answer now? (B), right? How do you know (B) is correct? You know the answer is (B) because of the clause "which earns over four million dollars each year." That clause gave you a clue as to what belonged in the blank. Let's change the question again.

ETS, which likes to trick test takers on hard questions, is ------- company.

(A) a nonprofit
(B) a wealthy
(C) a devious
(D) a cautious
(E) an enormous

The answer now is (C). What tells you the answer is (C)? The clue "which likes to trick test takers on hard questions."

On every single sentence completion, there must be a clue that tells you what belongs in the blank. Without a clue, there would be no right answer.

So, anytime you're coming up with your own word for the blank, look for the clue to help you out. In fact, often you can repeat the clue itself in the blank. For example, in the last question, you might have said, "ETS ... is a *tricky* company." *Tricky* is the word you came up with based on the clue.

Keep in mind that clues can show up anywhere in the sentence: at the beginning, in the middle, at the end. If you're having trouble finding the clue, look for the most descriptive part of the sentence. That's usually where the clue is. Try to identify the clue in the following example:

> Though some of her peers ------- the theoretical
> approach she had taken, no one could find
> fault with her conclusions: not only ------- but
> also profound.
>
> (A) disregarded . . . original
> (B) applauded . . . seminal
> (C) exhausted . . . penetrating
> (D) criticized . . . insightful
> (E) ridiculed . . . mundane

Let's start with the first blank. What word comes to mind after reading the sentence? The clue is "no one could find fault with her conclusions." Everybody liked her conclusions, but did everybody feel that way about her theoretical approach? Nope. Let's repeat the clue in the blank. Some of her peers *found fault with* her theoretical approach. Does (A) work? Not really. They had problems with her approach; they didn't ignore it. (B) definitely doesn't work, and (C) just doesn't make sense. What about (D) and (E)? They both could be matches for *found fault with*, so leave them both in.

Let's look at the second blank now. Her conclusions were something and profound. The clue for this blank is "profound." Well, for your own word, let's just repeat the clue again. Her conclusions were *profound* and profound. Is it okay to do this? Sure. The word won't be *profound* exactly, but it'll be something pretty close to it. You already eliminated (A), (B), and (C), so let's move on to (D). Does *insightful* match *profound*? Yes—it could work. What about (E)? Does *mundane* match *profound*? No—*mundane* means boring. So the best answer is (D).

TRIGGERS

Besides the clue, there are other parts of the sentence that tell you what should go in the blank. These other parts of the sentence are what we call triggers.

Triggers are, for the most part, small words. They're important, though, because they usually give structure to the sentence: They either keep the sentence going in the same direction, or they change the direction of the sentence.

Let's take a look at two classic triggers: *and* and *but*. Fill in the blank for each of the sentences below.

- I don't want to go to the party, and _____.

- I don't want to go to the party, but _____.

For the first sentence, you might have come up with something like: "I don't want to go to the party, and you can't make me go." For the second sentence, you might have had something along the lines of "I don't want to go to the party, but I'll go anyway."

Notice the function of *and* in the first sentence. It continues the flow of the sentence. In contrast, *but* in the second sentence changes the flow—it takes the sentence in the opposite direction.

Let's take a look at a question you've already seen to get an idea of how triggers work.

The actress, though portrayed by the media as an arrogant prima donna, was, in fact, both charming and -------.

(A) improvident
(B) gracious
(C) enthusiastic
(D) exceptional
(E) lithesome

First, let's stop and look for the clue. The most descriptive part of the sentence is "portrayed by the media as an arrogant prima donna." Now let's look for triggers. Do you see any?

There are not one, but two, triggers in this sentence. The first is the word "though" and the second is the word "and." The "though" tells you the sentence is going to change in direction. Therefore, what goes in the blank should be the opposite of "an arrogant prima donna." What about the second trigger? The "and" tells you the sentence is going to continue in the same direction. So what goes in the blank should be similar to "charming."

MORE TRIGGERS

Not all sentences have triggers, but the majority do. The chart below shows some of the most common triggers.

Same-Direction Triggers	Changing Direction Triggers
and	but, yet
since	though, although, even though
because	however
so	despite, in spite of
not only . . . but also	rather, instead
thus	whereas
therefore	while
consequently	notwithstanding
hence	ironically
:	however
;	

Triggers aren't always words. Note that the last two triggers in the same-direction column are punctuation marks. ETS loves to use the colon (:) and semicolon (;), so always be on the watch for them. Take a look at an example:

> Born of the blood of Uranus, the mythic Furies
> are ------- creatures: they punish those who
> have wronged blood relatives, regardless of
> the perpetrators' motivations.
>
> (A) vehement
> (B) unforgiving
> (C) gloomy
> (D) quarrelsome
> (E) caustic

The clue is everything that comes after the colon; the trigger is the colon itself. Therefore, you know that whatever goes in the blank should continue the direction of "they punish those who have wronged their blood relatives, regardless of the perpetrators' motivation."

Given the clue and the trigger, a good word for the blank is *vengeful*. You can eliminate (A) since *vehement* isn't a good match. (B) looks okay, but let's go through the rest of the answer choices just to make sure. (C) definitely isn't right, and neither is (D). (E) doesn't fit since *caustic* means sarcastic, so you're left with (B). It's the best answer.

QUIZ #2

In the following questions, underline the clue and circle any triggers. Then, use the clue and triggers to help you determine what word should go in the blank. Remember, the clue is typically the most descriptive part of the sentence. Also, don't forget you can often repeat a part of the clue as the word that goes in the blank

1. In the Bible, handwriting appeared on the wall at the feast of Belshazzar, a ------- of doom according to Daniel; that night, Babylon fell to Cypress.

2. Because the reclogging of an artery often occurs after balloon angioplasty, some physicians have turned to the use of such ------- techniques as laser angioplasty.
    MODERN

3. Even though the evidence produced did not ---- his guilt, the jury still believed in his -------.
    GUILT

4. Jane's naiveté was often charming, but her ------- all too easily led her to be -------.
    CANDOR   UNCHARMING
    WELL KNOWNED

5. The jealousy of the goddess Hera has been ------- in Greek mythology: numerous stories tell of her ------- Zeus and his philandering.
    OVER

6. Early ethologists classified animal behavior as either ------- or learned; current ethologists, however, believe there is an ------- genetically determined and environmental responses.
    NATURAL

7. It remains a mystery as to how the ------- EXPANSION of the early universe evolved into its present day diversity.

NO WORD OF YOUR OWN?

Together the clue and the triggers help you come up with your own word for the blank. There are times, however, when you won't be able to come up with your own word—even though you've found the clue and the triggers. What do you do then?

You can still use the clue and the triggers to help you. Even though you may not be able to come up with your own word, you can often tell if what goes in that blank is positive or negative. If you know the word is positive, then you can eliminate any answer choice that contains a negative word. If you know the word is negative, then you can eliminate any answer choice that contains a positive word.

This technique—Positive/Negative—is very powerful, but a word of caution: Don't use it as a crutch. It's going to be very tempting to use this technique instead of coming up with your own word, but you shouldn't. Your first goal is always to come up with your own word. Only if you can't do that should you move on to Positive/Negative. For those times when you do use Positive/Negative, remember that you still need to find the clue and triggers. Otherwise you won't know what should go in the blank. Let's try applying Positive/Negative to a question.

> Because he did not want to appear -------, the junior executive refused to dispute the board's decision, in spite of his belief that the decision would impair employee morale.
>
> (A) –
> (B) –
> (C) +
> (D) –
> (E) +

Let's say that you can't come up with your own word, which means you need to rely on Positive/Negative. What's the clue in the sentence? The most descriptive part is "refused to dispute." There's also the trigger "Because." Together, the clue and trigger tell you that a negative word belongs in the blank. So what can you eliminate? (C) and (E).

This is a good example why Positive/Negative can be a very powerful technique. You can't figure out exactly what should go in the blank, but you can still manage to eliminate two answer choices. If you were stuck after that, who cares? You now have a one-in-three chance of getting the question right.

Here's what the complete question looks like:

> Because he did not want to appear -------, the junior executive refused to dispute the board's decision, in spite of his belief that the decision would impair employee morale.
>
> (A) contentious
> (B) indecisive
> (C) solicitous
> (D) overzealous
> (E) steadfast

(C) and (E) are gone because they're positive words. You can't eliminate (A) if you don't know what *contentious* means. (B) doesn't work because the clue is "refused to dispute." That doesn't work with *indecisive*. For the same reason, (D) doesn't work either. So the best answer is (A). Even though you might not know *contentious*, you can still get to the right answer.

QUIZ #3

Find the clue and triggers in the following questions and determine whether the word in the blank should be positive or negative.

1. Though Californians claim to be ------- to *FAMILIAR +* earthquakes, the smallest of tremors are ------- to most people.
   TERRIFYING −

2. Even when injured, Steffi Graf has always been a ------- opponent; indeed, a *COMPETITIVE +* problematic back and foot did not ------- *− IMPEDE* her from winning several championships during the 1996 season.

3. The nouveau riche often strive for the same social standing as the established wealthy, but they usually find themselves left with only the ------- of affluence.

4. Joseph's ------- was misleading: his *IMAGE +* appearance suggested innocence and artlessness, but he was, in fact, quite -------.
   DIFFERENT −

5. Though it is important to stand by one's beliefs, it is also important not to cling ------- to them.
   +

6. It is not necessary for a scientific theory to be proved in order to be -------; rather, it *TRUE +* need only be ------- the best explanation *SIMPLY +* offered for a phenomenon at the time.

7. A pioneer in modern population study, Thomas Malthus was the first to suggest that ------- and distress are ------- because *CAUSED +* population increases more quickly than the means of subsistence.

TWO BLANKS

So far the majority of sentence completions we've looked at have been one-blank questions. However, not all sentence completions have only one blank. Some have two.

For those of you who hate sentence completions, you should thank your lucky stars that at least some have two blanks. Two-blank sentence completions are often easier than one-blank sentence completions because two-blank sentence completions tend to have more clues. After all, each blank in a sentence completion has to have a clue. (It is possible, however, for two blanks to share a clue.)

The key to two-blank sentence completions is to focus on one blank at a time. Two-blank questions are only hard when you try to do too much at once—i.e., try to work on both blanks at the same time. To make two-blank questions easy, focus on one blank and then focus on the other.

Which blank should you do first? It doesn't matter. Whichever one is easier. We will say, however, that you shouldn't always tackle the first blank first. The second blank can be easier at times because by the time you get to the second blank, you've got more information about the sentence. Let's try one:

> Though the statement released by the press secretary was deliberately ------- in neutral language, many people were ------- by its implications.
>
> (A) framed . . . bemused
> (B) discounted . . . enervated
> (C) couched . . . perturbed
> (D) phrased . . . nonplussed
> (E) confounded . . . incensed

Let's start with the second blank. The clue for the second blank is "neutral language" and the trigger is "Though." The statement had neutral language, but how did people respond? Not in a positive way, so a good word for the blank might be *angry*. (A) doesn't make sense if you know that *bemused* means confused. (B) doesn't make sense either if you know that *enervated* means weakened. (C) might work since *perturbed* could match *angry*, but (D) doesn't work because *nonplussed* means perplexed. *Incensed* means very angry, so (E) might work, too. You're left, then, with (C) and (E).

Now you can move on to the first blank. Remember, there's no need to look at (A), (B), and (D) because once one part of an answer choice is wrong, the entire answer choice is wrong. A good word for the first blank is *expressed*. (C) can still work, but (E) can't because *confounded* means baffled. The best answer, then, is (C).

It's really important that, for every two-blank sentence completion, you focus on one blank at a time. Don't get confused by trying to do too much at once. Once you figure out what should go in one blank, use POE *right away*. If you know one word in an answer choice is wrong, you know the entire answer choice is wrong. Don't even look at that answer choice when you come around to look at what should go in the second blank.

RELATIONSHIP BETWEEN THE BLANKS

There are a few two-blank questions where you won't know *exactly* what should go in the blanks. Why not? Because what you put in one blank has an effect on what you put in the other blank. On questions like these, determine the relationship between the blanks. For example, both blanks could contain positive words, or both blanks could hold negative words. It could go either way.

So what should you do? Go to each answer choice and look at the relationship between the two words. If you know the blanks could be both positive or both negative, then the right answer choice can never have one positive word along with one negative word. Similarly, if you know the relationship is such that one blank is positive and the other negative (or vice versa), the right answer choice can never have two positive words or two negative words. Let's take a look at the following example. What is the relationship between the two blanks?

> In spite of the numerous articles and books
> devoted to the works of William Shakespeare,
> there is no criticism so ------- that his plays and
> sonnets no longer ------- the academia of
> English literature.

Both blanks should have the same type of word—most likely, the words are both positive. So eliminate any answer choice that contains a positive word coupled with a negative word. Here are the answer choices:

> (A)   severe . . . interest
> (B)   exhaustive . . . engage
> (C)   demanding . . . engross
> (D)   comprehensive . . . effect
> (E)   astute . . . tax

You can eliminate (A), (C), and (E) because each contains one positive word and one negative word. At this point, if you're stuck, just guess. You have a 50 percent chance of getting the question right. The best answer turns out to be (B). Notice that the clue for the second blank is actually the word for the first blank. Anytime you come across a question where the clue for one blank is the other blank, focus on what the relationship between the two blanks is.

LAST RESORT

As a last resort—and we mean it when we say this is the *last* resort—pick the answer choice that contains the most difficult words. Why? Because chances are, if you're having a really hard time with a sentence completion, it's probably a hard question and hard questions tend to have hard answers. For example, let's say that you come across a question and that you're able to get it down to two answer choices.

    (A) exculpate . . . chary
    (B) vindicate . . . puzzled

If, after checking the clue and triggers one more time, you have no idea which one is better, then pick the one with the hardest (or the weirdest) words. (A), in this case, should be your choice.

This isn't to say that the answer choice with the hardest word or words is always right. It's just a good guessing technique when you're absolutely stuck.

IN SUMMARY...

A sentence completion is hard only when you get distracted by the answer choices and forget about the sentence itself. Focus on the sentence—that's where the clue and triggers are.

1. Cover up the answer choices. Remember, it's the sentence that's important.

2. Come up with your own word for the blank. If you're having trouble coming up with your own word, look for the clue and triggers.

3. If you can't come up with your own word, use the clue and triggers to determine if what goes in the blank is positive or negative.

4. If it's a two-blank sentence completion, focus on one blank at a time.

5. If the clue for one blank is actually the other blank, determine what the relationship between the blanks is.

6. As a last resort, pick the answer choice that contains the hardest (or weirdest) words.

QUIZ #1: ANSWERS

1. outraged . . . offense

2. acclaim . . . deify

3. insight . . . shared

4. advent . . . defensible

5. moist . . . hardy

6. belied

7. exacerbate

QUIZ #2: ANSWERS

1. In the Bible, handwriting appeared on the wall at the feast of Belshazzar, a ------- of doom according to Daniel; that night, Babylon fell to Cypress.

   portent

2. Because the reclogging of an artery often occurs after balloon angioplasty, some physicians have turned to the use of such ------- techniques as laser angioplasty.
   alternative

3. Even though the evidence produced did not ------- his guilt, the jury still believed in his -------.

   prove . . . culpability

4. Jane's naiveté was often charming, but her ------- all too easily led her to be deceived and therefore -------.

   credulousness. . . duped

5. The jealousy of the goddess Hera has been ------- in Greek mythology: numerous stories tell of her ------- Zeus and his philandering.

   well documented . . . resentment toward

6. Early ethologists classified animal behavior as either ------- or learned; current ethologists, however, believe there is an ------- genetically determined and environmental responses.

   instinctual . . . interaction between

7. It remains a mystery as to how the ------- of the early universe evolved into its present day diversity.

   homogeneity

GRE VERBAL WORKOUT

QUIZ #3: ANSWERS

1. (Though) Californians claim to be ------- to earthquakes, the smallest of tremors are ------- to most people.

+. .−

inured. .disconcerting

2. Even when injured, Steffi Graf has always been a ------- opponent; indeed, a problematic back and foot did not ------- her from winning several championships during the 1996 season.

+. . −

formidable . . . keep

3. The nouveau riche often strive for the same social standing as the established wealthy, (but) they usually find themselves left with only the ------- of affluence.

−

trappings

4. Joseph's ------- was misleading: his appearance suggested innocence and artlessness, (but) he was, in fact, quite -------.

neither + or −. . −

mien. .cunning

5. (Though) it is important to stand by one's beliefs, it is also important not to cling ------- to them.

−

dogmatically

6. It is not necessary for a scientific theory to be proved in order to be -------; (rather) it need only be ------- the best explanation offered for a phenomenon at the time.

+. .+

adopted . . . plausible

7. A pioneer in modern population study, Thomas Malthus was the first to suggest that ------- (and) distress are ------- because population increases more quickly than the means of subsistence.

−. . −

privation . . . ineluctable

PROBLEM SET #1

Directions: Each sentence below has one or two blanks, each blank indicating that something has been omitted. Beneath the sentence are five lettered words or sets or words. Choose the word or set of words for each blank that **best** fits the meaning of the sentence as a whole.

1. In science, ------- is only conjecture until it is proven or disproved by ------- experimentation.

   (A) a hypothesis . . . rigorous
   (B) a prediction . . . controversial
   (C) an abstraction . . . cursory
   (D) a theory . . . public
   (E) a deliberation . . . thorough

2. An experienced film critic is one who not only calls attention to the ------- of a particular feature, but also puts forth legitimate ------- that, if employed, would create a more satisfying product.

   (A) interpretations . . . observations
   (B) construction . . . synopses
   (C) allusions . . . complaints
   (D) inadequacies . . . recommendations
   (E) influences . . . modifications

3. Louis was so painfully shy that his friends had to cajole him not to ------- even the smallest social gathering.

   (A) confront
   (B) subdue
   (C) flout
   (D) shun
   (E) attend

4. The salmon was prepared with such care that even those who did not have ------- sea food found the meal to be delicious.

   (A) a contention with
   (B) an assurance of
   (C) a penchant for
   (D) a preconception of
   (E) an endorsement of

5. The movement in literature known as realism was so labeled because of its attempt to describe life without idealization or romantic subjectivity; similarly, the realist movement in art had as its intent the ------- of natural forms without -------.

   (A) portrayal . . . adulation
   (B) subjection . . . sentimentality
   (C) depiction . . . vulgarity
   (D) abstraction . . . refinement
   (E) rendering . . . embellishment

6. The field of science known as nonlinear dynamics may appear, at first, to be paradoxical: it attempts to reveal ------- in systems that are seemingly random and therefore -------.

   (A) imperfection . . . chaotic
   (B) structure . . . unpredictable
   (C) unity . . . unfathomable
   (D) definition . . . frenetic
   (E) organization . . . inimitable

7. It would be both unwise and unfair to criticize bell hooks's writings on the intersection of race and gender as either obscure or -------; though she often does discuss abstract ideas, in no way does she express them in ------- fashion.

   (A) contemplative . . . a practical
   (B) incomprehensible . . . a seminal
   (C) harried . . . an ingenuous
   (D) opprobrious . . . a theoretical
   (E) inaccessible . . . an abstruse

PROBLEM SET #2

Directions: Each sentence below has one or two blanks, each blank indicating that something has been omitted. Beneath the sentence are five lettered words or sets or words. Choose the word or set of words for each blank that best fits the meaning of the sentence as a whole.

1. In conducting field research, one must observe every detail, no matter how small, for it is often the seemingly unimportant that actually leads to scientific -------.

   (A) recessions
   (B) obstructions
   (C) incapacities
   (D) breakthroughs
   (E) dissolutions

2. Isaac Asimov's Foundation trilogy explores the idea of psychohistory, a science that disregards the ------- and focuses instead on the tendencies of masses to act in particular ways.

   (A) nonconformist
   (B) individual
   (C) revolutionary
   (D) trifling
   (E) legislator

3. Whereas the flexing of a muscle is viewed as a motion that requires ------- effort, breathing is considered an involuntary act.

   (A) careful
   (B) conscious
   (C) minimal
   (D) thoughtful
   (E) intensive

4. Thompson ------- the integrity of his paper by failing to cite the authors whose ideas he employed to reach his conclusions, thus making charges of ------- possible.

   (A) enhanced . . . imposture
   (B) debased . . . recidivism
   (C) moderated . . . audacity
   (D) compromised . . . plagiarism
   (E) expunged . . . deception

5. Although the formation of a union was not ------- by the management of the company, it was ------- that any effort on the part of employees to unionize would not be welcomed.

   (A) prevented . . . imperceptible
   (B) facilitated . . . infamous
   (C) barred . . . implicit
   (D) sundered . . . manifest
   (E) commandeered . . . calculated

6. The issue of capital punishment draws a highly charged response, each side refusing to see the merits of the other's position, unwilling to ------- or engage in ------- of any kind.

   (A) evaluate . . . imputations
   (B) demur . . . conversation
   (C) compromise . . . reprisals
   (D) advance . . . formulations
   (E) yield . . . discourse

7. Christopher Columbus Langdell was ------- in legal studies: as dean of Harvard's law school, he ------- the approach to law, introducing the case method to the curriculum and instituting the Socratic method in the classroom.

   (A) an innovator . . . extirpated
   (B) a patriarch . . . simplified
   (C) a pundit . . . facilitated
   (D) a pedagogue . . . invigorated
   (E) a pioneer . . . reconstructed

PROBLEM SET #3

1. It is ------- to argue that, because a superconductor permits a current to flow more easily, ------- electrical resistance, scientists should devote more time and effort to its study.

   (A) faulty . . . connected to
   (B) reasonable . . . unchecked by
   (C) singular . . . common to
   (D) hasty . . . hampered by
   (E) interesting . . . resigned to

2. Unless David decides to ------- himself from the rest of humanity and live as a hermit, he must learn how to compromise and -------.

   (A) distance . . . suppress
   (B) delude . . . initiate
   (C) seclude . . . cooperate
   (D) conceal . . . command
   (E) protect . . . collaborate

3. May's tendency to worry excessively over even the ------- of problems so confused her colleagues that they never knew whether her so-called plights were of a calamitous or a ------- nature.

   (A) slightest . . . trifling
   (B) most trivial . . . hapless
   (C) most relevant . . . deplorable
   (D) most unfeasible . . . grievous
   (E) profanest . . . inconsequential

4. Although Jonathan himself admitted that he had yet to master the piano, his ------- could not be doubted with the ------- with which he performed the concerto.

   (A) rectitude . . . ardor
   (B) competence . . . ineptitude
   (C) ungainliness . . . expression
   (D) proficiency . . . facility
   (E) virtuosity . . . simplicity

5. Although she conveyed the message calmly and without to-do, Lin's expression betrayed the message's ------- nature.

   (A) facetious
   (B) impartial
   (C) puerile
   (D) uncommunicative
   (E) dire

6. Shi-yu's art is to be admired not for its realism, but rather for its distortion of reality: he creates ------- of the world, exaggerating not only its beauty but also its meanness and pettiness.

   (A) a mockery
   (B) a personification
   (C) a caricature
   (D) a sublimation
   (E) an allegory

7. Though law is often perceived to be -------, it is not, in fact, expressive of objective truths: law is a contract created by society to regulate the interactions among its members, and as such, law is -------.

   (A) even-handed . . . a statute
   (B) expedient . . . an invention
   (C) universal . . . a construct
   (D) politic . . . an execution
   (E) logical . . . ratiocination

PROBLEM SET #4

1. It is common practice for a scientific journal to have several experts ------- an article's findings before publication in order to discourage scientists from reporting ------- assertions.

   (A) revise . . . conceptual
   (B) critique . . . unsubstantiated
   (C) expand . . . . false
   (D) verify . . . extreme
   (E) employ . . . unwarranted

2. Some scientists believe that certain human beings may be more ------- than others because the former possess a gene that predisposes them toward aggressive behavior.

   (A) reserved
   (B) timorous
   (C) self-possessed
   (D) uncouth
   (E) quarrelsome

3. During her lectures, Professor Hsing speaks as eloquently and effectively as she writes, thus earning from her students the moniker "queen of -------."

   (A) debate
   (B) logic
   (C) metaphor
   (D) bombast
   (E) rhetoric

4. Political parties must find a way to deal with the ------- a structure that permits no ------- and one that is inclusive, allowing for different mind-sets and appreciative of diversity.

   (A) appeal of . . . submission
   (B) hostility to . . . might
   (C) deliberation between . . . neutrality
   (D) inconsistency between . . . dissent
   (E) discreteness of . . . tradition

5. Professor Xavier was so well known for his radical experimentation with form and language, that his devotees responded to his most recent short story, characterized by a linear plot and traditional characters, with -------.

   (A) stupefaction
   (B) abashment
   (C) diffidence
   (D) aplomb
   (E) criticism

6. The class was purportedly an exhaustive study of Jane Austen's works, yet since it failed to include either *Emma* or *Pride and Prejudice* in its analysis, it was, by no means, -------.

   (A) prudent
   (B) acceptable
   (C) comprehensive
   (D) adequate
   (E) authoritative

7. After ------- for months without resolution, the parties agreed to defer to -------, a third party to evaluate each side and then settle the dispute.

   (A) engaging . . . a magistrate
   (B) recessing . . . an adjudicator
   (C) wrangling . . . an arbiter
   (D) feuding . . . a diplomat
   (E) haggling . . . a reprobate

4

PROBLEM SET #5

1. Some historians have portrayed the reformers of the Progressive era as people ------- seeking to improve the lives of the lower class; other historians, however, have interpreted the reformers' efforts at betterment as an attempt to control and -------.

   (A) intentionally . . . convert
   (B) consciously . . . amend
   (C) earnestly . . . confirm
   (D) surreptitiously . . . civilize
   (E) honestly . . . constrain

2. Although honesty is a trait to be valued, it is not always appropriate because when one is too forthright, one can often be -------.

   (A) objective
   (B) equitable
   (C) deluded
   (D) tactless
   (E) corrupt

3. Newspapers often lose money when their customers, who purchase two or three papers, discover articles being -------, and, not wanting to purchase the same item twice, ------- the number of papers to which they subscribe.

   (A) reproduced . . . reduce
   (B) repeated . . . appraise
   (C) censored . . . cut back on
   (D) abridged . . . settle on
   (E) copied . . . augment

4. Sexual harassment lawsuits often question whether the defendant ------- acted to discriminate against the plaintiff; however, this line of reasoning fails to ------- the fact that one can cause offense without having intended it.

   (A) rationally . . . challenge
   (B) precisely . . . discuss
   (C) conscientiously . . . uphold
   (D) hesitantly . . . disregard
   (E) purposefully . . . address

5. The scientific interest with which impressionist artists studied nature proved to be limiting; however, their movement produced an aesthetic revolution, successfully ------- the academic standards of the time.

   (A) promulgating
   (B) eschewing — *evitar, esquivar*
   (C) repudiating
   (D) objectifying
   (E) plundering

6. Unfortunately, Jeannie's shy demeanor was often misinterpreted by those who did not know her: indeed, strangers typically construed her ------- behavior as coyness.

   (A) unresponsive
   (B) supercilious
   (C) amenable
   (D) acquiescent
   (E) demure

7. The Reformation was, in large part,
responsible for the ------- of life, because it
rejected the hold of the church on society
and ------- instead the import of personal
responsibility and individual freedom.

   (A) sublimation . . . emphasized
   (B) appreciation . . . highlighted
   (C) revitalization . . . imbued
   (D) abnegation . . . imparted
   (E) secularization . . . cited

Problem Set #1: Explanations

1. *A* For a two-blank sentence completion, focus on one blank at a time. Start with the first blank since it has an easier clue. The clue for this blank is "only conjecture." If something is "only conjecture," then a good word for the blank is *guess*. *Hypothesis* in (A) and *prediction* in (B) could both mean *guess*, so leave them in. However, *abstraction* in (C) doesn't match *guess*, nor does *theory* in (D) or *deliberation* in (E). So cross them out.

    Now move on to the second blank. The clue for this blank is "until it is proven or disproved by." If a *guess* is to be "proven or disproved," then it has to be subject to a lot of experimentation. So a good word for the blank is *a lot of*. Since (C), (D), and (E) have already been eliminated, don't look at them a second time. Focus on (A) and (B). *Rigorous* in (A) could mean *a lot*. *Controversial* in (B) isn't a good match for *a lot*. Therefore, the best answer is (A).

2. *D* For a two-blank sentence completion, focus on one blank at a time. Start with the second blank because it has an easier clue. The clues for this blank are "legitimate" and "if employed, would create a more satisfying product." If the critic puts forth something legitimate that would improve the product, then she is making a *suggestion*. *Observations* in (A) and *synopses* in (B) don't mean *suggestion*, so cross them out. *Complaints* in (C) doesn't work either, so eliminate it. *Recommendations* in (D) and *modifications* in (E) could both mean *suggestion*, so leave them in.

    Now move on to the first blank. The clue for this blank is "not only calls attention . . . but also puts forth legitimate." Therefore, what goes in the first blank should be along the lines of *problems*—the critic is pointing out flaws *and* suggesting ways to make the film better. (Note the same-direction trigger "not only ... but also.") *Inadequacies* in (D) is a good match for *problems*; *influences* in (E) isn't. Therefore, the best answer is (D).

3. *D* The clue for this blank is very straightforward: "so painfully shy." If Louis is "painfully shy," is he going to want to attend social gatherings? Probably not. Therefore, what goes in the blank is a negative word—probably something like *avoid*. (A) and (B) are both negative, but they don't mean *avoid*, so eliminate them.

Don't cross out (C) if you don't know what *flout* means. (D) looks good, but don't forget to check out (E) just in case. *Attend* in (E) clearly doesn't work, so it's gone. You're left with a word you don't know in (C) and a word that works in (D). Go with what works. The best answer is (D).

4. **C** A good word for the blank is *a liking of* because of the clue "the salmon was prepared with such care that even those . . . found the meal to be delicious." Don't cross out (A) if you don't know what *contention* means. (B) doesn't really match *liking*, so cross it out. (C) does mean *liking*, so leave it in. (D) definitely doesn't match *liking*, so cross it out. (E) doesn't match *liking* quite as well as (C). You're left with (A) and (C). Go with what you know. The best answer is (C).

5. **E** For a two-blank sentence completion, focus on one blank at a time. Start with the second blank because the clue is easier to work with. The clue for this blank is "without idealization or romantic subjectivity." The triggers are the semicolon and "similarly." If you know that the realist movement in art was similar to the realist movement in literature, then a good word for the blank is *idealization*. *Adulation* in (A) isn't quite what you're looking for, so cross it out. *Sentimentality* in (B) could work, so leave it in. *Vulgarity* in (C) definitely doesn't work, so eliminate it. Both *refinement* in (D) and *embellishment* in (E) are okay, so leave them in.

Move on to the first blank. The clue for this blank is "the attempt to describe life." The triggers are, once again, the semicolon and "similarly." Again, because the movements are similar, a good word for the blank is *describing*. The only answer choices remaining are (B), (D), and (E). *Subjection* in (B) doesn't match *describing*, nor does *abstraction* in (D). Since (E) is the only answer choice left, it's got to be right. *Rendering* does match *describing*, so the best answer is (E).

6. **B** Start with the second blank because it's easier. The clue for the second blank is "seemingly random." The trigger "and" tells you that what goes in the second blank has to continue the direction of "seemingly random." Therefore, a good word for the blank is *random*. *Chaotic* in (A) could mean *random*, as could *unpredictable* in (B), so leave them in. *Unfathomable* in (C) isn't quite what

you're looking for, so cross it out. *Frenetic* in (D) could mean *random*, so keep it. If you don't know what *inimitable* in (E) means, you can't eliminate it.

Move on to the first blank. The clue for this blank is "paradoxical." If you know that nonlinear dynamics is paradoxical, then what goes in the blank has to be the opposite of "random." A good word might be *order*. *Imperfection* in (A) doesn't mean *order*, so cross it out. *Structure* in (B) could work, so leave it in. *Definition* in (D) isn't quite right, so cross it out. *Organization* in (E) could work, so keep it. You're down to (B) and (E). As always, go with what works. The best answer is (B).

7. **E** For a two-blank sentence completion, focus on one blank at a time. Start with the first blank because it's got a very strong clue. The clue for this blank is "obscure." Just repeat the clue as a good word for the blank—her writings shouldn't be criticized as "either obscure or" *obscure*. *Contemplative* in (A) doesn't match *obscure*, so cross it out. *Incomprehensible* in (B) could work, so leave it in. *Harried* in (C) doesn't work, so eliminate it. Don't cross out (D) if you don't know what *opprobrious* means. *Remote* in (E) is a pretty good match, so leave it in. You're down to (B), (D), and (E).

Move on to the second blank. The clue for this blank is the same as the clue for the first blank: "obscure." There is another clue as well: "she often does discuss abstract ideas." Therefore, what goes in the second blank is something like *obscure* and *abstract*. If you don't know what *seminal* means, you can't cross out (B). *Theoretical* in (D) matches *abstract*, but it's not really negative—which is what you want in the blank because of *obscure*. Cross it out. Don't cross out (E) if you don't know what *abstruse* means.

You're left with (B) and (E). What should you do now? You could go with the hardest word or words, but *seminal* and *abstruse* are both pretty tough. At this point, just guess. You've got a 50 percent chance of getting the question right. As it turns out, the best answer is (E). *Seminal* means creative or original; *abstruse* means difficult to comprehend.

Problem Set #2: Explanations

1. *D* Coming up with your own word should be fairly easy for this sentence completion because the clue is very direct. The clue is "the seemingly unimportant." Well, if the detail only seems unimportant, what is it actually? Very important. Therefore, a good word for the blank might be *wonders*. Does (A) match? No. (B) and (C) definitely don't match. (D) looks good—it's a very positive word—but don't forget about (E). (E) doesn't make any sense, so the best answer is (D).

2. *B* For this sentence completion, it's pretty easy to come up with your own word. The clue is "focuses instead on the tendency of the masses." If psychohistory is focusing on the masses, then what is it probably ignoring? The individual. A good word for the blank, then, is *individual*. (A) doesn't give you the sense of *individual*, so eliminate it. (B) is a perfect match, so definitely leave it in. (C) could look attractive only if you're moving too fast. If you remember the clue, you should know (C) can't be right. (D) isn't a good match, nor is (E). Therefore, the best answer is (B). (Keep in mind that even though (B) was a perfect match for your own word, you should still examine each and every answer choice.)

3. *B* It may be hard to come up with your own word at first, but if you find the clue, it shouldn't be a problem. The clue is "an involuntary act." There's also the changing-direction trigger "whereas." Together, the clue and trigger tell you that what goes in the blank is the opposite of "involuntary." So a good word for the blank is *voluntary*. (A) doesn't give you *voluntary*, so cross it out. (B) could mean *voluntary*, so leave it in. (C) doesn't match, and (D) isn't quite as good as (B)—eliminate both. Finally, (E) is no good. The best answer, then, is (B). This is a great example of why you should never plug and chug. If you go the route of plugging and chugging, guess what? Every answer choice *sounds* as if it could work.

4. *D* For a two-blank sentence completion, focus on one blank at a time. Start with the second blank because it's got a more direct clue. The clue for this blank is "failing to cite the authors whose ideas he employed." If Thompson did this, then he was basically stealing, right? A good word for the blank, then, is *stealing*. Is

imposture in (A) along the lines of *stealing*? Sort of. Leave (A) in for now. What about *recidivism* in (B)? You can't cross out (B) if you don't know what *recidivism* means. *Audacity* in (C) doesn't work, so eliminate it. *Plagiarism* in (D) looks good, so leave it in. *Deception* in (E) also looks good, so leave it in, too. You're down to (A), (B), (D), and (E).

Move on to the second blank. The clue for this blank is the same as the clue for the first blank: "failing to cite the authors whose ideas he employed." If Thompson did this, then what did he do to the integrity of his paper? He hurt it. A good word for the blank, then, is *hurt*. *Enhanced* in (A) doesn't work, so cross it out. *Debased* in (B) could work, so leave it in. *Compromised* in (D) looks okay, so leave it in. If you don't know what *expunged* in (E) means, you have to leave it in.

(B), (D), and (E) are the remaining choices. You have one answer choice that works and two that contain words you don't know. Go with what works. The best answer is (D).

5. **C** This sentence completion is a little tricky, but as long as you work methodically, you should be okay. Start off with the first blank. The clue for this blank is "any effort . . . to unionize would not be welcomed." There is also the changing-direction trigger "Although." What do you know about the management of the company, then? That even though it wouldn't welcome unionization, it wouldn't ban employees from forming one. A good word for the blank is *ban*. *Prevented* in (A) looks good, so leave it in. *Facilitated* in (B) only looks good if you didn't find the right clue. It doesn't match *ban*, so cross (B) out. *Barred* in (C) could work, so leave it in. If you don't know what *sundered* means, you can't eliminate (D). *Commandeered* in (E) definitely doesn't work, so cross it out. You're down to (A), (C), and (D).

Move on to the second blank. The clue for this blank is the same as the clue for the first blank. Also, the clue for this blank is, in part, the first blank itself. Given the clue, a good word for the second blank might be *clear*. *Imperceptible* in (A) doesn't give you *clear*, so cross it out. *Implicit* in (C) is okay, so leave it in. *Manifest* in (D) is also okay, so leave it in.

Only (C) and (D) are left. Again, go with what you know when you're left with an answer choice that works and one that contains words you don't know. (C) works, so pick (C). It's the best answer.

6. **E** For a two-blank sentence completion, focus on one blank at a time. Start with the first blank because it's a little more manageable. The clue for this blank is "each side refusing to see the merits of the other's position." If each side is so stubborn that it can't acknowledge anything good about the other side, then you know that the word in the first blank has to be positive. *Evaluate* in (A) isn't positive or negative, so cross it out. Don't cross out (B) if you don't know what *demur* means. *Compromise* in (C) and *advance* in (D) are both positive, so leave them in. *Yield* in (E) can be positive, so it's okay. You're down to (B), (C), (D), and (E).

   Move on to the second blank. The clue for this blank is also "each side refusing to see the merits of the other's position." Because of the clue, you can tell that the word in the second blank is also positive. *Conversation* in (B) is slightly positive, so leave it in. *Reprisals* in (C) is negative, so cross it out. *Formulations* in (D) isn't really positive or negative, so eliminate it. *Discourse* in (E) is slightly positive, so leave it in.

   (B) and (E) are the remaining answer choices. (B) contains a word you don't know; (E) works. Go with what works. The best answer is (E).

7. **E** For this sentence completion, the clue for the second blank is the other blank. This tells you that there is a relationship between the blanks. Are the words in the blanks going to be similar or dissimilar? Similar, in this case. So the correct answer choice has to have words that are similar to each other.

   You may not know what *extirpated* in (A) means exactly, but you probably know that it's a negative word. That means (A) contains dissimilar words. Cross it out. (B) has words that aren't really similar. Eliminate it. (C) has similar words, so you can leave it in. (D) has similar words, so leave it in, too. (E) also has similar words, so leave it in.

   You're down to (C), (D), and (E). What now? Take a look at the second blank. There's an additional clue for it: "introducing the case method . . . and instituting the Socratic method." A good word for the blank, then, is *changed*. Does *facilitated* in (C) mean *changed*? No. Does *invigorated* in (D)? No. Does *reconstructed* in (E)? Yes. Therefore, the best answer is (E).

Problem Set #3: Explanations

1. *B* For a two-blank sentence completion, focus on one blank at a time. Start with the second blank first because it's a little easier. The clue for this blank is "permits a current to flow more easily." If a superconductor makes it easier for the current to flow, what does it do to the resistance? It probably lessens the resistance. So a good word for the blank is *lessening*. Does *connected to* in (A) mean *lessening*? No. Eliminate (A). What about *unchecked by* in (B)? It could work. *Common to* in (C)? No. *Hampered by* in (D)? No. *Resigned to* in (E)? Definitely not. Therefore, the best answer is (B).

2. *C* For a two-blank sentence completion, focus on one blank at a time. Start with the first blank because it's easier. The clue for this blank is "live as a hermit." If David is going to "live as a hermit," then he's going to isolate himself from humanity. A good word for the blank, then, is *isolate*. Does *distance* in (A) match *isolate*? Sure. What about *delude* in (B)? No. *Seclude* in (C) works, as does *conceal* in (D). *Protect* in (E) doesn't quite work, so cross it out.

    The remaining answer choices are (A), (C), and (D). Move on to the next blank. The clue for this blank is "compromise." There is also the same-direction trigger "and." "And" tells you that what goes in the blank is similar to "compromise." For the purpose of convenience, just repeat the clue as the word for the blank: David has to compromise and *compromise*. Does *suppress* in (A) match *compromise*? No. *Cooperate* in (C) looks okay. *Command* in (D) doesn't work, so the best answer is (C).

3. *A* It's a two-blank sentence completion, so focus on one blank at a time. Start with the second blank since it's more direct. The clue for this blank is "so confused her colleagues that they never knew whether her so-called plights were of a calamitous." From the clue, you know that May's colleagues are confused. If they're confused, they don't know if one of her problems is "calamitous" or unimportant. A good word for the blank, then, is *unimportant*. Does *trifling* in (A) mean *unimportant*? Yes. What about *hapless* in (B)? No. *Deplorable* in (C) doesn't work, nor does *grievous* in (D). *Inconsequential* in (E) is a good match.

    You're left with (A) and (E). Move on to the first blank. The clue for this blank is "worry excessively over even" and "so-called plights." If something isn't a plight, then it's something unimportant. So a good word for the blank is *least important*. Does *slightest* in (A) work? Yes. What about *profanest* in (E)? No. The best answer, then, is (A).

4. **D** For this two-blank sentence completion, focus on the first blank first—it's a little easier to work with. The clue for the first blank is "he had yet to master." There is also the changing-direction trigger "Although." From the clue and trigger you know that Jonathan isn't a master but . . . But what? But he's still pretty good. Therefore, what goes in the first blank has to be a positive word—something like *talent*. *Rectitude* in (A) doesn't match *talent*, so eliminate it. *Competence* in (B) is okay. *Ungainliness* in (C) definitely doesn't work, but *proficiency* in (D) could. *Virtuosity* is a positive word, but it's too positive—it implies that David is a master. So get rid of (E).

You're left with (B) and (D). Go on to the second blank. The clue for this blank is really the first blank. You know Jonathan has *talent*, so he played the concerto well. A good word for the blank, then, is *talent*. *Ineptitude* in (B) doesn't match *talent*, but (D) could. The best answer, then, is (D).

5. **E** The clue for the blank is "conveyed the message calmly and without to-do." There is also the changing-direction trigger "although." Together the clue and trigger tell you that what goes in the blank is the opposite of calmness. A good word for the blank might be *serious*. (A) doesn't match, nor does (B). (C) you can't cross out if you don't know what *puerile* means. (D) doesn't work, but (E) does.

You're down to (C) and (E). When one answer choice has a word you don't know and the other works, go with what works. Pick (E). The best answer is, indeed, (E).

6. **C** The clue for this blank is really everything before the colon—which, don't forget, is a same-direction trigger. That means what goes in the blank should agree with "not for its realism, but rather for its distortion of reality." A good word for the blank, then, is *distortion*. Does (A) match *distortion*? No. What about (B)? No. (C) works, but (D) and (E) don't. The best answer is (C).

This question is a great example of why *not* to rush. If you don't stop to find the clue, then (A) becomes an attractive answer choice.

7. **C** For this two-blank sentence completion, focus on the first blank first—it's easier to deal with. The clue for this blank is "expressive of objective truths." If law has a claim to "objective truths," then a good word for the blank is *objective*. *Evenhanded* in (A) could mean *objective*. *Expedient* in (B) doesn't work. *Universal* in (C) is okay, but *politic* in (D) isn't. Finally, *logical* in (E) isn't a good match.

You're left with (A) and (C). Look at the second blank. The clue for this blank is "created by society." There is also a trigger, the colon, which keeps the sentence moving in the same direction. If law is a creation, then a good word for the blank is *creation*. Does *statute* in (A) mean *creation*? No. Does *construct* in (C)? Yes. The best answer is (C).

Problem Set #4: Explanations

1. **B** For two-blank sentence completions, focus on one blank at a time. Start with the second blank because it's a little easier. The clue for this blank is "to discourage scientists." Therefore, what goes in the second blank is something like *false*. *Conceptual* in (A) doesn't mean *false*, so eliminate it. *Unsubstantiated* in (B) is okay, so keep it. *False* in (C) is a perfect match, but you should still look at (D) and (E). *Extreme* in (D) isn't quite right, but *unwarranted* in (E) works.

You're left with (B), (C), and (E). Move on to the first blank. The clue for this blank is "several experts." The experts are somehow discouraging scientists from making false assertions, so the experts must be reviewing the articles. A good word for the blank, then, is *review*. *Critique* in (B) works, so leave it in. *Expand* in (C) doesn't, nor does *employ* in (E). The best answer is (B).

2. **E** The clue for the blank is "predisposes them toward aggressive behavior." Since some people have a gene that makes them aggressive, a good word for the blank is *aggressive*. (A) doesn't match *aggressive*, so cross it out. If you don't know what *timorous* means, you have to leave (B) in. (C) isn't a good match, nor is (D). (E), however, works.

You're down to (B) and (E). When you're left with one answer choice that contains a word you don't know and one that works, go with what works. (E) is the best answer.

3. **E** The clue for the blank is "speaks as eloquently and effectively as she writes." Just repeat the clue for the word in the blank. Professor Hsing is a queen of *eloquence*. Does (A) match *eloquence*? No. (B) and (C) don't work either. If you don't know what *bombast* means, then you can't eliminate (D). Finally, (E) works.

You're down to an answer choice that contains a word you don't know and one that works. Go with what works. The best answer is (E).

4. **D** For a two-blank sentence completion, focus on one blank at a time. Start with the first blank because it's easier. The clue for the first blank is "find a way to deal with." If political parties have to "find a way to deal with," then you can expect the word in the blank to be negative. *Appeal of* in (A) is positive, so eliminate it. *Hostility to* in (B) is negative, so it's okay. *Deliberation between* in (C) is either slightly positive or neither positive nor negative—either way, it needs to go. *Inconsistency between* in (D) is negative, as is *discreteness of* in (E), so leave them in.

You're left with (B), (D), and (E). Go on to the second blank. What goes in this blank largely depends on what belongs in the first blank. In (B), the word for the first blank is *hostility*. This suggests that what goes in the second blank should be something like *arguing*—one structure doesn't allow for *arguing* and the other structure, because it is "inclusive," does. *Might* in (B) doesn't mean *arguing*, so get rid of it. In (D), the word for the first blank is *inconsistency between*. This also suggests that what goes in the second blank should be something like *arguing*. *Dissent* in (B) could mean *arguing*, so leave it in. In (E), the word for the first blank is *discreteness*. As with (B) and (D), this suggests *arguing* should go in the second blank. Does *tradition* in (E) mean *arguing*? No. Therefore, the best answer is (D).

5. **A** The clue for this blank is "so well known for his radical experimentation." If Professor Xavier is typically radical, how would his fans react to something conventional? With surprise, naturally. A good word for the blank is *surprise*. Does (A) match? If you don't know what *stupefaction* means, you can't cross it out. Does (B) match? No—*abashment* means embarrassment. Does (C) match? No—*diffidence* means shyness. What about (D)? If you don't know what *aplomb* means, then you can't eliminate it. What

about (E)? No—be careful. Don't jump to any conclusions. The clue doesn't suggest anything about his fans being unhappy.

So you're down to (A) and (D), each of which contains a word you don't know. At this point, just guess. You have a 50 percent chance of getting the question right. As a last resort technique, pick the one with the hardest word. That would probably be (A), and (A) is indeed the best answer. *Stupefaction* is just another form of the word *stupefied*.

6. **C** This sentence completion is actually very easy as long as you take the time to find the clue. The clue for the blank is "purportedly an exhaustive study." The class was supposedly "exhaustive" but if it didn't talk about two of her major books, then what was it? Not exhaustive. Therefore, a good word for the blank is *exhaustive*. (Take note of the two triggers: "yet" and "since.")

Does (A) mean *exhaustive*? No. What about (B)? Not quite. (C)? It could. (D)? No—be careful. The clue doesn't mention anything about the class being bad—just not complete. And finally, what about (E)? It's not a good match. The best answer, then, is (C).

7. **C** For two-blank sentence completions, focus on one blank at a time. The second blank has a better clue, so start there first. The clue for the blank is "a third party to evaluate each side." A good word for the blank then is something like *mediator*. Does *magistrate* in (A) match *mediator*? No—a *magistrate* is just an official with authority of some sort. *Adjudicator* in (B) looks good, so leave it in. If you don't know what *arbiter* in (C) means, you have to leave it in. *Diplomat* in (D) isn't quite the right fit, so eliminate it. And finally (E)—you can't cross it out if you don't know what *reprobate* means.

The remaining answer choices are (B), (C), and (E). The clue for this blank is "settle the dispute." You know the parties were fighting; therefore, a good word for the blank is *fighting*. *Recessing* in (B) doesn't match, so throw it out. *Wrangling* in (C) could work, so leave it in. *Haggling* in (E) could also work, so keep it.

You're left with (C) and (E), each of which contains a word you don't know. If you really don't know anything about either *arbiter* or *reprobate*, just pick one and go. You have a 50 percent chance of getting the question right. However, if you know that *reprobate* is a negative word, then you know (E) can't be right. (C) is the best answer.

Problem Set #5: Explanations

1. *E* For two-blank sentence completions, focus on one blank at a time. Start with the second blank because it has an easier clue. The clue for this blank is "attempt to control." There is also the same-direction trigger "and." Together, the clue and trigger tell you that what goes in the blank is something similar to control. So just repeat the clue in the blank—a good word for the blank is *control. Convert* in (A) doesn't match *control*, so eliminate it. *Amend* in (B) doesn't match, so cross it out, too. *Confirm* in (C) doesn't work, nor does *civilize* in (D), so eliminate both. *Constrain* in (E) is the only answer choice that remains, and it's the only answer choice that works. Don't even worry about what should go in the first blank. The best answer has to be (E).

2. *D* The clue for this blank is "too forthright." One is "too forthright" when one takes honesty too far. Therefore, what goes in the blank has to be a negative word. (A) is either slightly positive or neither positive nor negative. In either case, throw it out. (B) is positive, so it can't be right. (C) is negative but it doesn't have anything to do with being honest or forthright. (D) is negative and certainly could explain what happens when one is "too forthright." (E) is negative, but it goes too far. (D) is the best answer.

3. *A* For two-blank sentence completions, focus on one blank at a time. Start with the second blank because it's a little easier to work with. The clue for this blank is "not wanting to purchase the same item twice." If customers don't want "to purchase the same item twice," then what would they do to the number of papers they subscribe? They would cut them down. So a good word for the blank is *cut down. Reduce* in (A) could mean *cut down*, so leave it in. *Appraise* in (B) doesn't match *cut down*, so eliminate it. *Cut back on* in (C) could work, so keep it. *Settle on* in (D) doesn't match, so cross it out. *Augment* in (E) is the opposite of what you're looking for, so eliminate it.

    You're left with (A) and (C). Go on to the first blank. The clue for this blank is also "not wanting to purchase the same item twice." If the customers don't want to buy the same item twice, then the item—the articles—are being repeated. A good word for the blank is *repeated. Reproduced* in (A) means *repeated*, so keep it. *Censored* in (C) doesn't match *repeated*, so it can't be right. The best answer is (A).

4. **E** For two-blank sentence completions, focus on one blank at a time. Start with the first blank since the clue is easier to work with. The clue for this blank is "one can cause offense without having intended it." So what goes in the blank might be a word like *intentionally*. *Rationally* in (A) doesn't work, so get rid of it. *Precisely* in (B) doesn't work either, so eliminate it. *Conscientiously* in (C) is a possible match, so leave it in. *Hesitantly* in (D) doesn't match, so eliminate it. *Purposefully* in (E) might work, so keep it.

    You're down to (C) and (E). Move on to the second blank. The clue for this blank is "fails to." If the line of reasoning fails, then it doesn't look at "the fact that one can cause offense without having intended it." So a good word for the blank is *look at*. *Uphold* in (C) doesn't work, so get rid of it. *Address* in (E) does work, so it has to be right. (E) is the best answer.

5. **C** The clue for this blank is "produced an aesthetic revolution." If the impressionist movement "produced an aesthetic revolution," then what did it do to "the academic standards of the time"? It went against them. So a good word for the blank is *went against*. If you don't know what *promulgating* means, then you can't get rid of (A). If you don't know what *eschewing* means, then you can't eliminate (B). (C) is a good match, so keep it. (D) isn't, so throw it out. (E) isn't quite right, so cross it out. You're left with (A), (B), and (C)—two contain words you don't know while the last one works. Go with what works. The best answer is (C).

6. **E** The clue for this blank is "shy demeanor was often misinterpreted." So what goes in the blank has to be something like *shyness*. (A) doesn't match, nor does (B), so cross them out. (C) doesn't work, so get rid of it, too. (D) isn't quite right, so eliminate it. (E) does work, so it has to be right. (E) is the best answer.

7. **E** For two-blank sentence completions, focus on one blank at a time. Start with the first blank because its clue is easier to work with. The clue for this blank is "rejected the hold of the church on society." If the church is less important, then life is more worldly. A good word for the blank, then, is *worldliness*. *Sublimation* in (A) doesn't work, so cross it out. *Appreciation* in (B) doesn't work either, so it's gone. *Revitalization* in (C) isn't quite right, so eliminate it. Don't eliminate (D) if you don't know what *abnegation* means. *Secularization* in (E) could work, so keep it.

You're down to (D) and (E). Take a look at the second blank. The clue for this blank is really "instead." Instead of having the church keep its hold on society, what did the Reformation do? It emphasized "the import of personal responsibility and individual freedom." A good word for the blank is *emphasized*. *Imparted* in (D) could work, as could *cited* in (E). So you're still left with (D) and (E). (D) contains a word you don't know, and (E) works. Go with what works. The best answer is (E).

CHAPTER

5

Analogies

THE GOAL: HOW TO RELATE

First things first: Here's what a typical analogy looks like

DEFILE : FILTHY ::

(A)   hasten : quick
(B)   detail : precise
(C)   level : flat
(D)   fume : angry
(E)   scrutinize : probing

The capitalized words are what we call the stem words. The answer choices are, of course, the answer choices.

Now that that's out of the way, what's the point of an analogy? It's to find the answer-choice words that have the same relationship as do the stem words. In short, the point of an analogy is to figure out how words relate to each other.

WHEN YOU KNOW THE STEM WORDS

We can divide analogies into two groups:

- Analogies where you know both of the stem words.

- Analogies where you don't know one or both of the stem words.

Let's start off with the first group: you know both of the stem words. If you know both of the stem words, make a sentence.

Now, "make a sentence" may sound easy, but don't get too confident yet. When we say "make a sentence," we mean make a sentence that defines one of the stem words in terms of the other. For example, let's think about what might be a good sentence for this stem pair:

KENNEL : DOG ::

What do you think of this sentence: When I go on vacation, a KENNEL is where I leave my DOG.

If you don't like this sentence, give yourself a pat on the back. This sentence does use both stem words, which is good, but it doesn't define one word in terms of the other, which is bad.

How about this sentence: a KENNEL is a house for a DOG.

Not bad, right? In fact, quite good. What's nice about this sentence is that it's concise and to the point. You don't want to write a novel when you make a sentence with a stem pair. Instead, "KISS."

Keep

It

Short and

Simple

Let's try to make a sentence with another stem pair:

PEBBLE : BOULDER ::

If you thought of something like "A PEBBLE is a little BOULDER," you're on the right track. Again, this sentence is good because it's short and simple. Now, you may be thinking, "But a PEBBLE isn't exactly a little BOULDER." True. However, the point of an analogy is to convey the relationship between the words. Does "little" get across the relationship between PEBBLE and BOULDER? Yes.

Apply Your Sentence

Once you've got a sentence for the stem pair, you want to apply that same sentence to each and every answer choice—then eliminate any that doesn't fit into your sentence. For example:

KENNEL : DOG ::

    (A)   pond : alga
    (B)   forest : mushroom
    (C)   branch : bird
    (D)   aquarium : fish
    (E)   field : sheep

The sentence we had for the stem words was: a KENNEL is a house for a DOG. To apply the sentence to the answer choices, just pretend there are blanks where the stem words are. In other words:

A _____ is a house for a _____.

(A) A *pond* is a house for an *alga*. Is that true? No.

(B) A *forest* is a house for a *mushroom*. Nope.

(C) A *branch* is a house for a *bird*. This definitely doesn't work.

(D) An *aquarium* is a house for a *fish*. Sure.

(E) A *field* is a house for a *sheep*. Not really.

The only answer choice that fit your sentence was (D). Therefore, (D) is the best answer. Pretty easy, right? Yes—as long as you can make a good sentence.

Note that we went through every single answer choice in the example above. That's what you should do for every analogy. Always check out (A) through (E), even if you've found the answer choice that you think is right. Remember, verbal is all about the *best* answer. You may think an answer choice is correct, but you may find an even better one further down.

MORE THAN ONE ANSWER CHOICE LEFT?

There may be times when you have a good sentence for the stem words and you apply your sentence to the answer choices, but guess what? You aren't able to eliminate all of the answer choices. If that's the case, then you need to make your sentence more specific. Take a look at the example below:

DISTANCE : KILOMETER ::

  (A) liquid : beaker
  (B) electricity : current
  (C) temperature : thermometer
  (D) length : perimeter
  (E) heat : calorie

A good sentence using the stem pair might be "A KILOMETER measures DISTANCE." Notice that we flipped the order of the stem words. Is that OK? Sure. Just remember to flip the order of the words in the answer choices, too. Try applying the sentence to the answer choices.

  (A) A *beaker* measures *liquid*. Maybe.

  (B) A *current* measures *electricity*. Nope—cross it out.

  (C) A *thermometer* measures *temperature*. Sure.

  (D) A *perimeter* measures *length*. Maybe.

  (E) A *calorie* measures *heat*. Yes.

With your sentence, you can only eliminate one answer choice. When you still have answer choices remaining after applying your sentence, you need to make your sentence more specific. How about "A KILOMETER is a unit that measures DISTANCE"?

(A)   A *beaker* is a unit that measures *liquid*. No.

(B)   Already eliminated.

(C)   A *thermometer* is a unit that measures *temperature*. No.

(D)   A *perimeter* is a unit that measures *length*. No.

(E)   A *calorie* is a unit that measures *heat*. Yes.

The best answer is (E).

QUIZ #1

On the following questions, make a sentence with each stem pair.

1. SHIRK : WORK ::

2. PENANCE : SORROW ::

3. SATIATE : SATISFY ::

4. TRICKLE : TORRENT ::

5. ELONGATE : LENGTH ::

6. AUTOMOBILE : GARAGE ::

7. IGNITE : FIRE ::

8. EXCESSIVE : MODERATION ::

9. INCONSPICUOUS : NOTICEABLE ::

10. MISER : FRUGAL ::

11. LURK : MOVEMENT ::

12. ANOMALY : NORM ::

13. MORTAL : DEATH ::

14. MUTE : SOUND ::

15. RÉSUMÉ : QUALIFICATION ::

16. SATIRE : SCORN ::

17. VORACIOUS : HUNGRY ::

18. DUBIOUS : CERTAINTY.

19. GUFFAW : LAUGH ::

20. SYLLABUS : COURSE ::

THE EVER-PREDICTABLE ETS

There isn't a lot of positive stuff we can say about ETS, but here's something that we do like. On analogies, ETS has certain relationships that it likes to use again and again and again. We like to say that ETS recycles relationships.

Below are ETS's top five recycled relationships. There's a good chance you may see some of them on the day of the GRE.

Type of

SOFA : FURNITURE ::
A SOFA is a type of FURNITURE.

POODLE : DOG ::
A POODLE is a type of DOG.

Function/Purpose

VEIL : COVER ::
The purpose of a VEIL is to COVER.

MEDAL : COMMEMORATE ::
The function of a MEDAL is to COMMEMORATE.

Degree

OBSEQUIOUS : ATTENTIVE ::
Someone OBSEQUIOUS is overly ATTENTIVE.

FOOLHARDY : BOLD
FOOLHARDY means very BOLD.

With/Has

ZEALOT : FERVOR ::
A ZEALOT is someone with FERVOR.

PERSPICACIOUS : INSIGHT ::
Someone PERSPICACIOUS has INSIGHT.

Without/Lacks

AMORPHOUS : SHAPE ::
Something AMORPHOUS lacks SHAPE.

FOOLPROOF : ERROR ::
Something FOOLPROOF is without ERROR.

Two notes: First, whenever you think two stem words are synonyms, it's likely that the words have a degree relationship. Second, whenever, you think two stem words are antonyms, it's likely that the words have a without/lacks relationship. It's very important that you *never* make a sentence using one word as the synonym or the antonym of the other. That type of sentence does not define one word in terms of the other.

QUIZ #2

On the following questions, make a sentence with the stem pair and then apply the sentence to the answer choices.

1. TRITE : ORIGINALITY ::

    (A) still : suppression
    (B) animated : interest
    (C) common : amazement
    (D) monotone : variation
    (E) notable : fame

2. WHISTLE : REFEREE ::

    (A) wood : lumberjack
    (B) needle : seamstress
    (C) gavel : judge
    (D) pulpit : preacher
    (E) stethoscope : physician

3. LUBRICATE : SLIPPERY ::

    (A) illuminate : radiant
    (B) humorous : funny
    (C) consecrate : sacred
    (D) desire : tempted
    (E) dilate : shut

4. BARTER : GOOD ::

    (A) conversation : idea
    (B) ration : provision
    (C) constitution : law
    (D) spoil : plunder
    (E) frugality : waste

5. HULL : COVERING ::

    (A) convention : discussion
    (B) spectacle : drama
    (C) freedom : liberty
    (D) compensation : payment
    (E) origin : beginning

6. ADROIT : SKILL ::

    (A) rueful : remorse
    (B) remarkable : memory
    (C) overstrung : temper
    (D) egotistical : impertinence
    (E) churlish : manners

7. IMPROVISED : REHEARSAL ::

    (A) lithe : inhibition
    (B) sloppy : care
    (C) preempted : appropriation
    (D) partial : favor
    (E) incurable : hope

8. INDECIPHERABLE : READ ::

    (A) unreal : envision
    (B) unstoppable : arrest
    (C) impolite : insult
    (D) untruthful : believe
    (E) incoherent : muddle

9. INTOXICANT : EXCITE ::

    (A) exercise : regroup
    (B) etiquette : behave
    (C) parody : ridicule
    (D) mirth : revel
    (E) contaminant : purify

WHEN YOU CAN'T MAKE A SENTENCE

So far, we've only looked at how to tackle analogies where you know both stem words. What about analogies where you know only one stem word? Or where you don't know either?

This is where a good vocabulary comes into play. The better your vocabulary, the more likely you are to know both stem words. And if you know both words in the stem, then you can make a sentence. In short, improve your vocabulary. It makes life on analogies much, much easier.

Still, there's no way you can learn every single word in the English language. The simple fact is that you're going to encounter words you don't know on the GRE. Luckily, we have a great technique to use on analogies when you don't know either one or both of the stem words.

When you don't know one or both of the stem words, you can't make a sentence, right? That much is clear. So what should you do? To answer this question, let's take a look at a stem pair that'll never show up on the real GRE:

DOG : COLD ::

Why won't this stem pair ever show up on the test? Well, let's think. We know both of the stem words, so let's try to make a sentence.

A DOG can be COLD.

A DOG can have a COLD nose.

Just about any DOG doesn't like the COLD.

Can you make a short and simple sentence that defines one word in terms of the other? No! Of course not. You can't because there is no relationship between the words.

Why did we show you this example, then? To point out to you that every single stem pair must have a relationship—what we call a "Clear and Necessary" relationship. By Clear and Necessary, we mean:

Clear   The words have a direct relationship.

Necessary   The words have a relationship that is always true.

Now, if the stem pair has a Clear and Necessary relationship, then the correct answer must also have a Clear and Necessary relationship. And, lucky for you, many of the wrong answer choices are wrong because they *don't* have Clear and Necessary relationships.

What does this mean to you? When you can't make a sentence, go to the answer choices and eliminate any that doesn't have a Clear and Necessary relationship.

PROVING CLEAR AND NECESSARY

How do you know whether an answer choice has a Clear and Necessary relationship? It's not too hard. All you have to do is make a sentence—a short, simple sentence that defines one word in terms of the other. Sound familiar? Let's try an example.

impartial : bias

Can you make a sentence with this answer choice pair? Sure. How about "Someone *impartial* lacks *bias*"? Therefore, this answer choice pair is Clear and Necessary. Try another one.

obvious : discover

Is this pair Clear and Necessary? If you can make a sentence, the answer is yes. What about "Something *obvious* is easy to *discover*?" Looks good. What about this one?

riot : illegal

Can you make a sentence that defines one word in terms of the other? No. Therefore, this pair is not Clear and Necessary. Here's another answer choice pair:

penchant : liking

Clear and Necessary? Yes. A good sentence that proves it: "*Penchant* means to have a strong *liking*." One more:

monitor: verify

Well? *Monitor* means to watch, and *verify* means to prove the truth of. You can't make a good sentence, so guess what? It's not Clear and Necessary.

Let's take a look at the following analogy. Eliminate those answer choice pairs that are not Clear and Necessary.

PRECIPITATE : HASTE ::

(A) meticulous : care
(B) sagacious : competence
(C) imminent : danger
(D) reticent : silence
(E) foreboding : quiet

Is answer choice (A) Clear and Necessary? Yes. A good sentence is: *meticulous* means marked by *care*. Therefore, leave (A) in.

Is answer choice (B) Clear and Necessary? No. *Sagacious* means discerning or wise—it has nothing to do with *competence*, so eliminate (B).

Is answer choice (C) Clear and Necessary? No. Don't work too quickly. *Imminent* means ready to take place. You've probably heard the phrase "*imminent* danger" before, but don't let this confuse you into thinking the words are related. Get rid of (C).

Is answer choice (D) Clear and Necessary? Sure. The sentence that proves it: *reticent* means inclined to *silence*. Leave (D) in.

Is answer choice (E) Clear and Necessary? No. *Foreboding* means ominous or menacing. Eliminate (E).

So, just by using Clear and Necessary, you can get the question down to two answer choices: (A) and (D). Not bad given that you don't even know what PRECIPITATE means. As it turns out, the best answer is (A). PRECIPITATE means marked by HASTE.

A ONE-WAY RELATIONSHIP (I.E., COVER IT UP)

If you're having trouble determining whether an answer choice pair is Clear and Necessary, here's a helpful tool. Let's say this is the answer choice pair you're looking at.

kennel : dog

Yes, we're using *kennel* and *dog* once again. Pretend that you don't know if this pair is Clear and Necessary. Cover up the word *dog*. If you look up *kennel* in the dictionary, is it going to mention *dog*? Yes. Therefore, you know the answer choice is Clear and Necessary.

Note that if you look up *dog* in the dictionary, you're not going to see *kennel*. Does that matter? No. To be Clear and Necessary, the relationship doesn't have to go both ways. A one-way relationship is perfectly fine. Let's try another one.

student : expel

If you look up *student* in the dictionary, would it say *expel*? Nope. But if you look up *expel*, is the dictionary going to say *student*? Yes—there's a pretty good chance. After all, *expel* means to kick out a *student*. Therefore, the answer choice pair is Clear and Necessary. Let's look at one more example.

strategic : analytical

It may be tempting to think the pair is related. But if you look up *strategic* in the dictionary, does it have to mention *analytical*? No. What about when you look up *analytical*—does *strategic* need to be there? No. Therefore, this answer choice pair does not have a Clear and Necessary relationship.

NO WISHY-WASHY SENTENCES

Again, to prove an answer choice is Clear and Necessary, all you have to do is make a sentence. If you find yourself coming up with a sentence that uses "can" or "may" or "might," you've just created a wishy-washy sentence. And wishy-washy sentences are a good sign that the words are not related. Remember, the rule says Clear and *Necessary*. Using "can," "may," or "might" is bad because these words conflict with the Necessary part of the rule.

> map : car

If I can have a *map* in my *car*, is the relationship Necessary? Nope.

> confident : successful

If someone is *confident*, he will be *successful*. Does that have to be true? Not necessarily. He *could* be successful, but he doesn't have to be.

QUIZ #3

Determine whether each of the following answer choice pairs is Clear and Necessary. If you think an answer choice pair is Clear and Necessary, prove it with a sentence that defines one word in terms of the other.

1. lassitude : energy

2. castigate : scold

3. nag : irritate

4. thought : logic

5. closet : shelves

6. castaway : discard

7. stockroom : supply

8. latent : manifest

9. charitable : amenable

10. ratify : approval

11. pilferage : deception

12. studious : sagacity

13. melee : confusion

14. terse : superfluous

15. inveterate : liar

16. charisma : charm

17. abrasive : irritation

18. entertain : enthrall

19. enchant : amuse

20. retain : lawyer

21. truncate : short

22. arduous : weaken

23. impertinent : forthright

24. inaugurate : beginning

25. satisfied : enjoyment

26. exert : muscle

27. wholesome : health

28. innocuous : harm

29. rationalize : reasonable

30. museum : art

QUIZ #4

On the following questions, use Clear and Necessary to get rid of wrong answer choices. Remember, you can't cross out an answer choice if it contains a word you don't know.

1. INCORRIGIBLE : REFORM ::

   (A) inefficient : effectiveness
   (B) ingenious : perfection
   (C) intemperate : violence
   (D) infallible : error
   (E) incidental : chance

2. OPALESCENT : MONOCHROMATIC ::

   (A) impervious : penetrable
   (B) discursive : rambling
   (C) complementary : mutual
   (D) profitable : opulent
   (E) infamous : shocking

3. TRANSMIGRATE : STATE ::

   (A) invert : logic
   (B) substitute : replacement
   (C) metamorphose : form
   (D) intimate : implication
   (E) deduce : reasoning

4. INTOXICANT : EXCITE ::

   (A) tonic : ameliorate
   (B) antidote : sterilize
   (C) sedative : cure
   (D) stimulant : dull
   (E) anesthetic : numb

5. INEXORABLE : AVOID ::

   (A) gleeful : contain
   (B) protean : versatile
   (C) baseless : defend
   (D) undeviating : swerve
   (E) magnanimous : respect

6. SALACIOUS : LUST ::

   (A) imperious : arrogance
   (B) anemic : vitality
   (C) pedantic : knowledge
   (D) dolorous : simplicity
   (E) capricious : resoluteness

7. OBFUSCATE : CONFUSE ::

   (A) juxtapose : contrast
   (B) decamp : depart
   (C) proscribe : affirm
   (D) routinize : steady
   (E) pacify : diminish

8. TUMID : SWELLING ::

   (A) lamentable : accusation
   (B) dubious : proclamation
   (C) oblique : clarity
   (D) elastic : resilience
   (E) insolent : provocation

9. GENUFLECT : RESPECT ::

   (A) brook : intolerance
   (B) coddle : complacency
   (C) brood : deliberation
   (D) sanction : acceptance
   (E) enfranchise : privilege

WORKING BACKWARDS

Let's take a step back and review before we go any further.

1. The first thing you do when you tackle an analogy is make a sentence.

2. If, after applying the sentence to the answer choices, you have more than one answer choice left, then you need to make the sentence more specific.

3. If you can't make any sentence whatsoever, then you go to the answer choices and eliminate those that do not have Clear and Necessary relationships.

After the third step, you may have more than one answer choice remaining. This is where the technique Working Backwards comes in.

Working Backwards really works hand-in-hand with Clear and Necessary. If an answer choice pair is not Clear and Necessary, you can eliminate it. If an answer choice pair *is* Clear and Necessary, then you Work Backwards.

What is Working Backwards? You prove an answer choice Clear and Necessary by making a sentence with the two words. Working Backwards entails taking that sentence and seeing if it could work with the stem words.

Let's look at the following answer choice pair. Is it Clear and Necessary?

remiss : negligent:

Yes. You know it's Clear and Necessary because you can make a sentence with the two words. "*Remiss* means *negligent* in duty." Take this sentence and try to apply it to the following stem pair.

??? : diligent

The question marks indicate that you don't know what the first word in the stem pair means. But that doesn't stop you from Working Backwards. Ask yourself: "Could a word exist that means DILIGENT in duty?" Sure. You don't have to know what the exact word is. The point is that such a word could exist. Therefore, the answer choice pair (remiss : negligent) could be the right answer. Take a look at another answer choice pair.

lionize : extol

Is this pair Clear and Necessary? Yes. The sentence that proves it: "*Lionize* means to *extol* someone." Now that you've got a good sentence, apply it to the following stem pair.

??? : cheat

Again, the question marks indicate you don't know one of the words in the stem pair. Ask yourself: "Could a word exist that means to CHEAT someone?" Definitely. Therefore, this answer choice could be the right answer. Let's look at one more answer choice pair.

debatable : dispute

Is the pair Clear and Necessary? Yes. A possible sentence is: "Something *debatable* is open to *dispute*." Apply the sentence to the following stem pair.

??? : LOYALTY

Ask yourself: "Could something that is something be open to LOYALTY?" No. It doesn't make a lot of sense. Therefore, what should you do? Eliminate this answer choice. It can't be the right answer.

To summarize: When you can't make a sentence with the stem words, go to the answer choices and use Clear and Necessary. Eliminate any answer choice that is not Clear and Necessary. For those answer choices that are Clear and Necessary, Work Backwards. Let's try an example:

DISABUSE : ERROR ::

(A) quell : submission
(B) liberate : domination
(C) foil : expulsion
(D) impair : health
(E) sidle : movement

Let's say that you don't know the word DISABUSE. Since you can't make a sentence, go to the answer choices and use Clear and Necessary along with Working Backwards.

Is answer choice (A) Clear and Necessary? Yes. You can make a sentence defining one word in terms of the other: *quell* means to reduce to *submission*. Since (A) is Clear and Necessary, you now need to Work Backwards. Could a word exist that means to reduce to ERROR? Doesn't make a lot of sense, does it? Therefore, eliminate this answer choice.

Is answer choice (B) Clear and Necessary? Yes. A good sentence: *liberate* means to free from *domination*. Since (B) is Clear and Necessary, you now need to Work Backwards. Could a word exist that means to free from ERROR? Sure. Therefore, leave this answer choice in. It could be right.

Is answer choice (C) Clear and Necessary? No. *Foil* means to thwart. If you look up *foil* in the dictionary, will you see *expulsion*? No. If you look up *expulsion* in the dictionary, will you see *foil*? No again. Therefore, (C) is not Clear and Necessary. Because (C) is not Clear and Necessary, you know it can't be the right answer. Eliminate it.

Is answer choice (D) Clear and Necessary? No. Don't be deceived. If you look up *impair* in the dictionary, does it have to say *health*? No. If you look up *health* in the dictionary, does it have to say *impair*? Definitely not. Therefore, (D) is not Clear and Necessary. Eliminate it.

Is answer choice (E) Clear and Necessary? Yes. The sentence to prove it: *sidle* is a type of *movement*. Since (E) is Clear and Necessary, you now need to Work Backwards. Could a word exist that means a type of ERROR? Possibly. Leave (E) in because it could be the right answer.

So you're down to (B) and (E). By using Clear and Necessary combined with Working Backwards, you have a 50% chance of getting the question right—even though you don't know what DISABUSE means. At this point, what should you do? How about guess? After all, you have a 50 percent chance. As it turns out, the best answer is (B). DISABUSE means to free from ERROR.

QUIZ #5

For each of the following questions, determine whether the answer choice pair is Clear and Necessary. If it is Clear and Necessary, then prove it by making a sentence. Finally, Work Backwards with that sentence and see if it can be applied to the stem pair. If the sentence can be applied, then leave the answer choice in. If the sentence can't be applied (i.e., it doesn't make sense), then cross it out. The question marks indicate that you don't know the meaning of the stem word.

1. ??? : TROOPS ::

    assemble : crowd

2. ??? : PROFIT ::

    arable : plowing

3. ??? : DISSOLUTE ::

    luminary : wealth

4. EXPEL : ??? ::

    touch : dab

5. ??? : CONDESCENSION ::

    kowtow : deference

6. ??? : DECLARE ::

    exhibit : display

7. ??? : FERMENTATION ::

    solvent : distillation

8. SADNESS : ??? ::

    word : laconic

9. ??? : TUMULTUOUS ::

    ruse : deceptive

QUIZ #6

On the following questions, use Clear and Necessary combined with Working Backwards to eliminate wrong answer choices. If an answer choice isn't Clear and Necessary, eliminate it. If an answer choice is Clear and Necessary, Work Backwards.

1. PECCADILLO : SIN ::

   (A) memorial : reminder
   (B) lapse : error
   (C) aptitude : intelligence
   (D) asperity : rigor
   (E) fortress : town

2. LAM : FLEE ::

   (A) bolt : swallow
   (B) suppress : revive
   (C) filch : deceive
   (D) ingratiate : dismiss
   (E) abstain : fulfill

3. LIBRETTO : OPERA ::

   (A) symphony : orchestra
   (B) prelude : event
   (C) buttress : stability
   (D) euphony : sound
   (E) script : play

4. CACHET : APPROBATION ::

   (A) discomfort : embarrassment
   (B) secret : disclosure
   (C) stockade : defense
   (D) malediction : dishonor
   (E) stigma : disgrace

5. NIP : NUMB ::

   (A) dally : playful
   (B) augment : greater
   (C) compel : pressing
   (D) tidy : proper
   (E) create : inventive

6. INDELIBLE : ERASE ::

   (A) irradicable : comprehend
   (B) incredible : doubt
   (C) indeterminate : fix
   (D) immobile : push
   (E) irredeemable : punish

7. HALE : VIGOR ::

   (A) hirsute : insight
   (B) craven : bravery
   (C) pitiless : vicious
   (D) circumspect : prudence
   (E) intransigent : concession

8. ODYSSEY : ADVENTURE ::

   (A) encyclopedia : book
   (B) condition : promise
   (C) chapter : unit
   (D) itinerary : trip
   (E) incivility : rudeness

9. DAUNTLESS : FEAR ::

   (A) licentious : freedom
   (B) stolid : emotion
   (C) fallible : liability
   (D) depraved : corruption
   (E) brazen : boldness

ABSOLUTELY STUCK

You should be picking up a lot of points by using Clear and Necessary combined with Working Backwards. However, if these techniques aren't getting you anywhere (and chances are they are), here're some last resorts.

SIDES OF THE FENCE

There may be times when you don't know the exact relationship between the stem words but you do know a little something about how they relate. That is, you can tell whether they're similar words or whether they're different words. Let's look at the following stem pair:

OVERWEENING : PRIDE ::

You may not know the exact relationship between OVERWEENING and PRIDE, but you may know that the two words are similar. In other words, they're on the "same side" of the fence. Take a look at the stem pair below. How is it different?

INGENUOUS : URBANE ::

These words are on "different sides" of the fence—that is, they don't share the same characteristics or qualities.

So how can Sides of the Fence help you? Well, if you know the stem words are on the same side of the fence, the correct answer must have words on the same side, too. Therefore, you can eliminate any answer choice that has words on different sides.

Similarly, if you know the stem words are on different sides, the correct answer must have words on different sides, too. Therefore, you can eliminate any answer choice that has words on the same side. Try the following example.

OBSTREPEROUS : CONTROL ::

(A) pugnacious : belligerence
(B) heterodox : convention
(C) euphoric : elation
(D) infallible : malfeasance
(E) precocious : maturity

OBSTREPEROUS and CONTROL are on different sides of the fence. Therefore, the right answer must be on different sides as well. Answer choice (A) has words on the same side, so it can't be correct. (B) has words on different sides, so leave it in. (C) has words on the same side, so eliminate it. (D) has words on different sides, so it's OK. (E) has words on the same side, so throw it out. (B) and (D) are the only possible choices, and if you look at (D) closely, you can see that the words aren't Clear and Necessary. The best answer is (B).

QUIZ #7

On the following questions, determine whether the words are on the same side or different sides of the fence.

1. nullify : invalid

2. prepossessing : unpleasant

3. litigious : lawsuit

4. altercation : dispute

5. nauseous : disgust

6. adversity : fortune

7. arbitrary : random

8. pacify : agitation

9. patent : obvious

10. penchant : disinclination

BREAD VS. MEAT

ETS likes to trick test takers by having them focus on the stem words themselves rather than on the relationship between the stem words. If you think of an analogy as a sandwich—the stem words are the pieces of bread and the relationship is the meat in between—ETS distracts test takers by using words in the answer choices that remind them of the bread. For example:

DEVOUT : PIETY ::

(A) reverent : righteousness
(B) prudent : discrimination
(C) virtuous : grace
(D) credulous : belief
(E) dolorous : grief

The pieces of bread are DEVOUT and PIETY. If you look at the answer choices, what words remind you of DEVOUT and PIETY? In (A), *reverent*; in (C), *virtuous*; and in (D), *belief*. These words are all associated with religion—just like DEVOUT and PIETY. Don't let the bread distract you. It's the meat—that is, the relationship—that matters.

The point is: Don't rush. Because if your work is dominated by speed, guess what's going to happen? You're going to look at the bread, not the meat.

By the way, the meat in the above example is "a _____ person expresses _____." The best answer, then, is (E).

THE HARDEST (OR WEIRDEST) WORDS

The very last resort for analogies is the same as the very last resort for sentence completions: Pick the answer choice that has the hardest (or weirdest) word or words. Again, it's not a foolproof method of guessing, but when you're absolutely stuck, it can give you some guidance.

IN SUMMARY

It's a step-by-step process you need to take to tackle analogies. The more vocabulary you know, the easier analogies are because you can make sentences with your stem words. But if you don't have the vocabulary, then Clear and Necessary along with Working Backwards are your salvation. The first three steps are the most important. By test time, these steps should be so ingrained in your mind that they're instinctive.

When you know both of the stem words . . .

1. Make a sentence. Then apply that sentence to the answer choices.

2. If you've applied your sentence and still have more than one answer choice left, make your sentence more specific.

When you know both of the stem words but can't make a sentence OR when you don't know one or both of the stem words . . .

3. Go to the answer choices and test for Clear and Necessary. Remember, you prove something is Clear and Necessary by making a sentence.

   a. If the answer choice pair is *not* Clear and Necessary, then eliminate it.

   b. If the answer choice pair *is* Clear and Necessary, Work Backwards immediately.

When you're absolutely stuck . . .

4. Use Sides of the Fence.

5. Watch out for words in the answer choices that remind you of the stem words.

6. Pick the answer choice that has the hardest (or the weirdest) words.

QUIZ #1: ANSWERS

1. SHIRK means to avoid WORK.

2. PENANCE is performed to show SORROW.

3. SATIATE means to SATISFY fully.

4. A TRICKLE is a little TORRENT.

5. ELONGATE means to increase in LENGTH.

6. A GARAGE is used to house an AUTOMOBILE.

7. IGNITE means to set on FIRE.

8. Something EXCESSIVE lacks MODERATION.

9. Something INCONSPICUOUS is not NOTICEABLE.

10. A MISER is a very FRUGAL person.

11. LURK is a type of MOVEMENT.

12. An ANOMALY goes against the NORM.

13. MORTAL means causing DEATH.

14. MUTE means to reduce the SOUND of.

15. A RÉSUMÉ shows one's QUALIFICATIONS.

16. A SATIRE's purpose is to SCORN.

17. Someone VORACIOUS is very HUNGRY.

18. Something DUBIOUS is without CERTAINTY.

19. A GUFFAW is a big LAUGH.

20. A SYLLABUS is a plan for a COURSE.

QUIZ #2: ANSWERS

1. *D* Something TRITE lacks ORIGINALITY.

2. *C* A WHISTLE is used by a REFEREE to keep order.

3. *C* LUBRICATE means to make SLIPPERY.

4. *A* BARTER means an exchange of GOODS.

5. *D* A HULL is a type of COVERING.

6. *A* ADROIT means having SKILL.

7. *B* IMPROVISED means done without REHEARSAL.

8. *B* You cannot READ something that is INDECIPHERABLE.

9. *C* The purpose of an INTOXICANT is to EXCITE.

QUIZ #3: ANSWERS

1. C&N: *lassitude* means a lack of *energy*.

2. C&N: *castigate* means *scold* a lot.

3. Not C&N.

4. Not C&N.

5. Not C&N.

6. C&N: a *castaway* is something you *discard*.

7. C&N: a *stockroom* contains *supplies*.

8. C&N: something *latent* does not *manifest* itself.

9. Not C&N.

10. C&N: *ratify* means to give *approval*.

11. Not C&N.

12. Not C&N.

13. C&N: a *melee* is marked by *confusion*

14. C&N: something *terse* is not *superfluous*.

15. Not C&N.

16. C&N: someone with *charisma* has a lot of *charm*.

17. C&N: something *abrasive* causes *irritation*.

18. Not C&N.

19. Not C&N.

20. Not C&N.

21. C&N: *truncate* means to cut *short*.

22. Not C&N.

23. Not C&N.

24. C&N: *inaugurate* means to bring about a *beginning*.

25. Not C&N.

26. Not C&N.

27. C&N: something *wholesome* promotes *health*.

28. C&N: something *innocuous* will not cause *harm*.

29. C&N: *rationalize* means try to make *reasonable*.

30. Not C&N.

QUIZ #4: ANSWERS

1. **D** Someone INCORRIGIBLE is incapable of REFORM
   Eliminate (B) and (C) because they are not C&N.

2. **A** Something OPALESCENT does not have the quality of being MONOCHROMATIC.
   Eliminate (C), (D), and (E) because they are not C&N.

3. **B** TRANSMIGRATE means to change STATE.
   Eliminate (A) and (E) because they are not C&N.

4. **E** The purpose of an INTOXICANT is to EXCITE
   Eliminate (A), (B), and (C) because they are not C&N.

5. **C** Something INEXORABLE is not possible to AVOID.
   Eliminate (A) and (E) because they are not C&N.

6. **A** Someone SALACIOUS possesses LUST.
   Eliminate (C) and (D) because they are not C&N.

7. **B** OBFUSCATE means to CONFUSE.
   Eliminate (A), (C), (D), and (E) because they are not C&N.

8. **D** Something TUMID is marked by SWELLING.
   Eliminate (A), (B), and (E) because they are not C&N.

9. **C** GENUFLECT is an action that indicates RESPECT.
   Eliminate (B), (D), and (E) because they are not C&N.

QUIZ #5: ANSWERS

1. **??? : TROOPS ::**
   assemble : crowd
   This answer choice pair is Clear and Necessary. The sentence that proves it: *assemble* means to gather together a *crowd*. Now Work Backwards with that sentence. Could something mean to gather together TROOPS? Yes. A word like that could exist. Leave this answer choice in—it could be the right answer.

2. **??? : PROFIT ::**
   arable : plowing
   This answer choice pair is Clear and Necessary. The sentence that proves it: *arable* means suitable for *plowing*. Now Work Backwards with that sentence. Could something mean suitable for PROFIT? The sentence doesn't make much sense. Therefore, this answer choice probably isn't right—cross it out.

3. **??? : DISSOLUTE ::**
   luminary : wealth
   This answer choice pair isn't Clear and Necessary. A *luminary* is a famous person— not necessarily a rich one. Therefore, this can't be the right answer. Cross it out.

4. **EXPEL : ??? ::**
   touch : dab
   This answer choice pair is Clear and Necessary. The sentence that proves it: *dab* means to *touch* gently or lightly. Now Work Backwards with that sentence. Could something mean to EXPEL gently or lightly? The sentence doesn't make sense

anymore. Therefore, this answer choice can't be right—cross it out.

5. ??? : CONDESCENSION ::
kowtow : deference
This answer choice pair is Clear and Necessary. The sentence that proves it: *kowtow* means to show *deference*. Now Work Backwards with that sentence. Could something mean to show CONDESCENSION? Sure. A word like that could exist. Leave this answer choice in—it could be the right answer.

6. ??? : DECLARE ::
exhibit : display
This answer choice pair is Clear and Necessary. The sentence that proves it: *exhibit* means to *display* publicly. Now work Backwards with that sentence. Could something mean to DECLARE publicly? Sure. A word like that could exist. Leave this answer choice in—it could be right.

7. ??? : FERMENTATION ::
solvent : distillation
This answer choice pair isn't Clear and Necessary. Therefore, it can't be right—cross it out.

8. SADNESS : ??? ::
word : laconic
This answer choice pair is Clear and Necessary. The sentence that proves it: someone *laconic* is sparing of *words*. Now Work Backwards with that sentence. Could someone something be sparing of SADNESS? The sentence doesn't make much sense. Therefore, this answer choice probably isn't right—cross it out.

9. ??? : TUMULTUOUS ::
ruse : deceptive
This answer choice pair is Clear and Necessary. The sentence that proves it: a *ruse* has the quality of being *deceptive*. Now Work Backwards with that sentence. Could something have the quality of being TUMULTUOUS? Sure. A word like that could exist. Leave this answer choice in—it could be right.

QUIZ #6: ANSWERS

1. *B*
(A) C&N: a *memorial* serves as a *reminder*. WB: could a PECCADILLO serve as a SIN? Probably not.
(B) C&N: a *lapse* is a small *error*. WB: could a PECCADILLO be a small SIN? Yes.
(C) Not C&N.
(D) C&N: *asperity* means *rigor*. WB: could a PECCADILLO mean a SIN? Yes.
(E) Not C&N.

2. *A*
(A) C&N: *bolt* means to *swallow* hastily. WB: could LAM mean to FLEE hastily? Yes.
(B) Not C&N.
(C) Not C&N.
(D) Not C&N.
(E) Not C&N.

3. *E*
(A) Not C&N.
(B) C&N: a *prelude* is the beginning of an *event*. WB: could a LIBRETTO be the beginning of an OPERA? Yes.
(C) C&N: a *buttress* provides *stability*. WB: could a LIBRETTO provide an OPERA? Probably not.
(D) C&N: *euphony* is a pleasing *sound*. WB: could a LIBRETTO be a pleasing OPERA? Probably not.
(E) C&N: a *script* is the text of a *play*. WB: could a LIBRETTO be the text of an OPERA? Yes.

4. *E*
(A) Not C&N.
(B) Not C&N.
(C) C&N: a *stockade* is a type of *defense*. WB: could CACHET be a type of APPROBATION? Yes.
(D) Not C&N.
(E) C&N: a *stigma* is a mark of *disgrace*. WB: could CACHET mean a mark of APPROBATION? Yes.

5. *B*

(A) C&N: *dally* means to act in a *playful* manner.
WB: could NIP mean to act in a NUMB manner? Probably not.

(B) C&N: *augment* means to make *greater*.
WB: could NIP mean to make NUMB? Yes.

(C) Not C&N.

(D) Not C&N.

(E) Not C&N.

6. *C*

(A) Not C&N.

(B) Not C&N.

(C) C&N: something *indeterminate* is impossible to *fix*.
WB: could something INDELIBLE be impossible to ERASE? Yes.

(D) Not C&N.

(E) Not C&N.

7. *D*

(A) Not C&N.

(B) C&N: someone *craven* lacks *bravery*.
WB: could someone HALE lack VIGOR? Yes.

(C) Not C&N.

(D) C&N: someone *circumspect* possesses *prudence*.
WB: could someone HALE possess VIGOR? Yes.

(E) C&N: someone *intransigent* will not make a *concession*.
WB: could someone HALE not make a VIGOR? Probably not.

8. *A*

(A) C&N: an *encyclopedia* is a series of *books*.
WB: could an ODYSSEY be a series of ADVENTURES? Yes.

(B) Not C&N.

(C) C&N: a *chapter* is a type of *unit*.
WB: could an ODYSSEY be a type of ADVENTURE? Yes.

(D) C&N: an *itinerary* is a plan for a *trip*.
WB: could an ODYSSEY be a plan for an ADVENTURE? Probably not

(E) C&N: an *incivility* is characterized by *rudeness*.
WB: could an ODYSSEY be characterized by an ADVENTURE? Yes.

9. *B*

(A) Not C&N.

(B) C&N: someone *stolid* shows no *emotion*.
WB: could someone DAUNTLESS show no FEAR? Yes.

(C) Not C&N.

(D) C&N: someone *depraved* is full of *corruption*.
WB: could someone DAUNTLESS be full of FEAR? Yes.

(E) C&N: someone *brazen* possesses *boldness*.
WB: could someone DAUNTLESS possess FEAR? Yes.

QUIZ #7: ANSWERS

1. same side

2. different sides

3. same side

4. same side

5. same side

6. different sides

7. same side

8. different sides

9. same side

10. different sides

PROBLEM SET #1

<u>Directions:</u> In each of the following questions, a related pair of words or phrases is followed by five lettered pairs of words or phrases. Select the lettered pair that best expresses a relationship similar to that expressed in the original pair.

8. AVIARY : BIRD ::

(A) stable : horse
(B) dam : beaver
(C) field : cow
(D) den : fox
(E) nest : hamster

9. METHANE : FUEL ::

(A) lathe : machine
(B) ether : tool
(C) drill : screw
(D) benzene : ring
(E) needle : sewing

10. RAMROD : RIGIDITY ::

(A) heretical : orthodoxy
(B) decorative : flamboyance
(C) luminous : transparency
(D) hectic : confusion
(E) brackish : strength

11. SHELTER : PROTECTION ::

(A) incentive : motivation
(B) shield : injury
(C) antiseptic : cure
(D) inoculation : longevity
(E) inundation : flood

12. IMPREGNABLE : ATTACK ::

(A) phlegmatic : calm
(B) salutary : health
(C) immortal : death
(D) ephemeral : brevity
(E) iridescent : color

13. DOCILITY : INTRACTABLE ::

(A) insurgency : oppressive
(B) desolation : alone
(C) anticipation : satisfied
(D) victory : conquered
(E) intrepidity : fearful

14. CORONATION : ROYAL ::

(A) enlistment : soldier
(B) excursion : adventurer
(C) trial : mediator
(D) commencement : student
(E) frocking : cleric

15. SYLLOGISM : SPECIOUS ::

(A) perversion : conventional
(B) distillation : intense
(C) conceit : fanciful
(D) contingency : certain
(E) truism : sincere

16. MAWKISH : SENTIMENT ::

(A) overt : secrecy
(B) rakish : codification
(C) meretricious : simplicity
(D) paramount : suspicion
(E) carping : criticism

PROBLEM SET #2

Directions: In each of the following questions, a related pair of words or phrases is followed by five lettered pairs of words or phrases. Select the lettered pair that best expresses a relationship similar to that expressed in the original pair.

8. EYEGLASSES : VISION ::

   (A) anvil : metal
   (B) attraction : desire
   (C) heat : warmth
   (D) solution : beaker
   (E) spice : flavor

9. SMITH : METAL ::

   (A) jeweler : gold
   (B) meteorologist : weather
   (C) hunter : rifle
   (D) carpenter : wood
   (E) gymnast : vault

10. SUITCASE : CLOTHING ::

    (A) kitchen : pantry
    (B) parasol : fringe
    (C) attaché : brief
    (D) envelope : letter
    (E) encyclopedia : volume

11. HURL : PITCH ::

    (A) flag : tire
    (B) carp : fault
    (C) truckle : attend
    (D) pore : meditate
    (E) seize : take

12. RECONDITE : COMPREHEND ::

    (A) illegible : decipher
    (B) fastidious : care
    (C) treacherous : trick
    (D) credulous : believe
    (E) unforgiving : condone

13. UNEQUIVOCAL : QUESTION ::

    (A) officious : reprimand
    (B) staid : deride
    (C) insuperable : overcome
    (D) contiguous : abut
    (E) belated : delay

14. OXYMORON : INCONGRUOUS ::

    (A) polemic : conciliatory
    (B) alliteration : rhythmic
    (C) transport : pleasurable
    (D) phantasm : imaginative
    (E) subjunction : biased

15. TRANSMIT : SIGNAL ::

    (A) emend : correction
    (B) fulminate : invective
    (C) exaggerate : hyperbole
    (D) affront : humanity
    (E) trespass : property

16. DESCRY : DETECT ::

    (A) titter : grin
    (B) champ : chew
    (C) stutter : speak
    (D) slurp : sip
    (E) counterfeit : imitate

PROBLEM SET #3

8. DRUM MAJOR : BAND ::

    (A) preacher : congregation
    (B) architect : designer
    (C) dancer : corps
    (D) adept : beginner
    (E) painter : viewer

9. SONATA : MOVEMENT ::

    (A) lampoon : ridicule
    (B) novel : prologue
    (C) tableau : stage
    (D) poem : stanza
    (E) fable : narrative

10. VIGILANCE : ALERT

    (A) flippancy : serious
    (B) garrulity : verbose
    (C) skepticism : doubting
    (D) judiciousness : merciful
    (E) sentience : attentive

11. WEALTH : INCOME ::

    (A) salary : performance
    (B) appetite : hunger
    (C) health : medicine
    (D) feeling : affection
    (E) wind : hurricane

12. EXTRINSIC : BELONG ::

    (A) submissive : resign
    (B) incontrovertible : challenge
    (C) evanescent : endure
    (D) protuberant : intrude
    (E) stigmatic : isolate

13. RECANT : BELIEF ::

    (A) reclaim : rescue
    (B) recoil : adoration
    (C) exact : requisition
    (D) repeal : law
    (E) calibrate : rectitude

14. PENURIOUS : FRUGALITY ::

    (A) philanthropic : grace
    (B) vainglorious : pettiness
    (C) priggish : integrity
    (D) lecherous : decency
    (E) perspicacious : insight

15. OBLOQUY : ABUSIVE ::

    (A) panegyric : laudatory
    (B) slander : inflammatory
    (C) diatribe : accusatory
    (D) calumny : criminal
    (E) travesty : contemptuous

16. LURID : MELODRAMA ::

    (A) redolent : fragrance
    (B) determinate : definition
    (C) alien : distinction
    (D) metaphysical : spirit
    (E) fortuitous : intention

PROBLEM SET #4

<u>Directions:</u> In each of the following questions, a related pair of words or phrases is followed by five lettered pairs of words or phrases. Select the lettered pair that best expresses a relationship similar to that expressed in the original pair.

8. LOSS : RECOUP ::

    (A) tale : recount
    (B) damage : recompense
    (C) document : record
    (D) health : recuperate
    (E) generosity : reciprocate

9. APATHY : INDIFFERENT ::

    (A) melancholy : sad
    (B) enthusiasm : zealous
    (C) stoicism : emotional
    (D) talent : adequate
    (E) discretion : secretive

10. SHEEP : FLEECE ::

    (A) duck : bill
    (B) insect : arthropod
    (C) lion : courage
    (D) kangaroo : pouch
    (E) fish : scale

11. REBATE : FORCE

    (A) tax : demand
    (B) blunt : sharpness
    (C) glean : information
    (D) appease : calm
    (E) cleave : division

12. TAMBOURINE : INSTRUMENT ::

    (A) scene : tableau
    (B) ship : yacht
    (C) chaise : vehicle
    (D) agenda : meeting
    (E) solution : chemistry

13. ANODYNE : ASSUAGE ::

    (A) diet : lighten
    (B) antiseptic : promote
    (C) vitamin : invigorate
    (D) drug : prevent
    (E) catalyst : hasten

14. APHORISM : CONCISE ::

    (A) eulogy : cursory
    (B) effigy : slanderous
    (C) sophism : veracious
    (D) provocation : irritating
    (E) camp : banal

15. INCONTINENT : RESTRAINT ::

    (A) impudent : suavity
    (B) naive : deception
    (C) impenitent : sin
    (D) covetous : desire
    (E) impolitic : tact

16. CHARY : TRUSTFUL ::

    (A) munificent : stinting
    (B) pragmatic : irrational
    (C) mulish : forgiving
    (D) treacherous : deceiving
    (E) cynical : quibbling

PROBLEM SET #5

Directions: In each of the following questions, a related pair of words or phrases is followed by five lettered pairs of words or phrases. Select the lettered pair that best expresses a relationship similar to that expressed in the original pair.

8. WOLF : CANINE ::

   (A) alligator : crocodile
   (B) shrimp : crustacean
   (C) tadpole : frog
   (D) horse : hock
   (E) goose : gaggle

9. SENTRY : GUARD ::

   (A) judge : legislate
   (B) student : learn
   (C) producer : finance
   (D) fireman : save
   (E) conductor : direct

10. DANDY : FOPPISH ::

    (A) ingenue : naive
    (B) elocutionist : public
    (C) martyr : melancholy
    (D) recreant : disagreeable
    (E) mercenary : avaricious

11. MOVE : MEANDER ::

    (A) think : concentrate
    (B) talk : ramble
    (C) run : lope
    (D) stammer : mutter
    (E) work : labor

12. PAEAN : TRIBUTE ::

    (A) hymn : catholicism
    (B) elegy : grief
    (C) canticle : purity
    (D) psalm : gravity
    (E) eulogy : devotion

13. EPAULET : DECORATION ::

    (A) cameo : image
    (B) epée : rapier
    (C) cavalry : unit
    (D) lapel : jacket
    (E) medal : ornament

14. PERORATION : SPEECH ::

    (A) conference : discussion
    (B) itinerary : travel
    (C) epilogue : play
    (D) letter : alphabet
    (E) destruction : life

15. ABHOR : DISLIKE ::

    (A) venerate : esteem
    (B) procrastinate : delay
    (C) testify : affirm
    (D) condone : neglect
    (E) detract : dismiss

16. TOTTER : GAIT ::

    (A) furrow : brow
    (B) simper : smile
    (C) canter : gallop
    (D) stutter : speech
    (E) deduction : thought

PROBLEM SET #1: EXPLANATIONS

8. *A* Make a sentence with the stem words. An AVIARY is a house for a BIRD. Now apply the sentence to the answer choices. Is a *stable* a house for a *horse*? Yes. However, don't forget to check the remaining answer choices just to make sure. Is a *dam* a house for a *beaver*? Yes again. Is a *field* a house for a *cow*? No. Is a *den* a house for a *fox*? Sure. Is a *nest* a house for a *hamster*? No. You're left with (A), (B), and (D).

    When you have more than one answer choice remaining after you apply the sentence, what should you do? Make the sentence more specific. How about: an AVIARY is a manmade house for a BIRD. Is a *stable* a manmade house for a *horse*? Yes. Is a *dam* a manmade house for a *beaver*? No. Is a *den* a manmade house for a *fox*? No. The best answer, then, is (A).

9. *A* Make a sentence with the stem words. METHANE is a type of FUEL. Now apply the sentence to the answer choices. Is a *lathe* a type of *machine*? If you don't know what a *lathe* is, you have to leave (A) in. Is *ether* a type of *tool*? No—*ether* is a gas. Is a *drill* a type of *screw*? No. Is *benzene* a type of *ring*? Not in the way you're looking for. Is a *needle* a type of *sewing*? No. Even though you don't know what *lathe* means, (A) is the only answer choice remaining. (A) is the best answer.

10. *D* Most likely, you can tell that RAMROD and RIGIDITY are similar words, but if you're not absolutely positive what RAMROD means, you can't make a sentence. Go to the answer choices and check for Clear and Necessary. Is (A) Clear and Necessary? Yes. The sentence that proves it: something *heretical* goes against *orthodoxy*. Now Work Backwards with that sentence. Could RAMROD mean going against RIGIDITY? Maybe. Leave (A) in for now. Is (B) Clear and Necessary? No. Just because something is *decorative* doesn't mean it possesses *flamboyance*. Similarly, just because something has *flamboyance* doesn't mean it's *decorative*. Cross out (B). Is (C) Clear and Necessary? No. If you look up *luminous* in the dictionary, it'll say something about giving off light—not *transparency*. Similarly, if you look up *transparency* in the dictionary, you won't see anything about *luminous*. Eliminate (C). Is (D) Clear and Necessary? Yes. The sentence that proves it:

something *hectic* is marked by *confusion*. Now Work Backwards with that sentence. Could something RAMROD be marked by RIGIDITY? Sure. Leave (D) in. Is (E) Clear and Necessary? If you don't know what *brackish* means, you have to leave it in.

You're left with (A), (D), and (E). Now, you sort of know that RAMROD and RIGIDITY are similar words. Therefore, (A) can't be right. (D) could still work. (E) you still don't know anything about. At this point, guess. When you're left with something that works and something you don't know, go with what works. The best answer is (D).

11. **A** Make a sentence with the stem words. A SHELTER provides PROTECTION. Now apply that sentence to the answer choices. Does an *incentive* provide *motivation*? Yes. Does a *shield* provide *injury*? No. Does an *antiseptic* provide a *cure*? No—be careful. An *antiseptic* sterilizes; it doesn't necessarily *cure*. Does an *inoculation* provide *longevity*? If you don't know what *inoculation* means, you can't cross (D) out. Does an *inundation* provide a *flood*? No—an *inundation* is a *flood*. You're down to (A) and (D). As always, go with what works. (A) is the best answer.

12. **C** Make a sentence with the stem words. Something IMPREGNABLE is not susceptible to ATTACK. Is something *phlegmatic* not susceptible to *calm*? If you don't know what *phlegmatic* means, you have to leave (A) in. Is something *salutary* not susceptible to *health*? No—*salutary* has something to do with *health*. Is something *immortal* not susceptible to *death*? Looks good, but go through the remaining answer choices. Is something *ephemeral* not susceptible to *brevity*? No. Is something *iridescent* not susceptible to *color*. No—*iridescent* has something to do with *color*. You're left with (A) and (C). Go with what you know. The best answer is (C)

13. **E** If you can't make a sentence, go to the answer choices and test for Clear and Necessary. Is (A) Clear and Necessary? No. If you look up *insurgency*, you won't see anything about *oppressive*, and if you look up *oppressive*, you won't see anything about *insurgency*. Cross out (A). Is (B) Clear and Necessary? Yes. The sentence that proves it: someone in his *desolation* is all *alone*. Now Work Backwards with the sentence. Could someone in his DOCILITY be all INTRACTABLE? Maybe. Leave (B) in. Is (C)

Clear and Necessary? No. If you look up *anticipation*, you won't see anything about *satisfied*, and vice-versa. Eliminate (C). Is (D) Clear and Necessary? Yes. The sentence that proves it: you have a *victory* over something that is *conquered*. Now Work Backwards with that sentence. Could you have DOCILITY over something that is INTRACTABLE? Not really. How can you have DOCILITY over something? Eliminate (D). Is (E) Clear and Necessary? If you don't know what *intrepidity* means, you can't cross out (E).

You're down to (B) and (E). Go with what works—pick (B). In this case, however, the best answer is actually (E). INTRACTABLE means stubborn, and *intrepidity* means fearlessness. Someone in his DOCILITY is not INTRACTABLE, and someone in his *intrepidity* is not *fearful*.

Note that even though you missed the question, you're doing the right thing. You followed the techniques and, at the end, had a 50% chance of getting the question right—even though you didn't know what INTRACTABLE means.

14. *E* You probably know both words, but if you can't make a good sentence, go to the answer choices and test for Clear and Necessary. Is (A) Clear and Necessary? Yes. The sentence that proves it: *enlistment* is the enrollment of a *soldier*. Now Work Backwards with the sentence. Could CORONATION mean the enrollment of a ROYAL? No—you can't really enroll into royalty, can you? Eliminate (A). Is (B) Clear and Necessary? No. Be careful—if you look up *excursion*, do you have to see something about an *adventurer*? No. If you look up *adventurer*, do you have to see something about an *excursion*? No. Cross out (B). Is (C) Clear and Necessary? No. If you look up *trial*, you don't have to see *mediator*, and if you look up *mediator*, you don't have to see *trial*. Eliminate (C). Is (D) Clear and Necessary? Yes. The sentence that proves it: *commencement* is the graduation of a *student*. Now Work Backwards with that sentence. Could CORONATION mean the graduation of a ROYAL? Clearly not. Cross out (D). Is (E) Clear and Necessary? If you don't know what *frocking* means, you can't eliminate (E). In fact, you shouldn't eliminate (E) because it's the only answer choice remaining. (E) is the best answer—*frocking* is the making of a *cleric* just as CORONATION is the making of a ROYAL.

15. **C** Chances are you don't know what SYLLOGISM or SPECIOUS means, so go to the answer choices and use Clear and Necessary. Is (A) Clear and Necessary? Yes. The sentence that proves it: a *perversion* goes against what is *conventional*. At this point, you would usually Work Backwards with the sentence. However, you can't in this case because you don't know what either stem word means. So go on to (B). Is (B) Clear and Necessary? Not quite. *Distillation* is the process of purifying. Is (C) Clear and Necessary? It may not seem so because usually *conceit* means something like arrogance. But be careful. ETS often likes to test secondary definitions of words. Leave (C) in for now. Is (D) Clear and Necessary? No. A *contingency* is likely to happen—not *certain*. Is (E) Clear and Necessary? No. A *truism* doesn't have to be *sincere*.

So you're down to (A) and (C). Because you have no idea what the stem words mean, just guess. You have a 50 percent chance of getting the question right. Go with a last resort—pick the one that has the hardest word or words. In this case, that's (C). And guess what? (C) is the best answer. A SYLLOGISM has the quality of being SPECIOUS, and a *conceit* has the quality of being *fanciful*.

Always be on the watch for secondary meanings. It's clear that a secondary definition is being used in (C) because it would be too obvious that the words are not related if the primary definition were used.

16. **E** When you can't make a sentence, go to the answer choices and use Clear and Necessary. Is (A) Clear and Necessary? Yes. The sentence that proves it: Something *overt* lacks *secrecy*. Now Work Backwards with the sentence. Could something MAWKISH lack SENTIMENT? Sure. Leave (A) in. Is (B) Clear and Necessary? If you don't know what *rakish* means, you have to leave (B) in. Is (C) Clear and Necessary? If you don't know what *meretricious* means, you have to leave (C) in. Is (D) Clear and Necessary? No. *Paramount* means superior to all others, so if you look up *paramount*, you won't see anything about *suspicion*. Similarly, if you look up *suspicion*, you won't see anything about *paramount*. Cross out (D). Is (E) Clear and Necessary? If you don't know what *carping* means, you have to leave (E) in.

You're left with (A), (B), and (E). Go with what works—pick (A). As it turns out, however, the best answer is (E). MAWKISH means prone to excessive SENTIMENT, and *carping* means prone to excessive *criticism*.

As stated in a previous question, it's okay to miss a question. Ultimately, you want to get as many questions right as possible, but for now, as long as you're following the techniques, you're doing the right thing. Remember, you did some great POE for this question—you had a 50 percent chance of getting the question right even though you didn't know what MAWKISH means.

PROBLEM SET #2: EXPLANATIONS

8. *E* You know both of the stem words, so make a sentence. EYEGLASSES enhance VISION. Now apply that sentence to the answer choices. Does an *anvil* enhance *metal*? No. Does *attraction* enhance *desire*? Not necessarily. Does *heat* enhance *warmth*? Not really—it provides *warmth*. Does a *solution* enhance a *beaker*? Definitely not. Does a *spice* enhance *flavor*? Yes. (E) is the best answer.

9. *D* When you know both of the stem words, make a sentence. A SMITH works with METAL. Now apply that sentence to the answer choices. Does a *jeweler* work with *gold*? Not necessarily. Does a *meteorologist* work with *weather*? Sort of. Does a *hunter* work with a *rifle*? Not necessarily. Does a *carpenter* work with *wood*? Yes. Does a *gymnast* work with a *vault*? Not necessarily.

    You're down to (B) and (D). If you have more than one answer choice remaining, make the sentence more specific. A SMITH works with METAL with his hands. Does a *meteorologist* work with *weather* with his hands? No. Does a *carpenter* work with *wood* with his hands? Yes. The best answer is (D).

10. *D* You know both of the stem words, so make a sentence. A SUITCASE contains CLOTHING. Now apply that sentence to the answer choices. Does a *kitchen* contain a *pantry*? Not necessarily. Does a *parasol* contain a *fringe*? No. Does an *attaché* contain a *brief*? Not necessarily—be careful. Does an *envelope* contain a *letter*? Yes. Does an *encyclopedia* contain a *volume*? No. The best answer is (D).

11. *B* You know both of the stem words, so make a sentence. HURL means to PITCH. Now apply that sentence to the answer choices. Does *flag* mean to *tire*? Yes. Does *carp* mean to *fault*? Yes. Does *truckle* mean to *attend*? If you don't know what *truckle* means, you

can't eliminate (C). Does *pore* mean to *meditate*? No. Does *seize* mean to *take*? Yes.

You're left with more than one answer choice—(A), (B), (C), and (E)—so make the sentence more specific. HURL means to PITCH with force. Does *flag* mean to *tire* with force? No. Does *carp* mean to *fault* with force? No. Does *truckle* mean to *attend* with force? You may not know what *truckle* means, but you do know that you can't *attend* with force. Does *seize* mean to *take* with force? Yes. The best answer is (E).

12. **A** Most likely, you don't know what RECONDITE means. When you can't make a sentence, go to the answer choices and test for Clear and Necessary. Is (A) Clear and Necessary? Yes. The sentence that proves it: Something *illegible* is hard to *decipher*. Now Work Backwards with that sentence. Could something RECONDITE be hard to COMPREHEND? Sure. Is (B) Clear and Necessary? Yes. The sentence that proves it: *Fastidious* means you *care* excessively. Could RECONDITE mean you COMPREHEND excessively? Doesn't make sense, so eliminate (B). Is (C) Clear and Necessary? No. If you look up *treacherous*, you won't necessarily see *trick*, and vice-versa. Is (D) Clear and Necessary? Yes. The sentence that proves it: someone who is *credulous* has a tendency to *believe*. Now Work Backwards with that sentence. Could someone RECONDITE have a tendency to COMPREHEND. Maybe. Is (E) Clear and Necessary? No. If you look up *unforgiving*, you won't see *condone*, and if you look up *condone*, you won't see *unforgiving*.

You're left with (A) and (D). Which sentence do you feel is stronger? Probably (A). It doesn't make complete sense to say that someone has a tendency to COMPREHEND. (A) is a good guess—it's the best answer.

13. **C** If you don't know what UNEQUIVOCAL means, you can't make a sentence. Therefore, go to the answer choices and use Clear and Necessary. Is (A) Clear and Necessary? No. Just because someone is *officious* doesn't mean he *reprimands*. Is (B) Clear and Necessary? No. If you look up *staid*, you don't see *deride*, and when you look up *deride*, you don't see *staid*. Is (C) Clear and Necessary? Yes. You cannot *overcome* something that is *insuperable*. Now Work Backwards with that sentence. You cannot

QUESTION something that is UNEQUIVOCAL. That could make sense. Is (D) Clear and Necessary? Don't eliminate it if you don't know what *abut* means. Is (E) Clear and Necessary? Yes. The sentence that proves it: Something *belated* has been *delayed*. Now Work Backwards. Something UNEQUIVOCAL has been QUESTIONED. That makes sense.

You're left with (C), (D), and (E). What now? Do you know whether UNEQUIVOCAL and QUESTION are on the same side of the fence or different sides? UNEQUIVOCAL is a positive word, so the stem words are on different sides. The correct answer, then, must also be on different sides. Does (C) contain words on different sides? Yes. You don't know about (D) since it has a word you don' know. What about (E)? The words are on the same side, so cross it out.

The remaining answer choices are (C) and (D). Go with what works over what you don't know. The best answer is (C).

14. **C** If you can't make a sentence, go to the answer choices and use Clear and Necessary. Is (A) Clear and Necessary? You can't eliminate it if you don't know what *polemic* means. Is (B) Clear and Necessary? No. If you look up *alliteration*, you don't see *rhythmic*, and if you look up *rhythmic*, you don't see *alliteration*. Is (C) Clear and Necessary? Be careful—it looks as if *transport* has a secondary definition that you don't know. Leave it in. Is (D) Clear and Necessary? No. If you look up *phantasm*, it doesn't have to say *imaginative*, and vice-versa. Is (E) Clear and Necessary? If you don't know what *subjunction* means, you can't cross it out.

You're down to (A), (C), and (E)—each answer choice contains a word you don't know. What now? You can't use Sides of the Fence since you don't know what some of the words in the answer choices mean. At this point, then, guess. You have a one-in-three chance of getting the question right, which isn't bad, especially if you aren't sure what OXYMORON means. How about pick the answer choice that has the hardest word or words? That would probably be (A) or (C). As it turns out, the answer is (C). An OXYMORON has the quality of being INCONGRUOUS, and a *transport* has the quality of being *pleasurable*.

Always be on the watch for secondary meanings. It's clear that a secondary definition is being used in (C) because *transport* is being used as different part of speech than normal.

15. **B** If you can't make a good sentence, go to the answer choices and use Clear and Necessary. Is (A) Clear and Necessary? You can't eliminate (A) if you don't know what *emend* means. Is (B) Clear and Necessary? You can't eliminate (B) if you don't know what *fulminate* or *invective* means. Is (C) Clear and Necessary? Yes. When you make a *hyperbole*, you *exaggerate* a lot. Now Work Backwards with the sentence. When you make a SIGNAL, do you TRANSMIT a lot? Doesn't make a lot of sense, so eliminate (C). Is (D) Clear and Necessary? No. Don't get stuck on the phrase "an *affront* to *humanity*." *Affront* means offense. If you look it up, you won't see anything about *humanity*, or vice-versa. Eliminate (D). Is (E) Clear and Necessary? Yes. The sentence that proves it: *Trespass* means to invade *property*. Now Work Backwards with the sentence. Does TRANSMIT mean to invade SIGNAL? Doesn't make a lot of sense, so cross out (E).

You're down to (A) and (B). As a last resort, go with the hardest word or words. Pick (B). As it turns out, (B) is the best answer. TRANSMIT means to send forth a SIGNAL, and *fulminate* means to send forth an *invective*.

16. **B** If you don't know what DESCRY means, you can't make a sentence. Therefore, go to the answer choices and use Clear and Necessary. Is (A) Clear and Necessary? No. *Titter* means laugh in a nervous way. Is (B) Clear and Necessary? If you don't know what *champ* means, you can't cross it out. Is (C) Clear and Necessary? Yes. *Stutter* means to *speak* in an indistinct way. Now Work Backwards with that sentence. Could DESCRY mean to DETECT in an indistinct way? Doesn't make a lot of sense. Eliminate it. Is (D) Clear and Necessary? No. *Slurp* means to eat or drink in a noisy way. Is (E) Clear and Necessary? Yes. The sentence that proves it: *Counterfeit* means to *imitate* with the intent to deceive. Now Work Backwards with that sentence. Could DESCRY mean to DETECT with the intent to deceive? Probably not. You're left with (B)—a choice that contains a word you don't know. But that's okay. It's fine to pick (B) if you're able to eliminate the other answer choices by using Clear and Necessary

along with Working Backwards. (B) is the best answer. DESCRY means to DETECT, and *champ* means to *chew*.

PROBLEM SET #3: EXPLANATIONS

8. *A* When you know both of the stem words, make a sentence. A DRUM MAJOR leads or guides a BAND. Now apply that sentence to the answer choices. Does a *preacher* lead or guide a *congregation*? Yes. Does an *architect* lead or guide a *designer*? No. Does a *dancer* lead or guide a *corps*? If you don't know what *corps* means, you can't cross it out. Does an *adept* lead or guide a *beginner*? Not necessarily. Does a *painter* lead or guide a *viewer*? No.   You're left with (A) and (C)—an answer choice that works and an answer choice that contains a word you don't know. Go with what you know. The best answer is (A).

9. *D* You probably know both of the stem words, but if you're not sure how the stem words relate, don't make a sentence. Instead, go to the answer choices and test for Clear and Necessary. Is (A) Clear and Necessary? Yes. The sentence that proves it: A *lampoon* is a work of *ridicule*. Now Work Backwards with that sentence. Could a SONATA be a work of MOVEMENT? Doesn't make a lot of sense. Is (B) Clear and Necessary? Yes. The sentence that proves it: The beginning of a *novel* is the *prologue*. Now Work Backwards with that sentence. Could the beginning of a SONATA be a MOVEMENT? Maybe. Is (C) Clear and Necessary? Yes. The sentence that proves it: A *tableau* is presented on a *stage*. Now Work Backwards with that sentence. Could a SONATA be presented on a MOVEMENT? No. Is (D) Clear and Necessary? Yes. The sentence that proves it: A *poem* is made up of *stanzas*. Now Work Backwards with that sentence. Could a SONATA be made up of MOVEMENTS? Yes. Is (E) Clear and Necessary? No. If you look up *novel*, you won't necessarily see *narrative*, and if you look up *narrative*, you won't necessarily see *novel*.

You're left, then, with (B) and (D). Which one is better? Well, which is more likely: The beginning of a SONATA is a MOVEMENT, or a SONATA is made up of MOVEMENTS? Just pick one—you have a 50 percent chance of getting the question right. The best answer is (D).

10. *C*   You know both of the stem words, so you can probably make a
sentence. How about VIGILANCE means being very ALERT?
Now that you have a sentence, apply it to the answer choices.
Does *flippancy* mean being very *serious*? No. Does *garrulity* mean
being very *verbose*? No—be careful. Just because someone is
talkative doesn't mean he's wordy. Does *skepticism* mean being
very *doubting*? Yes. Does *judiciousness* mean being very *merciful*?
Not necessarily. Does *sentience* mean being very *attentive*? No.
The best answer, then, is (C).

11. *B*   You know both of the words, so try to make a sentence. How
about: INCOME determines WEALTH? Apply that sentence to
the answer choices. Does *performance* determine *salary*? Not
necessarily. Does *hunger* determine *appetite*? Yes. Does *medicine*
determine *health*? Not always. Does *affection* determine *feeling*?
No. Does *hurricane* determine *wind*? Not quite. The best answer is
(B).

This analogy is a good example of why you shouldn't rush.
Carefully applying the sentence gets you to (B). Speed makes
both (A) and (C) attractive.

12. *C*   When you can't make a sentence, go to the answer choices and
use Clear and Necessary. Is (A) Clear and Necessary? No. If you
look up *submissive*, you don't have to see *resign*, and if you look
up *resign*, you don't have to see *submissive*. Is (B) Clear and
Necessary? Yes. The sentence that proves it: You can't *challenge*
something that is *incontrovertible*. Now Work Backwards with that
sentence. You can't BELONG something that is EXTRINSIC.
Huh? (B) can't be right. Is (C) Clear and Necessary? Yes. The
sentence that proves it: Something *evanescent* does not *endure*.
Now Work Backwards with that sentence. Something EXTRINSIC
does not BELONG. Makes sense, right? Is (D) Clear and
Necessary? No something that is *protuberant* doesn't have to
intrude. Is (E) Clear and Necessary? Yes. The sentence that proves
it: Something *stigmatic isolates* you. Now Work Backwards with
that sentence. Does something EXTRINSIC BELONG you?
Doesn't make sense. The best answer, then, is (C).

13. *D*   When you're not sure about a sentence, go to the answer choices
and use Clear and Necessary. Is (A) Clear and Necessary? Yes.
The sentence that proves it: *reclaim* means to carry out a *rescue*.

Now Work Backwards with that sentence. Could RECANT mean to carry out a BELIEF? Yes. Is (B) Clear and Necessary? No. *Recoil* means to shrink away or withdraw—not necessarily from *adoration*. Is (C) Clear and Necessary? No. If you look up *exact*, you won't see anything about *requisition*, and vice-versa. Is (D) Clear and Necessary? Yes. The sentence that proves it: *Repeal* means to take back a *law*. Now Work Backwards with that sentence. Could RECANT mean to take back a BELIEF? Yes. Is (E) Clear and Necessary? No. If you look up *calibrate*, you don't see *rectitude*, and if you look up *rectitude*, you don't see *calibrate*.

You're left with (A) and (D). What now? Well, try Sides of the Fence. (A) has words on the same side, while (D) has words on different sides. Are RECANT and BELIEF on the same side or different sides? Different. Since the stem words are different, the correct answer has to have different words, too. So the best answer is (D).

14. *E* When you can't make a sentence with the stem words, go to the answer choices and use Clear and Necessary. Is (A) Clear and Necessary? No. Someone *philanthropic* doesn't have to possess *grace*. Is (B) Clear and Necessary? You can't cross it out if you don't know what *vainglorious* means. Is (C) Clear and Necessary? No. If you look up *priggish*, you won't see *integrity*, and if you look up *integrity*, you won't see *priggish*. Is (D) Clear and Necessary? Yes. The sentence that proves it: Someone *lecherous* lacks *decency*. Now Work Backwards with that sentence. Could someone PENURIOUS lack FRUGALITY? It's possible. Is (E) Clear and Necessary? If you don't know what *perspicacious* means, you can't cross it out.

You're down to (B), (D), and (E). As always, go with what works. Pick (D). As it turns out, however, (E) is the best answer. Someone PENURIOUS is characterized by a lot of FRUGALITY, and someone *perspicacious* is characterized by a lot of *insight*.

If you missed this problem, but got it down to (B), (D), and (E), you're on the right track. For now, you want to be concerned with whether you're applying techniques correctly. And remember—you had a one-in-three chance of getting the problem right even without knowing what PENURIOUS means.

15. **A** Chances are you don't know what OBLOQUY means, so you can't make a sentence. Since that's the case, go to the answer choices and use Clear and Necessary. Is (A) Clear and Necessary? You can't eliminate it if you don't know what *panegyric* means. Is (B) Clear and Necessary? No. *Slander* can be *inflammatory*, but it doesn't have to be. Is (C) Clear and Necessary? You can't eliminate it if you don't know what *diatribe* means. Is (D) Clear and Necessary? You can't eliminate it if you don't know what *calumny* means. Is (E) Clear and Necessary? No. If you look up *travesty*, you won't see *contemptuous*, and if you look up *contemptuous*, you won't see *travesty*.

You're left with (A), (C), and (D)—each of which contains a word you don't know. At this point, guess. A good last resort to use is to pick the choice that has the hardest words. That's (A), and indeed, (A) is the best answer.

16. **A** You may know what both stem words mean, but if you're not sure about the relationship, don't make a sentence. Use Clear and Necessary instead. Is (A) Clear and Necessary? Yes. The sentence that proves it: Something *redolent* is full of *fragrance*. Now Work Backwards with that sentence. Could something LURID be full of MELODRAMA? Yes. Is (B) Clear and Necessary? No. Something *determinate* is fixed; it doesn't have to have *definition*. Is (C) Clear and Necessary? No. If you look up *alien*, you won't see *distinction*, and if you look up *distinction*, you won't see *alien*. Is (D) Clear and Necessary? You can't eliminate it if you don't know what *metaphysical* means. Is (E) Clear and Necessary? You can't eliminate it if you don't know what *fortuitous* means.

You're left with (A), (D), and (E). One answer choice works and the other two contain words you don't know. Go with what works. The best answer is (A).

PROBLEM SET #4: EXPLANATIONS

8. **D** When you know both of the stem words, make a sentence. RECOUP means to regain a LOSS. Since you flipped the stem words in making the sentence, be sure to flip the words in the answer choices when you apply the sentence. Does *recount* mean to regain a *tale*? No. Does *recompense* mean to regain *damage*? No.

Does *record* mean to regain *document*? No. Does *recuperate* mean to regain *health*? Yes. Does *reciprocate* mean to regain *generosity*? Not quite. The best answer is (D).

9. **A** When you know both of the stem words, make a sentence. Someone with APATHY is INDIFFERENT. Now apply that sentence to the answer choices. Someone with *melancholy* is *sad*. That's true. Someone with *enthusiasm* is *zealous*. Not necessarily. Someone with *stoicism* is *emotional*. No. Someone with *talent* is *adequate*. Not quite. Someone with *discretion* is *secretive*. Not necessarily. The best answer is (A).

10. **E** When you know both of the stem words, make a sentence. If you're not sure what part of speech FLEECE is, check the second word in each of the answer choices—each is a noun. Therefore, FLEECE is a noun. So a good sentence using the stem words might be the following: A SHEEP is covered with FLEECE. Now apply the sentence to the answer choices. Is a *duck* covered with a *bill*? No. Is an *insect* covered with an *arthropod*? If you don't know what *arthropod* means, then you can't cross it out. Is a *lion* covered with *courage*? No. Is a *kangaroo* covered with a *pouch*? No. Is a *fish* covered with *scales*? Yes. (B) contains a word you don't know, and (E) works. Go with what works. The best answer is (E).

11. **B** If you're not sure what REBATE means, then you can't make a sentence. Go to the answer choices, then, and test for Clear and Necessary. Is (A) Clear and Necessary? Yes. The sentence that proves it: *Tax* means to make a *demand* on. Now Work Backwards with that sentence. Could REBATE mean to make a FORCE on? Probably not. Is (B) Clear and Necessary? Yes. The sentence that proves it: *Blunt* means to reduce the *sharpness* of. Now Work Backwards with that sentence. Could REBATE mean to reduce the FORCE of? Sure. Is (C) Clear and Necessary? Yes. The sentence that proves it: *Glean* means to gather *information*. Could REBATE mean to gather FORCE? Sure. Is (D) Clear and Necessary? Yes. The sentence that proves it: *Appease* means to make *calm*. Now Work Backwards with that sentence. Could REBATE mean to make FORCE? Doesn't make sense. Is (E) Clear and Necessary? Yes. The sentence that proves it: *Cleave* means to make a *division*. Now Work Backwards with that sentence. Could REBATE mean to make a FORCE? Not likely.

The remaining answer choices are (B) and (C). What can you do now? Try using Sides of the Fence. If you sort of know what REBATE means, then you might know REBATE and FORCE are on different sides. The right answer, then, has to be on different sides. *Blunt* and *sharpness* in (B) are on different sides, so leave it in. *Glean* and *information* are on the same side, so it can't work. The best answer is (B).

12. **C** When you know both of the stem words, make a sentence. A TAMBOURINE is a type of INSTRUMENT. Now apply that sentence to the stem words. Is a *scene* a type of *tableau*? Not necessarily. Is a *ship* a type of *yacht*? Again, not necessarily. Is a *chaise* a type of *vehicle*? If you don't know what *chaise* means, don't cross it out. Is an *agenda* a type of *meeting*? No. Is a *solution* a type of *chemistry*? No. The best answer has to be (C) because it's the only remaining answer choice.

13. **E** If you don't know what ANODYNE means, then you can't make a sentence. Go to the answer choices, then, and use Clear and Necessary. Is (A) Clear and Necessary? No. Be careful. You might think a *diet*'s purpose is to *lighten*, but it isn't. We often use *diet* in association with losing weight, but the definition of the word is actually food or drink that is regularly consumed. Eliminate (A). Is (B) Clear and Necessary? No. If you look up *antiseptic*, you won't see *promote*, and if you look up *promote*, you won't see *antiseptic*. Is (C) Clear and Necessary? No—a *vitamin* doesn't necessarily *invigorate*. Is (D) Clear and Necessary? No. A *drug* doesn't have to *prevent*. For example, a *drug* could ease. Is (E) Clear and Necessary? Yes. The sentence that proves it: The purpose of a *catalyst* is to *hasten*. Now Work Backwards with that sentence. Could the purpose of an ANODYNE be to ASSUAGE? Yes. (E) is the only answer choice that is Clear and Necessary— and Work Backwards-able—so it has to be the best answer.

14. **E** If you can't make a sentence, then go to the answer choices and use Clear and Necessary. Is (A) Clear and Necessary? If you're not sure what *cursory* means, then you can't eliminate it. Is (B) Clear and Necessary? No—an *effigy* is a crude representation of a person, usually one who is hated, but an *effigy* doesn't have to be *slanderous*. Is (C) Clear and Necessary? If you don't know what *sophism* means, then you can't cross it out. Is (D) Clear and

Necessary? No. A *provocation* incites—so it doesn't necessarily have anything to do with *irritating*. Is (E) Clear and Necessary? If you're not sure what *camp* means, then you can't cross it out.

You're left with (C) and (E), each of which contains a word you don't know. At this point, just guess. Try picking the answer choice with the hardest word or words. It's really a toss as to which one contains the hardest word or words. So just pick a choice and go. As it turns out, the best answer is (E). An APHORISM has the quality of being CONCISE, and *camp* has the quality of being *banal*. Note the use of *camp*'s secondary definition.

15. *E* If you're not sure what INCONTINENT means, then go to the answer choices and use Clear and Necessary. Is (A) Clear and Necessary? No. If you look up *impudent*, you're not going to see *suavity*, and if you look up *suavity*, you're not going to see *impudent*. Is (B) Clear and Necessary? Yes. The sentence that proves it: someone *naive* is an easy prey for *deception*. Now Work Backwards with that sentence. Could someone INCONTINENT be an easy prey for RESTRAINT? Doesn't make a lot of sense. Is (C) Clear and Necessary? Yes. The sentence that proves it: Someone *impenitent* does not have regret for his *sins*. Now Work Backwards with that sentence. Could someone INCONTINENT not have regret for his RESTRAINT? Again, doesn't make a lot of sense. Is (D) Clear and Necessary? Yes. The sentence that proves it: Someone *covetous* possesses *desire*. Now Work Backwards with that sentence. Could someone INCONTINENT possess RESTRAINT? Sure. Is (E) Clear and Necessary? Yes. The sentence that proves it: Someone *impolitic* lacks *tact*. Now Work Backwards with that sentence. Could someone INCONTINENT lack RESTRAINT? Yes.

You're down to (D) and (E). At this point, think about Sides of the Fence. (D) has words on the same side; (E) has words on different sides. So ask yourself: Are INCONTINENT and RESTRAINT on the same side or different sides? The answer: Different sides. Therefore, the answer is (E).

16. *A* If you don't know what CHARY means, then you can't make a sentence. Go to the answer choices, then, and test for Clear and Necessary. Is (A) Clear and Necessary? Yes. The sentence that

proves it: Someone *munificent* is not *stinting*. Now Work Backwards with that sentence. Could someone CHARY be not TRUSTFUL? Yes. Is (B) Clear and Necessary? No. Be careful—if you look up *pragmatic*, you won't see *irrational*, and if you look up *irrational*, you won't see *pragmatic*. Is (C) Clear and Necessary? *Mulish* means stubborn—and just because you're stubborn, doesn't mean you can't be forgiving. Is (D) Clear and Necessary? No. Just because someone is *treacherous* doesn't mean he is also *deceiving*. Is (E) Clear and Necessary? No. If you look up *cynical*, you won't see *quibbling*, and if you look up *quibbling*, you won't see *cynical*. The only answer choice that works is (A). (A) is the best answer.

PROBLEM SET #5: EXPLANATIONS

8. *B* When you know both of the stem words, make a sentence. A good sentence might be: A WOLF is a type of CANINE. Now apply that sentence to the answer choices. Is an *alligator* a type of *crocodile*? No. Is a *shrimp* a type of *crustacean*? Yes. Is a *tudpole* a type of *frog*? No. Is a *horse* a type of *hock*? No. Is a *goose* a type of *gaggle*? No. The best answer is (B).

9. *E* When you know both of the words, make a sentence. A SENTRY's job is to GUARD. Now apply that sentence to the answer choices. Is it a *judge*'s job to *legislate*? No. Is it a *student*'s job to *learn*? Not quite. Is it a *producer*'s job to *finance*? It doesn't have to be. Is it a *fireman*'s job to *save*? Again, it doesn't have to be. Is it a *conductor*'s job to *direct*? Yes. The best answer is (E).

10. *A* If you're not quite sure what the relationship is between the stem words, don't make a sentence. Go to the answer choices and test for Clear and Necessary. Is (A) Clear and Necessary? If you're not sure what *ingenue* means, then you can't eliminate it. Is (B) Clear and Necessary? If you don't know what *elocutionist* means, then you can't eliminate it. Is (C) Clear and Necessary? No. A *martyr* doesn't have to be *melancholy*. Is (D) Clear and Necessary? If you're not sure what *recreant* means, then you can't eliminate it. Is (E) Clear and Necessary. No—just because a *mercenary* works for money doesn't mean he's *avaricious*.

You're left with (A), (B), and (D). What now? Try Sides of the Fence. DANDY and FOPPISH are on the same side of the fence. If you know a little something about *ingenue*, then you might know it's on the same side of the fence as *naive*. Leave (A) in. If you don't know what *elocutionist* means at all, then you can't do anything with (B). If you know a little something about *recreant*, you know it's on the same side of the fence as *disagreeable*. Leave (D) in.

So you're still left with (A), (D), and (E). At this point, just guess. You've managed to eliminate two answer choices, so you've got a pretty good chance of getting the question right. Pick the one that has the hardest word or words. (A), (D), and (E) are all good choices—each has a tough word. As it turns out, the best answer is (A). A DANDY has the quality of being FOPPISH, and an *ingenue* has the quality of being *naive*.

11. *B* When you know both of the stem words, make a sentence. MEANDER means to MOVE. Now apply that sentence to the answer choices. Does *concentrate* mean to *think*? Not quite. Does *ramble* mean to *talk*? Yes. Does *lope* mean to *run*? Yes. Does *mutter* mean to *stammer*? No. Does *labor* mean to *work*? No. You're left with more than one answer choice, so now what? Make the sentence more specific. MEANDER means to MOVE aimlessly. Does *ramble* mean to *talk* aimlessly? Yes. Does *lope* mean to *run* aimlessly? No. The best answer is (B).

12. *B* If you're no sure what PAEAN means, then don't make a sentence. Go to the answer choices instead and test for Clear and Necessary. Is (A) Clear and Necessary? No. If you look up *hymn*, you don't have to see *catholicism*, and if you look up *catholicism*, you don't have to see *hymn*. Is (B) Clear and Necessary? Yes. The sentence that proves it: An *elegy* is a song of *grief*. Now Work Backwards with that sentence. Could a PAEAN be a song of TRIBUTE? Sure. Is (B) Clear and Necessary? No. If you look up *canticle*, it doesn't have to say *purity*, and if you look up *purity*, it doesn't have to say *canticle*. Is (C) Clear and Necessary? No. If you look up *psalm*, you don't have to see *gravity*, and if you look up *gravity*, you don't have to see *psalm*. Is (E) Clear and Necessary? No. A *eulogy* is a speech of praise—not of *devotion*. The only answer choice that is Clear and Necessary is (B), so it has to be the right answer. And it is—(B) is the best answer.

13. **C** When you can't make a sentence, go to the answer choices and look for Clear and Necessary. Is (A) Clear and Necessary? Yes. The sentence that proves it: A *cameo* shows an *image*. Now Work Backwards with that sentence. Could an EPAULET show a DECORATION? Probably not—it doesn't make a lot of sense. Is (B) Clear and Necessary? No. An *epée* is a sword, as is a *rapier*, but the words are not related. Is (C) Clear and Necessary? Yes. The sentence that proves it: A *cavalry* is a military *unit*. Now Work Backwards with that sentence. Could an EPAULET be a military DECORATION. Possibly. Is (D) Clear and Necessary? Yes. The sentence that proves it: A *lapel* is a part of a *jacket*. Now Work Backwards with that sentence. Could an EPAULET be a part of a DECORATION? It could. Is (E) Clear and Necessary? No. A *medal* is supposed to honor—it doesn't have to be an *ornament*.

You're left, then, with (C) and (D). Both are Clear and Necessary, and both are Work Backwards-able. So what now? At this point, just guess. You've got a 50% chance of getting the right answer. Pick the one that has the hardest word or words. As it turns out, the answer is (C).

14. **C** If you don't know what PERORATION means, then don't make a sentence. Go to the answer choices instead and test for Clear and Necessary. Is (A) Clear and Necessary? Yes. The sentence that proves it: A *conference* is meeting for *discussion*. Now Work Backwards with that sentence. Could a PERORATION be a meeting for SPEECH? Doesn't make a lot of sense. Is (B) Clear and Necessary? Yes. The sentence that proves it: An *itinerary* is a plan for *travel*. Now Word Backwards with that sentence. Could a PERORATION be a plan for a SPEECH? Possibly. Is (C) Clear and Necessary? Yes. The sentence that proves it: An *epilogue* is the end of a *play*. Now Work Backwards with that sentence. Could a PERORATION be the end of a SPEECH? Yes. Is (D) Clear and Necessary? Yes. The sentence that proves it: *Letters* make up the *alphabet*. Now Work Backwards with that sentence. Could PERORATIONS make up a SPEECH? Sure. Is (E) Clear and Necessary? No. *Destruction* doesn't have to deal with the ruin of a *life*.

The remaining answer choices are (B), (C), and (E). If you don't know anything else about PERORATION, then just guess—you have a one-in-three chance of getting the question right. Pick the answer choice that has the hardest word or words. That would be either (B) or (C). Either is a good guess. As it turns out, the best answer is (C). A PERORATION is the end of SPEECH.

15. **A** When you know both of the stem words, make a sentence. ABHOR means to DISLIKE a lot. Now apply that sentence to the answer choices. Does *venerate* mean to *esteem* a lot? It could. Does *procrastinate* mean to *delay* a lot? No—it just means to *delay*. Does *testify* mean to *affirm*? No. Does *condone* mean to *neglect* a lot? No—it means to *neglect* or overlook purposefully. Does *detract* mean to *dismiss*? No. The best answer is (A).

16. **D** When you know both of the stem words, make a sentence. TOTTER is a type of GAIT. Now apply that sentence to the answer choices. Is a *furrow* a type of *brow*? No. Is a *simper* a type of *smile*? Yes. Is a *canter* a type of *gallop*? No. Is a *stutter* a type of *speech*? Yes. Is a *deduction* a type of *thought*? No. Be careful—a *deduction* is a type of reasoning, not *thought*.

Since you're left with more than one answer choice, make the sentence more specific. TOTTER is an unsteady GAIT. Is a *simper* an unsteady *smile*? No. Is a *stutter* an unsteady *speech*? Yes. The best answer is (D).

CHAPTER

6

Reading

Comprehension

THE TERRAIN OF THE MUNDANE

Practically every test taker in the world hates reading comprehension, and for a very good reason: it's incredibly boring. Well, take heart. Though we can't make the passages any less dull, we can try to make the time spent here a little less painful.

How can we do that? Well, let's talk about how Joe Bloggs approaches reading comprehension. First, he reads the passage. That means he reads the *entire* passage—each and every word. He tries to digest this information as much as possible as he reads, and then he moves on to the questions. For each question, he reads the question, goes back to the passage to find the answer, rereads the part of the passage that contains the answer, and only then goes on to the answer choices. Finally, after reading all of the answer choices, he picks the one he thinks is best.

What's wrong with this approach? There's too much reading going on. Basically, the typical person reads the passage at least twice—a big waste of time. Why is reading and rereading passages a bad idea? In order to do well on reading comprehension, you don't need to read that much. It's not *how much* you read that's important; it's *what* you read.

WHICH PASSAGE FIRST?

Before we discuss how you should approach reading comprehension, let's talk about which passage you should do first. On the computer test, you don't have a choice. The passage you do first is the passage that appears first—you can't control the order. On the paper test, things are a little different.

For the paper test, you have one long passage and one short passage for each verbal section. The passage you want to tackle first is the long one. Why? Because the long passage has more questions, and therefore more potential points to gain. If you don't have time to get to the short passage, who cares? It only has three or four questions. Comparatively, the long passage has seven or eight.

TYPES OF PASSAGES

Subject matter for reading comprehension is going to vary from test to test, but you can expect to see three major categories represented.

- Science
- Humanities
- Social studies

For the paper test, you typically have one science passage and one humanities or social studies passage for each verbal section. For the computer test, it's not so rigid. You might see one science passage, one humanities passage, and one social studies passage. Or you might see two science passages and two social studies passages. We can't predict what's going to show up exactly because you can have anywhere from to two to four passages on the verbal section of the computer test.

In the end, it doesn't really matter what the subject matter of a passage is. The important thing is not to let a particular category scare you. For example, if you hate science and haven't taken a science class since high school, don't think that a science passage is necessarily going to be a killer. Often, a science passage is relatively easy. Though the jargon may be hard to get past, all the information contained in the passage is factual. Therefore, there's no need for you to do any interpreting or analyzing. The passages ETS selects are pretty cut-and -dried.

POLITICALLY CORRECT

That said, there is one type of passage in which subject matter may count—and that's when ETS uses what we call a PC (or politically correct) passage. Most of the time a PC passage falls into either the humanities or social studies category. We call it a PC passage because it deals with a topic such as women, African Americans, Native Americans, or even the environment.

What can you expect about a PC passage? Everything in the passage is going to be either neutral or positive (sometimes even inspirational) in tone. In no way can a correct answer for a question be un-PC. For example: "Women should not work in the public sphere because they are not as rational as men." That sentence is *very* un-PC, and therefore could never be the right answer. So anytime you have a passage that has a subject matter such as women or minorities, you already know a little something. You know that every right answer must be PC and that any answer choice that is not PC must be wrong.

Keep in mind that ETS, for the most part, is always PC—obviously so on a PC passage, but also on other passages that aren't explicitly PC. Think of it this way: Does ETS want to say anything that's going to be controversial? No. Why not? Lawsuit, lawsuit, lawsuit. ETS's whole goal is to make money. Lawsuits mean losing money. If anyone was in any way offended by anything, ETS could be subject to a lawsuit. Think of what the National Organization for Women might say if it read the sentence "Women should not work in the public sphere . . . " on the GRE. ETS ain't stupid—so it's not going to do anything stupid.

WHAT'S THE BIG IDEA?

Okay, we've established that Joe Bloggs wastes time because he reads too much. Quite simply, there's no need to read so much. In fact, reading comprehension only becomes hard when you do read too much. Remember, it's not *how much* you read that counts. It's *what* you read.

So what should you do? Well, what's the primary goal the first time you see a passage? All you really want is a general idea of what the passage is about, right? You want the gist of the passage—that is, the main idea. You don't really care about the specifics, at least not yet. In order to get the main idea of a passage, do you really need to read the entire thing? No, of course not. To find the main idea of a passage, all you have to do is read a few sentences:

- The first two sentences of the first paragraph

- The first sentence of each following paragraph

- The final sentence of the entire passage

That's it. These sentences alone are sufficient to give you the main idea. Why can these sentences alone tell you the main idea? You need to consider what good writing is—or rather, how good writing is organized. Good writing is well structured. That means for every paragraph there has to be a *topic sentence*. A topic sentence is a sentence that tells you what's going to happen in a particular paragraph. Technically, a topic sentence can be located anywhere in a paragraph, but usually, it's the first (sometimes the second) sentence of a paragraph.

So if a topic sentence tells you what's going to take place in a paragraph, then guess what? To get the main idea, all you really need to do is read the topic sentence of each paragraph in a passage. We make you read a little more at the beginning because it's the introductory paragraph, and a little at the very end because it often provides some sort of conclusion.

REALLY?

At this point, you're probably thinking, "There's no way that I can read so few sentences and actually get the main idea." You can. But you have to practice using this technique because you're not going to be comfortable with it at first—and therefore, you're not going to like it. But trust us, it works. After reading the first sentence in a paragraph, ask yourself: "Does what I've read give me enough information that I can *anticipate* what's going to be discussed?" If not, then it's okay to read one or two more sentences. But don't go hog-wild. The whole point is to save valuable time by not reading so much the first time around. Remember, the very first time you see a passage, you don't need to know specifics. All you want to do is find out what is the main idea.

COGITATE AND MASTICATE

In other words, think and chew. Once you've read the topic sentences, stop for a second. Don't leap ahead and start tackling the questions. Ask yourself: "What did I just read?" And then, in your own words, *state the main idea of the passage*. You don't have to articulate a beautiful sentence for the main idea. You just need to say what the main idea is in a short, simple sentence or phrase. It could be: "Macroeconomists good, microeconomists bad."

It is incredibly important that you state the main idea before you go on to the questions. By stating the main idea, you ensure that you understand the sentences that you read. If you aren't able to state the main idea, then you know something isn't right.

(Note: There is, on occasion, a passage that is made up of only one paragraph. In this case, you may need to do a little more reading than usual. However, don't lose sight of the fact that you should stop reading once you have enough information to anticipate what's going to happen in the rest of the paragraph.)

THE QUESTIONS

After you've got the main idea in your head, you can move on to the questions. For the purpose of simplicity, we break down all questions into three types:

- General

- Specific

- Weird

POE

To answer any of these question types, there's one thing you have to do: POE.

Finding the right answer is often hard to do on reading comprehension. Well, if you can't make it through the front door—that is, find the right answer; then try the back door: In short, find the wrong answers first and get rid of them. It's usually much easier to identify wrong answers over right ones because, after all, there are more wrong answers than there are right ones on any question. Also, don't forget that verbal is really about the best answer, not the right one. Sometimes that means finding the least bad answer, and to find the least bad answer, you have to look for the ones that are *really* horrible first.

(Note that since reading comprehension is largely about POE, you must—as on all verbal questions—look at each and every single answer choice.)

EXTREME WORDING

The first thing to watch out for on reading comprehension is extreme wording. Typically, extreme wording in an answer choice will make that answer choice wrong. Take a look at the following sentence:

> Everyone loves chocolate ice cream.

ETS would never have this sentence be part of the correct answer. Why? Because it's too easy to prove wrong. All you have to say is "I hate chocolate ice cream."

The following provides a list of words that usually go "too far" in the land of ETS.

> everyone
>
> no one
>
> only
>
> never
>
> always
>
> must
>
> impossible

Keep in mind that, at first glance, some words may not look as if they are extreme. For example, the word *is*. Consider the following sentence:

> It is the answer.

Does ETS know for sure that it is? How can ETS prove it without a doubt? Or think about the word *will*:

> The United States will buy more imports in the
> next ten years.

Is ETS capable of predicting the future? This isn't to say that, if an answer choice contains *is* or *will*, it's wrong. Just remember that, in certain contexts, words can take on extreme meanings. Here's a list of words that ETS uses on the reading comprehension section that can often be extreme:

> resolve
>
> reconcile
>
> prove
>
> define
>
> trace

Well, if extreme wording is bad, then guess what? Wishy-washy wording is good. Words like *can, may, most, some, sometimes, possible, seldom, few*.

So, the general rule of thumb: Answer choices that contain extreme wording are usually wrong. Answer choices that contain wishy-washy wording or are moderate in tone are usually right.

COMMON SENSE

The second POE tool to use on reading comprehension is common sense. Use it! Just because something's in print doesn't mean it's plausible. Indeed, ETS often includes ridiculous answer choices on reading comprehension. For example:

> According to the passage, the author believes the purpose of children's literature to be which of the following?
>
> (A) Expose children to the cruelties of life
> (B) Instruct children on the difference between right and wrong

Which is the better answer? Clearly (B). You don't have to read anything to know that (A) is wrong. All you have to is exercise a little common sense.

PARAPHRASE, PARAPHRASE, PARAPHRASE

Finally, the most important POE tool on reading comprehension is to paraphrase. The right answer to a question is never going to be a direct quote from the passage. Rather, the right answer is going to be a paraphrase; that is, a restatement of what's in the passage. Which is why there's one thing you should always do for every question, no matter what type it falls into: Always state the answer to a question in your own words *before* you look at the answer choices. It's the same kind of thinking as coming up with your own word on sentence completions.

When you state the answer to a question in your own words, what you're doing is paraphrasing. And once you know what you're looking for, it's much easier to be discerning and figure out what's a bad answer choice. Not taking the time to paraphrase and rushing to the answer choices is one of the worst mistakes people make on reading comprehension.

GENERAL QUESTIONS

Okay—let's go back and talk about the question types. Let's start off with general questions. These are questions that ask you to provide "big picture" information about the passage. Below are some examples of how general questions can be worded:

Main Idea

The primary purpose of the passage is to
The main idea of the passage is
The passage focuses primarily on which of the following?
The passage is primarily concerned with
Which of the following best states the central idea of the passage?

Organization/Structure

Which of the following best describes the organization of the passage as a whole?
Which of the following is the most accurate description of the organization of the passage

Other

Which of the following titles best describes the content of the passage?
Which of the following is the best title for the passage?
The passage would most likely be found in
The passage would be most likely to appear as part of

Tone

The author's attitude toward . . . can best be described as
The author's attitude toward . . . is best described as which of the following?

To answer any general question, focus on the main idea. Typically, an answer to a general question contains some sort of paraphrased version of the main idea. Also, don't forget about your tools for POE. As mentioned earlier, be wary of answer choices that:

1. Contain extreme wording.

2. Don't make common sense.

3. Don't match your paraphrase (i.e., the main idea you came up with).

Also, watch out for answer choices that:

1. *Mention something you haven't read about.* If it isn't mentioned at all in the topic sentences, there's no way it can be right.

2. *Are too detailed or specific.* People often miss general questions because they read the entire passage and get caught up in the specifics. That is, in reading the entire passage, they lose sight of the main idea. Therefore, they end up picking an answer choice that contains information from the passage, but that isn't the main idea.

3. *Are too general or beyond the scope of the passage.* Sometimes ETS is too vague. For example, if the main idea was about eighteenth-century *female poets*, an overly general answer choice would say something about eighteenth-century *writers*.

SPECIAL NOTE ON TONE QUESTIONS

Tone questions are a gift. Occasionally, they can be specific questions—that is, they ask about how the author feels about a particular paragraph rather than how he or she feels about the entire passage. But the approach to tone questions, whether general or specific, is basically the same. Take a look at the following answer choices:

     (A)   overwhelming support
     (B)   unabashed admiration
     (C)   qualified appreciation
     (D)   profound ambivalence
     (E)   deep-rooted hostility

What's the right answer? Without reading the passage, you know it has to be (C). Why? Think of extremes. ETS doesn't like extremes, right? Therefore, the right answer to a tone question is never going to be extremely positive or extremely negative. It's going to be somewhere in between. An author can be neutral or objective. He or she can be appreciative or slightly critical. But the author is never going to love something to death or hate something completely. Again, extreme is bad; moderation is good.

(Note that *apathetic* or *indifferent* are always wrong answers on tone questions. If the author didn't care about something, why would he or she write about it?)

QUIZ #1

For each of the following passages, find the main idea.

Passage #1

If my colleagues and I are right, we may soon be saying good-bye to the idea that our universe was a single fireball created in the big bang. We are exploring a new theory based on
5 a 15-year-old notion that the universe went through a stage of inflation. During that time, the theory holds, the cosmos became exponentially large within an infinitesimal fraction of a second. At the end of this period,
10 the universe continued its evolution according to the big bang model. As workers refined this inflationary scenario, they uncovered some surprising consequences. One of them constitutes a fundamental change in how the
15 cosmos is seen. Recent versions of inflationary theory assert that instead of being an expanding ball of fire the universe is a huge, growing fractal. It consists of many inflating balls that produce more balls, which in turn
20 produce more balls, ad infinitum.

Cosmologists did not arbitrarily invent this rather peculiar vision of the universe. Several workers, first in Russia and later in the U.S., proposed the inflationary hypothesis that is the
25 basis of its foundation. We did so to solve some of the complications left by the old big bang theory. In its standard form, the big bang theory maintains that the universe was born about 15 billion years ago from a cosmological
30 singularity—a state in which the temperature and density are infinitely high. Of course, one cannot really speak in physical terms about these quantities as being infinite. One usually assumes that the current law of physics did not apply
35 then. They took hold only after the density of the universe dropped below the so-called Planck density, which equals about 10^{94} grams per cubic centimeter.

As the universe expanded, it gradually
40 cooled. Remnants of the primordial cosmic fire still surrounds us in the form of the microwave background radiation. This radiation indicates that the temperature of the universe has dropped to 2.7 kelvins. The 1965 discovery of
45 this background radiation proved to be the crucial evidence in establishing the big bang theory as the preeminent theory of cosmology. The big bang theory also explained the abundances of hydrogen, helium and other
50 elements in the universe.

As investigators developed the theory, they uncovered complications. For example, the standard big bang theory, coupled with the modern theory of elementary particles, predicts
55 the existence of many super heavy particles carrying magnetic charge—that is, objects that have only one magnetic pole. These magnetic monopoles would have a typical mass 10^{16} times that of the proton, or about 0.00001 milligram.
60 According to the standard big bang theory, monopoles should have emerged very early in the evolution of the universe and should now be as abundant as protons. In that case, the mean density of matter in the universe would be
65 about 15 orders of magnitude greater than its present value, which is about 10^{-29} gram per cubic centimeter.

19. Which of the following best expresses the main idea of the passage?

(A) Scientists have proven the big bang theory to be inaccurate and replaced it with the concept that the universe inflated over time.

(B) Because the big bang theory cannot account for the actual state of the universe, it is possible that the universe actually evolved through inflation.

(C) The big bang theory cannot be discounted completely, but the inflationary theory is also plagued by inconsistencies.

(D) The big bang theory is incorrect because of the absence of magnetic monopoles in the universe.

(E) Cosmologists have combined the big bang theory with the inflationary theory to produce a new picture of the universe's evolution.

Passage #2

Over the last decade surrealism has returned with a vengeance, the subject of many exhibitions, symposia, books, and articles. Lest I merely add another line to the list, I
5 want to begin with a reflection on the past repression and present recovery of this movement. For not so long ago surrealism was played down in Anglo-American accounts of modernism (if not in French ones). In effect
10 it was lost twice to such art history: repressed in abstractionist histories founded on cubism (where it appears, if at all, as a morbid interregnum before abstract expressionism), it was also displaced in neo-avant-garde
15 accounts focused on dada and Russian constructivism (where it appears, if at all, as a decadent version of vanguardist attempts to integrate art and life).

In Anglo-American formalism surrealism
20 was considered a deviant art movement: improperly visual and impertinently literary, relatively inattentive to the imperatives of form and mostly indifferent to the laws of genre, a paradoxical avant-garde concerned
25 with infantile states and outmoded forms, not properly modernist at all. For neo-avant-garde artists who challenged this hegemonic three decades ago, its very deviance might have made surrealism an attractive object. But
30 such was not the case. Since this formalist model of modernism was staked on the autonomy of modern art as separate from social practice and grounded in visual experience, its antagonist, the neo-avant-garde
35 account of modernism, stressed the two movements, dada and constructivism, that appeared most opposed to this visualist autonomy—that sought to destroy the separate institution of art in an anarchic attack
40 on its formal conventions, as did dada, or to transform it according to the materialist practices of a revolutionary society, as did constructivism. Again surrealism was lost in the shuffle. To the neo-avant-gardists who
45 challenged the formalist account in the 1950s and 1960s, it too appeared corrupt: technically kitschy, philosophically subjectivity, hypocritically elitist. Hence when artists involved in pop and minimalism turned away
50 from the likes of Picasso and Matisse, they turned to such figures as Duchamp and Rodchenko, not to precedents like Ernst and Giacometti.

Obviously times have changed. The
55 formalist idea of optical purity has long since fallen, and the avant-gardist critique of

categorical art is fatigued, at least in practices that limit "institution" to exhibition space and "art" to traditional media. A space for
60 surrealism has opened up: an *impensé* within the old narrative, it has become a privileged point for the contemporary critique of this narrative. And yet for the most part art history has filled this new space with the same old
65 stuff. Despite its redefining of the image, surrealism is still often reduced to painting; and despite its confounding of reference and intention, surrealism is still often folded into discourses of iconography and style. One
70 reason for this art-historical failure is a neglect of the other principal precondition for the return of surrealism as an object of study: the dual demands of contemporary art and theory.

1. The author is primarily concerned with

   (A) comparing surrealism with other movements in art such as dada and constructivism
   (B) challenging the traditional view of surrealism as confined to the realm of art
   (C) examining surrealism's place in the history of modern art movements
   (D) exploring the reasons why surrealism has long been ignored as an object of study
   (E) refuting the claim that surrealism focused on the literary over the visual

SPECIFIC QUESTIONS

These are questions that ask about particular details in the passage. Like general questions, specific questions can be phrased in several ways. For example:

The author suggests that . . .

According to the passage, . . .

The author mentions . . .

According to the author, . . .

Since specific questions ask you about details from the passage, there's one thing you must do for every specific question:

> Refer back to the passage

No ifs, ands, or buts. You must do this. Never, never, never rely on your memory. Your memory is your worst enemy. That being said, let's talk about the two major groups of specific questions: Line reference and lead word.

Line Reference

Line reference questions are easy to identify because they always contain a line reference. For example:

The author mentions T. H. White (line 40) in order to . . .

Which of the following situations is most analogous to the situation described by the author as . . . (line 15-19)?

You get the idea. Line reference questions are great because they tell you where you should go in the passage to find the information. But they're also a little tricky because the information you're looking for typically isn't contained exactly in the line reference. Rather, it's usually a little bit before the line reference or a little bit after. Therefore, here's your approach to any line reference question:

1. Use the line reference to guide you to the right area of the passage.

2. Read roughly five lines above the line reference and roughly five lines below.

3. Answer the question based on what you've read in your own words (i.e., paraphrase) before moving on to the answer choices.

Lead Word

Lead word questions are basically line reference questions without the line reference. Well, if you don't have the line reference, how do you know where in the passage to look for the information? The answer is: The lead word.

The lead word is a word or phrase that's easy to skim for. Usually, the lead word stands out in the question because it's the most important or the most specific. What's the lead word in the following question:

It can be inferred that, during the 1840s, the abolitionist movement did which of the following?

The lead word is *1840s*. *Abolitionist movement* could be a lead word(s), but only if the entire passage were not about the abolitionist movement. If the main idea were the abolitionist movement, would *abolitionist movement* be easy to skim for? Nope. *1840s* is a good lead word because it's specific and it's very easy to skim for. Numbers, words that have capital letters at the beginning, and italicized words are all good lead words because they're easy to skim for.

Once you've identified the lead word in a question, here's your approach.

1. Skim (not read) the passage for the lead word.

2. Once you find the line that contains the lead word, read roughly five lines before and five lines after.

3. Based on what you've read, answer the question in your own words (i.e., paraphrase). Do this before moving on to the answer choices.

Keep in mind that the lead word may appear more than once in the passage. So if you read the lines surrounding the lead word and don't find the answer to the question, skim the rest of the passage for another appearance of the lead word.

Also keep in mind that the lead word in the question won't necessarily be perfectly represented in the passage. For example, if the lead word in the question is "governmental intrusion," you may find the passage talking about "intrusive actions by the government."

POE FOR SPECIFIC QUESTIONS

Paraphrasing is the key to specific questions. However, you also have some POE tools to help you out as well. As always, watch out for answer choices that:

1. Contain extreme wording

2. Don't make common sense

3. Don't match your paraphrase

Also, watch out for answer choices that:
1. Contain information that's true according to the passage but that doesn't answer the question
2. Misrepresent information found in the same area of the passage as the correct answer

QUIZ #2

For each of the following questions, locate the answer in the passage by using either a line reference or a lead word. Make sure you paraphrase the answer to the question before looking at the answer choices.

The feminists of revolutionary France were not the only persons hoping that the current paroxysm of social change would bring about improvement of their state. A most singular
5 category of men, the public executioners, had thought that the advent of a new regime would transform that peculiar disdain in which society held them. For hundreds of years, the post of Master of the High Works in France's
10 major cities was held by men from ten or so dynastic families, members of an abominable elite that had developed as a consequence of social prejudice: anyone who had ever been a *bourreau* could never hope to find another job,
15 nor could he aspire to marry any woman not herself the daughter of a colleague. In this way the dreadful dynasties developed. The best known recipients of this peculiar distinction were the Sanson family, who
20 operated in Paris and Versailles from 1688 to 1847; the diary kept by Charles Henri Sanson, executioner of Paris during the Terror, provides details of the deaths of many illustrious victims.
25 Several passages in the Sanson diary suggest that professional executioners did not particularly like having to kill women. This chivalrous repugnance later spread through the Court d'Assizes; while women were
30 regularly condemned to death in the late nineteenth and early twentieth centuries, in fact they were almost always reprieved. A roughly contemporaneous reluctance to execute women in the United States has been
35 explained by recent American feminists as evidence of women's almost non-existent social status at that time; to compensate for legal inegality the men who were women's judges, prosecutors, jurors adopted a 'protective'
40 stance, frequently acquitting women who, in modern retrospect, seem guilty. In France the egalitarian practices of earlier centuries were ultimately reinstated, which guillotined five women.
45 This temporary preservation of execution as an exclusively male domain—a thing too necessary and revolting to be inflicted on or endured by half the population—apparently did not strike legislators as being intolerably
50 illogical, or as being rather a back-handed sort

of compliment to men. Proper equality would have involved either equal rights and equal punishment for men and women, or else abolition. However, arguments against the
55 death penalty tend rather to develop from general humanitarian principles, and less from the putative equality of women.
Chivalry, indeed, would seem to have been the nineteenth century's solution to the
60 problems posed to the authorities by 'female' executions. But more importantly, chivalry enabled society to observe a version of that logic set forth in 1791 by Olympe de Gouges, a logic echoed later in the United States by
65 Wendell Phillips, who bluntly declared 'You have granted that women may be hung; therefore you must grant that woman may vote.' In not executing women, the judiciary body was able to sidestep these irritating
70 formulations: if women did not receive equal punishment under law, perhaps they need not be assured of equal rights.

1. Which of the following best describes the author's attitude toward the formation of public executioner dynasties?

   (A) Qualified appreciation
   (B) Studied neutrality
   (C) Tempered disapproval
   (D) Vehement condemnation
   (E) Resigned acceptance

2. According to the passage, the unwillingness of men to condemn women to death in the United States during the late nineteenth century was

   (A) a reflection of the influence of the Court d'Assizes on the judicial system in the United States

   (B) in accordance with women's low standing in society and their lack of legal rights

   (C) a result of a popular movement promoting the chivalrous idea that women should be protected from harm

   (D) a misinterpretation on the part of modern historians, who believed many of the women to be guilty

   (E) a reaction to the excesses of the French Revolution and the large number of women who were guillotined

3. The passage suggests that, during the French Revolution, popular arguments against the death penalty did which of the following?

   (A) Emphasized the failure of the death penalty to suppress dissent.

   (B) Asserted that the defense of the death penalty was based upon faulty logic.

   (C) Supported indirectly the notion that men were equal to women.

   (D) Addressed only the needs of men, at the expense of those of women.

   (E) Failed to employ the reasoning that men and women should have equal rights.

WEIRD QUESTIONS

Finally . . . weird questions. We call these questions weird because they have special formats. They're also weird because they tend to be more time-consuming than usual. The three types of weird questions are:

Roman Numeral

> All of the following are stated by the author as the advantages of hydroponics EXCEPT

> According to the passage, neutrinos are NOT

> It can be inferred from the passage that which of the following is LEAST compatible with Graham's approach to dance?

Except/Least/Not

> Which of the following can be inferred from the passage about the earliest observations of Mars?
>
> I.   Though Aristotle correctly placed Mars further from the earth than the moon, he drew this conclusion based upon a faulty assumption.
> II. Ptolemaeus' writings were based in large part on the work done by Hipparchus, though the two disagreed on the relationship of the earth to the universe.
> III. The recognition of Mars as a planet and not simply a star could not be confirmed until the development of the telescope.
>
> (A) I only
> (B) III only
> (C) I and III only
> (D) II and III
> (E) I, II, and III

Questions in the Answer Choices

> The passage supplies information to answer which of the following questions?

Except/Least/Not

Often these questions are not that difficult, but they tend to consume a lot of time. Also, they can be a little tricky. What makes these questions easy to miss is the fact that you're trying to find information that's *incorrect* according to the passage—and usually, it's your job to find out the correct information. To sidestep this pitfall, here's how to approach EXCEPT/LEAST/NOT questions.

1. For each answer choice, ask yourself if it is true according to the passage or false.

2. If the answer choice is true, put a Y next to it; if the answer choice is false, put a N next to it.

3. After going through all the answer choices, you should have four Ys and one N. The answer is the one that doesn't belong—the N.

As long as you follow these steps, you should be okay. Just remember, you're looking for information that's *not* true.

Roman Numeral

Roman numeral questions, as you can probably tell, all too easily eat up a lot of time. And that's because these questions actually have three questions for every one.

To save yourself a little time, here's the approach you should take.

1. Focus on one Roman numeral at a time.

2. If you discover that a certain Roman numeral is false, immediately go to the answer choices and cross out any that contains that Roman numeral. Similarly, if you discover that a certain Roman numeral is true, immediately go to the answer choices and cross out any that doesn't contain that Roman numeral.

By using this process, you can often avoid looking at all three Roman numerals. Instead, you may only have to investigate two of them.

QUESTIONS IN THE ANSWER CHOICE

These questions are also time-consuming, particularly because there's nothing like a line reference or a lead word to help you out. The approach you need to take on these questions:

1. Look for a lead word in each answer choice.

2. Use that lead word to guide you to the right part of the passage.

3. Ask yourself if the question is answered by that part of the passage.

QUESTION ORDER AND CHRONOLOGY

On the computer test, you can't decide which questions to do first: general, specific, or weird. On the paper test, however, you can. Take advantage of this. You can control the question order, not ETS. We recommend that you do general questions first, then specific, and finally, weird.

1. Do general questions first because once you've read the topic sentences and found the main idea, you've got the information to answer the general questions. Also, remember that wrong answer choices on general questions are often too detailed or specific. You won't fall into this trap if you get all of the general questions out of the way before even looking at specific questions.

2. Do specific questions next because you can find all of the answers quickly by using line references and lead words. Don't forget to paraphrase the answer to a specific question before moving on to the answer choices.

3. Save weird questions for last simply because they take up a lot of time.

As an additional note for paper- test takers, specific questions are typically arranged in chronological order. So if you're having trouble finding a lead word, keep in mind that the first half of the specific questions usually ask about the first half of the passage and the last half of the specific questions usually ask about the last half.

IN SUMMARY . . .

For reading comprehension, it's the approach that counts. Break bad habits. Don't rely on your memory. Always paraphrase. The bottom line is that reading comprehension is an open-book test. All of the answers are in the passage. It's your job to hunt them down, and you can do that most effectively through POE—that is, getting rid of bad answer choices first.

Finally, don't forget that reading a lot isn't necessarily a good thing. It's not how much you read, it's what you read. We hope that with our approach you're not reading as much as you were before. However, just because you're reading less doesn't mean you can afford to read quickly. You're not reading a lot anymore, so take the time to make sure you understand what you do read.

1. Before you answer any questions, always find the main idea. You can find the main idea by reading the first two sentences of the first paragraph, the first sentence of each succeeding paragraph, and the last sentence of the entire passage. Be sure to state the main idea in your own words.

2. Don't forget that POE is the best way to get the right answer on reading comprehension. Be wary of any answer choice that
   a) contains extreme wording,
   b) doesn't make common sense, or
   c) doesn't match your paraphrase.

3. General questions. These questions ask about "big picture" information such as what's the main idea or how is the passage organized or what's the author's tone. To answer general questions, focus on the main idea. Watch out for answer choices that
   a) mention something you haven't read,
   b) are too detailed or specific, or
   c) are too general or go beyond the scope of the passage.

4. Specific questions. These questions ask about particular details in the passage. Use either line references or lead words to guide you to the part of the passage that contains the answer. Always remember to read five lines before and five lines after. Watch out for answer choices that
   a) contain information that's true according to the passage but that doesn't answer the question, or
   b) misrepresent information found in the same area of the passage as the correct answer.

5. Weird questions. These questions are the most time-consuming. For EXCEPT/LEAST/NOT questions, play the Y/N game. For Roman numeral questions, focus on one Roman numeral at a time. For questions in the answer choices questions, look for a lead word in each answer choice to take you to the right part of the passage.

6. Above all . . . never rely on your memory. Always refer back to the passage. And always, always paraphrase. Paraphrasing helps you see which answer choices are bad because it makes sure you understood what you just read.

Quiz #1: Answers

Passage #1

To find the main idea, here's all you need to read:

- If my colleagues and I are right, we may soon be saying good-bye to the idea that our universe was a single fireball created in the big bang. We are exploring a new theory based on a 15-year-old notion that the universe went through a stage of inflation.

- Cosmologists did not arbitrarily invent this rather peculiar vision of the universe.

- As the universe expanded, it gradually cooled.

- As investigators developed the theory, they uncovered complications.

- In that case, the mean density of matter in the universe would be about 15 orders of magnitude greater than its present value, which is about 10^{-29} gram per cubic centimeter.

Given these sentences, how might you paraphrase the main idea? That the big bang theory may be wrong and that the inflationary theory may be right. Now you can go to the answer choices.

Eliminate (A) because it's too extreme. Scientists haven't *proven* the big bang theory wrong. Leave (B) in because it's a good match for your paraphrase. Also, note how moderate (B) is. Eliminate (C) because it says the inflationary theory is bad. Remember, it's the big bang theory that's problematic, not the inflationary theory. Eliminate (D) because it mentions stuff (magnetic monopoles) you didn't read about. Eliminate (E) because it suggests the big bang theory is okay. The best answer, then, is (B).

Passage #2

To find the main idea, here are the sentences you need to read:

- Over the last decade surrealism has returned with a vengeance, the subject of many exhibitions, symposia, books, and articles. Lest I merely add another line to the list, I want to begin with a reflection on the past repression and present recovery of this movement

- In Anglo-American formalism surrealism was considered a deviant art movement: improperly visual and impertinently literary, relatively inattentive to the imperatives of form and mostly indifferent to the laws of genre, a paradoxical avant-garde concerned with infantile states and outmoded forms, not properly modernist at all.

- Obviously times have changed.

- One reason for this art-historical failure is a neglect of the other principal precondition for the return of surrealism as an object of study: the dual demands of contemporary art and theory.

From these sentences alone, you can come up with the main idea. What is the main idea? To paraphrase: that surrealism is no longer being ignored as it once was.

Now that you've stated the main idea, go to the answer choices. Eliminate (A) because you didn't read anything about dada or constructivism. Eliminate (B) because you didn't read anything about surrealism being limited to art. Eliminate (C) because you didn't read anything about surrealism's place in history. Keep (D) for now because it says something about surrealism being ignored. Eliminate (E) because it's too specific—only the topic sentence of the second paragraph mentions the literary over the visual. The best answer, then, is (D).

Quiz #2: Answers

1. **C** This tone question is specific, not general. Regardless, for any tone question, extreme answer choices are bad. What answer choices are too extreme here? Definitely (D), so cross it out. The other answer choices are fairly moderate, so leave them in for now. What now? Use "dynasties" as your lead word. That takes you to the first paragraph. How does the author feel about the formation of the dynasties? Not too good: she calls them an "abominable elite that had developed as a consequence of social prejudice." So what's the best answer? Something that's slightly negative. Eliminate (A) because it's positive. Eliminate (B) because it's not negative at all. Keep (C) for now because it's slightly negative. Finally, leave in (E) because it's slightly negative.

The remaining answer choices are (C) and (E). Which one is better? Well, does the author dislike the formation of the dynasties or is she resigned to it? She dislikes it, right? So the best answer is (C).

2.   *B*   This is a specific question. Use "United States" as your lead word. Once you find the lead word, remember to read about five lines above and five lines below. So where is "United States"? In the second paragraph. What does the passage say about men in the United States? That they took a "'protective' stance" toward women to compensate them for their "non-existent social status." Always make a paraphrase of the answer before moving on to the answer choices.

Eliminate (A) because who cares about the Court d'Assizes. Keep (B) because it looks like a pretty good match for your paraphrase. Eliminate (C) because you didn't read anything about a popular movement. Eliminate (D) because who cares about the modern historians. Eliminate (E) because you didn't read anything about lots of French women being guillotined. The best answer is (B).

3.   *E*   This is a specific question. Use "death penalty" as your lead word. Once you find the lead word, don't forget to read about five lines above and five lines below. So where is "death penalty"? In the third paragraph. What does the passage say about popular arguments against the death penalty? That they focus on humanitarian principles and that they don't focus on equal rights. In other words, men and women are equal, so if women aren't subject to capital punishment, then men shouldn't be either. It's important that you paraphrase the answer to the question before moving on to the answer choices.

Eliminate (A) because it doesn't talk about humanitarian principles or equal rights. Eliminate (B) for the same reason. Eliminate (C) because it misinterprets information in the passage. Popular arguments *failed* to incorporate equal rights. Eliminate (D) because it also misrepresents information in the passage. It's the men that are getting killed, not the women. Keep (E) because it's a good match for your paraphrase. (E) is the best answer.

PROBLEM SET #1

The passage below is followed by questions based on its content. After reading the passage, choose the best answer to each question. Answer all questions on the basis of what is *stated* or *implied* in that passage.

Political parties today are consciously non-ideological, but in the 1840's and 1850's ideology made its way into the heart of the political system. Political sociologists have
5 pointed out that the stable functioning of a political democracy requires a setting in which parties represent broad coalitions of varying interests, and that the peaceful resolution of social conflict takes place most easily when the
10 major parties share fundamental values. Such a view implies that the peaceful operation of the political system is the highest social value, an implication which, under certain circumstances, may be justly questioned. But it
15 does contain important insights about the normal functioning of the American polity. Government by majority rule, Carl Becker observed many years ago, works best when political issues involve superficial problems,
20 rather than deep social divisions. The minority can accept the victory of the majority at the polls, because both share many basic values, and electoral defeat does not imply "a fatal surrender of . . . vital interests." Before the
25 1850's, the second American party system conformed to this pattern—largely because sectional ideologies and issues were consciously kept out of politics. In this sense, the party system had a certain artificial quality.
30 Its divisions rarely corresponded to the basic sectional divisions which were daily becoming more and more pronounced. The two decades before the Civil War witnessed the development of conflicting sectional ideologies,
35 each viewing its own society as fundamentally well-ordered, and the other as both a negation of its most cherished values and a threat to its existence. The development of the two
40 ideologies was in many ways interrelated; each grew in part as a response to the growth of the other. Thus, as southerners were coming more and more consciously to insist on slavery as the very basis of civilized life, and to reject the
45 materialism and lack of cohesion in northern society, northerners came to view slavery as the antithesis of the good society, as well as a threat to their own fundamental values and interests. The existing political system could
50 not contain these two irreconcilable ideologies,
and in the 1850's each national party—Whigs, Know-Nothings, and finally Democrats—disintegrated. And in the end the South seceded from the Union rather than accept the
55 victory of a political party whose ideology threatened everything southerners most valued.
At the center of the Republican ideology was the notion of "free labor." This concept
60 involved not merely an attitude toward work, but a justification of ante-bellum northern society, and it led northern Republicans to an extensive critique of southern society, which appeared both different from and inferior to
65 their own. Republicans also believed in the existence of a conspiratorial "Slave Power" which had seized control of the federal government. Two profoundly different and antagonistic civilizations, Republicans thus
70 believed, had developed within the nation, and were competing for control of the political system.

1. The primary purpose of the passage is to

    (A) discuss the requirements for a stable political system, in particular, a democracy

    (B) present a cause for the breakdown in relations between North and South that led, ultimately, to the Civil War

    (C) explain the reason why political parties seek to avoid introducing ideology into their platforms

    (D) analyze the effect of the Civil War on the political party system in the United States

    (E) propose the theory that the Republican party was responsible for the South's secession from the Union

2. It can be inferred from the passage that political parties today

    (A) do not differ from each other markedly in terms of interests
    (B) consider freedom from conflict the most important social concern
    (C) keep their distance from ideology because of its potential to divide
    (D) look to the Civil War as a lesson on how to maintain national unity
    (E) address only problems of little weight and rarely dispute one another

3. The author mentions Carl Becker in order to

    (A) challenge the position popularly held by political sociologists regarding the power of ideology
    (B) argue that a democracy is characterized by the peaceful transition of power from one party to another
    (C) promote the notion that it is better for a democracy to address only issues that are not divisive
    (D) suggest that, in order for a democracy to flourish, the political system must represent diverse interests
    (E) lend credence to the assertion that political stability is founded upon the absence of ideological confrontation

4. The passage states the party system in the years preceding the Civil War did which of the following?

    (A) Did not accurately reflect the tensions existing between North and South.
    (B) Was responsible for the conflicting northern and southern ideologies.
    (C) Failed to acknowledge its inability to reconcile the North with the South.
    (D) Exacerbated the differences among the Whigs, Know-Nothings, and Democrats.
    (E) Could not suppress the dissent voiced by the Republicans.

5. According to the passage, the antagonism of the North and South was, at heart, a result of

    (A) the South's insistence on an economy based on slave labor
    (B) the failure of the political parties to find common ground
    (C) the North's rejection of slavery as an immoral institution
    (D) the perception that "free labor" and slave labor were diametrically opposed
    (E) the Republican belief in a Southern plot to overthrow the federal government

6. The passage suggests that the concept of free labor

    (A) instigated immediately the secession of the South from the Union
    (B) was a creation of the North to define itself as distinct from the South
    (C) allowed the North to justify its condemnation of the South's secession
    (D) was an encapsulation of northern values and concerns
    (E) represented the materialist interests of the North

7. The author's attitude toward the Republican party of the mid-nineteenth century can best be described as

    (A) admiring
    (B) appreciative
    (C) sympathetic
    (D) objective
    (E) vehement

PROBLEM SET #2

The passage below is followed by questions based on its content. After reading the passage, choose the best answer to each question. Answer all questions on the basis of what is *stated* or *implied* in that passage.

How do we know what we believe we know? What we know is generally considered to be the result of our exploration and understanding of the real world, of the
5 way things really are. After all, common sense suggests that this objective reality can be discovered. How we know is a far more vexing problem. To solve it, the mind needs to step outside itself, so to speak, and observe
10 itself at work; for at this point we are no longer faced with facts that apparently exist independently of us in the outside world, but with mental processes whose nature is not at all self-evident. If what we know depends on
15 how we came to know it, then our view of reality is no longer a true image of what is the case outside ourselves, but is inevitably determined also by the processes through which we arrived at this view.

1. The author implies that an "objective reality" (line 5) ("After all, common sense . . . ") is

   (A) a necessary part of life, even it may not exist, because without it our existence would lack order and structure

   (B) accurate only if we take into account how we know and not what we know

   (C) not possible because knowledge is a result not only of concrete experience but also abstract thought processes

   (D) a false image that we construct so that we might come to some sort of understanding of the world outside us

   (E) a reflection of our inner reality, that is, the world inside us governed by mental processes

2. According to the passage, we tend to believe what we know is a product of our

   (A) imagination as well as our contact with other people

   (B) daily experiences with the outside world

   (C) analytical and logical reasoning

   (D) mental and physical activity combined

   (E) education, both formal and informal

3. The passage suggests that the author would be most likely to agree with which of the following statements?

   (A) We can only come "to know" through a rigorous examination of our customs and prejudices.

   (B) We can never determine with complete certainty whether something is true.

   (C) At the very best, our knowledge of the outside world is vague and incomplete.

   (D) So complex are our minds that we cannot, at times, discern the difference between the real and fantasy.

   (E) Our perception of reality can be inaccurate at times, but overall, we are rational beings.

PROBLEM SET #3

The passage below is followed by questions based on its content. After reading the passage, choose the best answer to each question. Answer all questions on the basis of what is *stated* or *implied* in that passage.

E. M. Forster is an Edwardian in point of time, and he is equally so in spirit. His outlook on the world and his literary manner were already thoroughly developed in that
5 epoch and have passed through the subsequent years of turbulence and cataclysm with remarkably little modification. The various modern revolutions in physics, in psychology, in politics, even in literary style,
10 have not escaped his intelligent notice, but they can scarcely be said to have influenced him deeply. His response to the explosion of the Victorian dream of benevolent progress has been a modest and orderly retreat to safer
15 ground—to a tolerant individualism now unmixed with Utopian dreams, but nevertheless closer to Victorian ideals than to any of the popular creeds of today. Rather than conform to bad times, Forster prefers to
20 remind us cheerfully that his views are atavistic.

The strength of Forster's resistance to the twentieth century is especially apparent when we place him beside some of his fellow
25 writers. If Joyce, Lawrence, Pound, and the early Eliot represent the main current of the modern literary movement in English, we must admit that Forster's private stream runs in an older channel. These others were radical
30 iconoclasts whose rejection of bourgeois-democratic life was violent and shattering. Equally shattering was their fragmentation of the polite cadences of Victorian literature. In seeing the falseness of the old psychology,
35 they conceived a scorn for the *hypocrite lecteur*; their role as apocalyptic prophets, as nay-sayers to the boredom and specious rationality of modern life, demanded that they be obscure
40 and idiosyncratic. Forster, in contrast, unashamedly calls himself a bourgeois and remains faithful to the tradition of calm intelligibility. He is anti-apocalyptic in both his politics and his literary sense. To some
45 degree his novels return us to the congenial Victorian relationship between writer and reader, with its unspoken agreement over the usefulness of the sociable virtues and its apotheosis of the happy family. Though
50 Forster's heroes struggle against "society" as a

body of inhibitions, their revolt is never truly radical. And Forster's ironical style, though it is unsparing in its probing at shams and half-truths, presupposes a confidence in the reader's
55 sympathy and good judgment—a confidence that seemed quite archaic to the other writers named.

Forster's resistance to modernity may account for the fact that his novels, though they are
60 almost universally esteemed, have never won his a cult of fanatical disciples. With a few exceptions, critics have tended to explicate and admire his works without becoming heated over the possible merit of his ideas. Yet Forster
65 decidedly *is* a novelist of ideas, and didactic moral content is hardly less conspicuous in his work than in Lawrence's. Forster's persistent "moral" is that the life of affectionate personal relations, disengaged from political and
70 religious zeal by means of a tolerant eclecticism, is supremely valuable. This is not a stirring creed; in fact, it is a warning against allowing oneself to be stirred by any creed.

1. The author's primary purpose in this passage is to

   (A) discuss E.M. Forster and his writing, particularly in the context of his reaction to modernity

   (B) compare E.M. Forster to other writers of the twentieth century such as Joyce and Lawrence

   (C) affirm that E.M. Forster is a much as novelist of ideas as other modern writers

   (D) suggest that E.M. Forster's writing is a reflection of not only Victorian ideals but also Edwardian

   (E) analyze E.M. Forster's response to the revolutions in science and art and how it affected his work

2. According to the passage, Forster's relationship to Victorianism is which of the following?

   (A) He believed Victorian ideals were preferable to those of modernity.
   (B) He did not believe in Victorian ideals but nevertheless clung to them.
   (C) He considered Victorian ideals to be not only oppressive but also false.
   (D) He rejected Victorian ideals, but not so completely as other modern writers.
   (E) He incorporated Victorian ideals into his own personal ideals.

3. The author most likely refers to Forster's "views as atavistic" (line 18) in order to

   (A) make a case for the importance of individualism to Forster and his work
   (B) isolate Forster as a writer unconnected to the revolutions of the modern world
   (C) emphasize that Forster was an atypical modern writer
   (D) suggest that Forster was an ardent supporter of the popular beliefs of his time
   (E) point out Forster's inherent belief in Victorianism

4. According to the passage, the literary style of modern writers

   (A) maintained the Victorian trust in the judgment of the reader
   (B) was revolutionary in its rejection of all beliefs and ideals
   (C) was ironical as well as difficult to decipher
   (D) was eccentric in nature and characterized by vagueness
   (E) lacked any structure and was riddled with ambiguity

5. It can be inferred from the passage that Lawrence's novels

   (A) condemn the life of the bourgeoisie, at the expense of destroying personal relations
   (B) are similar to Forster's as both men valued the relationship between reader and writer
   (C) are more conciliatory to Victorianism than Joyce's novels
   (D) have elicited much impassioned debate among critics
   (E) express ideas that are antithetical to those found in Forster's novels

6. The author's reaction to Forster's novels can best be described as one of

   (A) disparagement
   (B) skepticism
   (C) neutrality
   (D) appreciation
   (E) enthusiasm

7. The passage suggests that the author would be likely to agree with which of the following statements about Forster's works?

   I. The characters in Forster's writings often rebel against a confining and restrictive society.
   II. Forster's works ultimately fail to be radical and stand out as an aberration in the modern literary movement.
   III. Literary critics, though respectful of Forster's writings, tend to believe his works lack moral tension.
   IV. Forster's works reflect his belief in the need for individuals to value personal relations.

   (A) I and IV only
   (B) II and III only
   (C) II and IV only
   (D) I, III, and IV only
   (E) I, II, III, and IV

PROBLEM SET #4

The passage below is followed by questions based on its content. After reading the passage, choose the best answer to each question. Answer all questions on the basis of what is *stated* or *implied* in that passage.

Natural selection is an immensely powerful yet beautifully simple theory that has held up remarkably well, under intense and unrelenting scrutiny and testing, for 135 years. In essence,
5 natural selection locates the mechanism of evolutionary change in a "struggle" among organisms for reproductive success, leading to improved fit of populations to changing environments . . .
10   Yet powerful though the principle may be . . . natural selection is not fully sufficient to explain evolutionary change. First, many other causes are powerful, particularly at levels of biological organization both above and below
15 the traditional Darwinian focus on organisms and their struggles for reproductive success. At the lowest level of substitution in individual base pairs of DNA, change is often effectively neutral and therefore random. At higher
20 levels, involving entire species or faunas, punctuated equilibrium can produce evolutionary trends by selection of species based on their rates of origin and extirpation, whereas mass extinctions wipe out substantial
25 parts of biotas for reasons unrelated to adaptive struggles of constituent species in "normal" times between such events.
     Second . . . no matter how adequate our general theory of evolutionary change, we also
30 yearn to document and understand the actual pathway of life's history. Theory, of course, is relevant to explaining the pathway . . . But the actual pathway is strongly *underdetermined* by our general theory of life's evolution. This
35 point needs some belaboring . . . Webs and chains of historical events are so intricate, so imbued with random and chaotic elements, so unrepeatable in encompassing such a multitude of unique (and uniquely interacting) objects,
40 that standard models of simple prediction and replication do not apply.
     History can be explained, with satisfying rigor if evidence be adequate, after a sequence
45 of events unfolds, but it cannot be predicted with any precision beforehand . . . History includes too much chaos, or extremely sensitive dependence on minute and unmeasurable differences in initial conditions, leading to
50 massively divergent outcomes based on tiny

and unknowable disparities in starting points. And history includes too much contingency, or shaping of present results by long chains of unpredictable antecedent states, rather than
55 immediate determination by timeless laws of nature.
     Homo sapiens did not appear on the earth, just a geologic second ago, because evolutionary theory predicts such an outcome based on
60 themes of progress and increasing neural complexity. Humans arose, rather, as a fortuitous and contingent outcome of thousands of linked events, any one of which could have occurred differently and sent
65 history on an alternative pathway that would not have led to consciousness . . .
     Therefore, to understand the events and generalities of life's pathway, we must go beyond principles of evolutionary theory to a
70 paleontological examination of the contingent pattern of life's history on our planet—the single actualized version among millions of plausible alternatives that happened not to occur. Such a view of life's history is highly
75 contrary both to conventional deterministic models of Western science and to the deepest social traditions and psychological hopes of Western culture for a history culminating in humans as life's highest expression and
80 intended planetary steward.

1. The primary purpose of the passage is to

   (A) suggest that the natural selection theory is no longer applicable to today's world

   (B) point out the limitations of natural selection at the lower and higher levels

   (C) propose changes to the natural selection theory to improve its accuracy

   (D) discuss the reasons why natural selection is not a complete evolutionary theory

   (E) expose problems with the natural selection theory in light of recent historical studies

2. According to the passage, natural selection does not take into account the

(A) tendency of certain species to evolve successfully due to isolation
(B) dependence of some organisms on the successful evolution of other organisms
(C) eradication of a species for reasons other than a failure to reproduce successfully
(D) continuation of specific organisms and species due to human intervention
(E) difficulty of successful reproduction for organisms at the lower and higher levels

3. It can be inferred that the author believes the study of history is

(A) problematic
(B) impossible
(C) futile
(D) not worthwhile
(E) untenable

4. The author mentions *Homo sapiens* primarily in order to

(A) highlight the short period during which humans have lived on the earth
(B) suggest the notion that the pathway to consciousness was a long-term process
(C) support the idea that the pathway of life is determined, in large part, by random events
(D) explain evolution through natural selection by employing a specific species as an example
(E) emphasize the intricacy of events that leads to the evolution of an organism or species

5. According to the passage, we might be reluctant to let go of traditional evolutionary theory because to do so would

(A) refute the ideas of the long-venerated scientist Darwin
(B) suggest that life cannot be ordered or structured
(C) challenge the way we understand the world
(D) throw other scientific theories into question as well
(E) compel us to reexamine both biology and history

6. Which of the following statements is supported by information given in the passage?

(A) The study of history will never be completely satisfactory.
(B) The theory of natural selection addresses the possibility of random events.
(C) The evolution of life does not follow a fixed or determined path.
(D) It is possible to determine with a fair degree of accuracy historical events.
(E) Theories will always be inadequate because they are at best predictions.

7. Which of the following best describes the organization of the passage?

(A) A theory is rejected, and new theories are suggested to replace it.
(B) A theory is considered, and conditions are stated under which the theory can apply.
(C) A theory is explained, and observations are made that both support and contradict it.
(D) A theory is described, and its limitations are noted and then further explored.
(E) A theory is outlined, and its relevance questioned by employing it in a different field of study.

PROBLEM SET #5

The passage below is followed by questions based on its content. After reading the passage, choose the best answer to each question. Answer all questions on the basis of what is *stated* or *implied* in that passage.

Occupations foster gender differences among workers in a variety of ways, one of the most pervasive being "internal stratification." That is, men and women in the same occupation
5 often perform different tasks and functions. Even in those occupations that appear sexually integrated, the aggregate statistics often mask extreme internal segregation. Although the proportion of female bakers increased from 25
10 percent in 1970 to 41 percent in 1980, for example, the majority of female bakers are found in highly automated baking industries, while their male counterparts are located in less-automated bakeries. The same
15 phenomenon has been detected among pharmacists, financial managers, and bus drivers—all groups where the influx of women workers suggests a diminution of sex segregation
20 Another strategy used to maintain gender differences in supposedly integrated occupations is the use of sumptuary and etiquette rules. When women enter male-dominated occupations, certain rules are often
25 introduced to govern their dress and demeanor. In office settings, for instance, dress codes—either formal or implicit—are not unusual; female employees may be required to wear dresses, nylons, and high-heeled shoes to
30 enhance their femininity. So it is for female marines and males nurses, both of whom are required to dress differently from their male and female counterparts. Male nurses never wear the traditional nursing cap; female
35 marines never sport the standard Marine Corps garrison cap.
Informal practices also play a role in constituting femininity in female marines and masculinity in male nurses. As members of
40 visible minority groups, they stand out at work and receive far more than their fair share of attention. This phenomenon was first documented by Rosabeth Moss Kanter, who
45 found that women in corporations, simply by virtue of their numerical rarity, were noticed and scrutinized more than their male counterparts. This added pressure may actually result in different job performances
50 from men and women in nontraditional

occupations and exacerbate gender differences. Kanter's corporate women, for example, became more secretive, less independent, and less oppositional in response to their greater
55 visibility — all traits that have traditionally been associated with femininity.
Another informal technique that enhances gender differences is practiced by supervisors who evaluate men and women differently. The
60 very qualities that are highly praised in one sex are sometimes denigrated in the other. Thus, a man is "ambitious," a woman, "pushy"; a woman is "sensitive," a man, "wimpy."
But it would be a mistake to claim that all
65 gender differences are forced on people. In addition to the external pressures I have just described, male nurses and female marines actively construct their own gender by redefining their activities in terms of traditional
70 masculine and feminine traits. For example, women in the Marine Corps insist that their femininity is intact even as they march cadence in camouflage units. Likewise, male nurses contend that their masculinity is not at all
75 threatened while they care for and nurture their patients.

1. The author is primarily concerned with

(A) explaining how femininity and masculinity can be reconstructed for specific careers

(B) examining jobs that, at first glance, seem to be nontraditional for men and women

(C) proving that discrimination based on gender is pervasive in all workplaces

(D) exploring the reasons why gender differences cannot be ignored in any occupation

(E) discussing practices that serve to perpetuate gender differences in the work place

2. Which of the following best describes the organization of the first paragraph?

(A) A specific case is presented, its particulars are analyzed, and a conclusion is drawn from it.
(B) A generalization is made, a clarification is put forth, and specific examples are offered in support.
(C) An observation is made, specific situations that are applicable are cited, and a generalization is derived.
(D) A hypothesis is presented, evidence to support it is given, and its implications are discussed.
(E) A criticism is made, a specific problem is noted, and ways to rectify the problem are suggested.

3. The author suggests which of the following about internal stratification?

(A) Although women now work in industries once dominated by men, they find it difficult, if not impossible, to be promoted to managerial positions.
(B) As women enter the work force in greater numbers, men feel their jobs are threatened and their hostility results in increased tension on the job.
(C) Because men and women rarely engage in the same activities on the job, certain specialties can be feminine-identified and others masculine-identified.
(D) Since men and women are segregated in the work place, men tend not to value the work carried out by women.
(E) Even when men and women are given the same tasks to perform, women continue to receive less pay than do their male counterparts.

4. The primary purpose of the last paragraph is to

(A) emphasize the importance of outside forces in establishing gender differences
(B) point out that men and women act to enforce gender differences themselves
(C) provide an example of men and women who defy the typical perceptions of masculinity and femininity
(D) demonstrate that, even in a nontraditional context, conventional definitions of "masculine" and "feminine" are preserved
(E) describe the tension that men and women feel when their sexuality is questioned

5. The passage supplies information to answer which of the following questions?

(A) Do women favor rules that dictate how they should dress and behave?
(B) Is internal stratification a worldwide phenomenon?
(C) Why do corporate women feel undue pressure on the job?
(D) Why do supervisors uphold gender differences in the work place?
(E) How do male nurses cope with a job that challenges their masculinity?

6. The author specifically mentions all of the following as methods to maintain gender differences in the work place EXCEPT

(A) a manager's use of particular words for men and particular words for women although describing the same quality

(B) the designation of dress codes so that the physical differences between men and women are highlighted

(C) the internal pressure men and women feel to be traditionally masculine or feminine

(D) pressure from coworkers to behave in a conventionally masculine or a feminine way

(E) the assignation of different duties for men and women in the same occupation

7. Which of the following statements could most logically follow the last sentence of the passage?

(A) Both groups redefine femininity and masculinity in their daily lives, which also reinforces gender differences.

(B) However, both groups recognize their inability to change the mind sets of those who see masculinity and femininity in rigid terms.

(C) And so, each group internalizes the need to be masculine or feminine to such a degree that their lives are in a constant state of conflict.

(D) In the end, internal pressures prove to be even greater than external pressures in maintaining gender differences.

(E) This leads to the question: How can one defy gender differences when even these groups try to sustain them?

PROBLEM SET #6

Although III-1 has caused hundreds of thousands of meningitis cases, it does not appear to be uniquely virulent. Now that it is possible to perform clonal analysis of
5 meningococcal strains, it is clear that other clones have caused similar epidemics in Africa and Asia. These findings do suggest, however, that the introduction of a potentially epidemic clone under the right circumstances can be
10 devastating. Two explanations have been given for this process: epidemic clones randomly expand as they progress through a population, or they survive by escaping herd immunity. As an analogy to influenza
15 outbreaks, it has been proposed that epidemics might result from what are called antigenic shifts. Although all serogroup A meningococci share the same polysaccharide, individual clones differ in the other antigens exposed on
20 the cell surface. Once immunity to the shared antigens wanes, a new clone with sufficiently different surface antigens might escape immune surveillance and start an epidemic. Epidemiologists following disease patterns will
25 then see an "antigenic shift" as new clones supersede older clones.

1. Which of the following best summarizes the content of the passage?

   (A) Meningitis: What Are Its Causes?
   (B) How an Epidemic Can Result from a Meningitis Strain
   (C) A Scientific Overview of an Antigenic Shift
   (D) Problems Confronting an Outbreak of Meningitis
   (E) An Analysis of the Meningitis Clone III-1

2. The author uses each of the following devices in the passage EXCEPT

   (A) provide an explanation
   (B) make a comparison
   (C) suggest a cause for an effect
   (D) provide a definition
   (E) make an inference

3. According to the passage, an antigenic shift takes place when

   (A) an epidemic causes specific clones to alter their surface antigens so that they are undetectable
   (B) shared antigens begin to be outnumbered by different antigens, thus allowing certain clones to pass through a population
   (C) certain clones are able to sidestep a weakened herd immunity and advance through a population
   (D) clones no longer randomly progress through a population but rather direct themselves toward the weakest elements
   (E) certain clones build resistance to herd immunity and share this ability with other clones through their antigens

PROBLEM SET #7

The passage below is followed by questions based on its content. After reading the passage, choose the best answer to each question. Answer all questions on the basis of what is *stated* or *implied* in that passage.

New York stood at the center of the momentous processes that recast American society in the nineteenth century. Once a modest seaport, the city early took the lead in
5 developing new forms of commerce and mass production; by 1860 it was both the nation's premier port and its largest manufacturing city. The appearance of new social classes was both cause and result of industrial development and
10 commercial expansion. Wealth from investments in trade and manufacturing ventures supported the emergence of an urban bourgeoisie; the expansion of capitalist labor arrangements brought into being a class of
15 largely impoverished wageworkers. The resulting divisions fostered, on each side, new and antagonistic political ideas and social practices.

We know most about the male participants in
20 these conflicts, workingmen and employers. Politically, bourgeois men upheld their right to protect, improve upon and increase the private property on which rested, they believed, their country's welfare. In return, many
25 workingmen affirmed a belief in the superior abilities of those who worked with their hands —as opposed to the idle, acquisitive, parasitical owners of property—to direct American society in accordance with republican values of social
30 equality, civil virtue and yeomanry that they inherited from the Revolution.

Class transformation was related to, but not synonymous with, the thorough-going transformation of the gender system in the first
35 half of the nineteenth century: that is, the changes in all those arrangements of work, sexuality, parental responsibilities, psychological life, assigned social traits and
40 internalized emotions through which the sexes defined themselves respectively as men and women. Women of the emerging bourgeoisie articulated new ideas about many of these aspects of their lives. Designating themselves
45 moral guardians of their husbands and children, women became the standard-bearers of piety, decorum and virtue in Northern society. They claimed the home as the sphere of society where they could most effectively
50 exercise their power. In their consignment to

the household as the sole domain of proper female activity, women suffered a constriction of their social engagements; at the same time, they gained power within their families that also
55 vested them with greater moral authority in their own communities.

While the cult of domesticity spoke to female interests and emerged from altered relations between men and women, it also contained
60 within it conflicts of class. As urban ladies increased their contacts with the working poor through Protestant missions and charity work, they developed domestic ideology as part of a vision of a reformed city, purged of the
65 supposed perfidies of working-class life. Domesticity quickly became an element of bourgeois self-consciousness. In confronting the working poor, reformers created and refined their own sense of themselves as social and
70 spiritual superiors capable of remolding the city in their own image. From the ideas and practices of domesticity they drew many of the materials for their ideal of a society that had put to rest the disturbing conflicts of class.

1. The author of the passage is primarily concerned with discussing

    (A) the authority possessed by middle-class women in New York both in the public and private

    (B) the transformation of New York into an industrial and commercial center of activity

    (C) social conflict in New York, in terms of class and gender, as a result of economic expansion

    (D) the social values of the middle class in New York, particularly the cult of domesticity

    (E) the attempt of the middle class in New York to reform the working class

2. The author states "We know most about the male participants in these conflicts" (line 19) primarily in order to

   (A) challenge past studies because they have largely ignored the female participants

   (B) preface a debate over the motivating factors for class conflict

   (C) propose possible reasons as to why only men's roles have been examined

   (D) emphasize the impact that class conflict had on industrial development

   (E) allude to a later discussion of the women who were active in such conflicts

3. According to the passage, middle-class men were similar to working-class men in that each group

   (A) perceived the other to be an obstruction to industrial and commercial expansion

   (B) placed a great deal of weight on private ownership and the entrepreneurial spirit

   (C) responded to the changing economy with both excitement and aversion

   (D) felt threatened by the activity of women who sought to lay claim to the home

   (E) considered itself responsible for the well-being and prosperity of the country

4. According to the passage, bourgeois women did which of the following by taking charge of the home?

   (A) Both enlarged the scope of their authority and circumscribed their power

   (B) Portrayed their challenge to male authority as an act necessary to preserve morality

   (C) Reconstructed the duties of parents as well as the role of children

   (D) increased their missionary activity intended to assist the working class

   (E) Set out to reform the city, in particular the working class

5. According to the passage, the cult of domesticity did which of the following?

   (A) Oppressed women as their activities were now confined to the realm of the home

   (B) Represented values cherished by northerners, particularly working-class women

   (C) Drew from the tradition of republicanism in its promotion of reform

   (D) Engendered increased tensions between the middle class and working class

   (E) Encouraged women to speak out on behalf of female interests and issues

6. The passage suggests that middle-class reformers attempted to do which of the following?

   (A) Convert the poor of the working class to Protestantism

   (B) Promote domesticity as a means to gain power over the working class

   (C) Ameliorate class tensions by advocating citywide changes

   (D) Encourage women to participate in public activities such as missionary work

   (E) Compel the working class to adopt bourgeois values

7. According to the author, the changing economy in New York was

   (A) responsible for the increased reformist activity
   (B) both a cause and an effect of class divisions
   (C) able to temper somewhat conflict between the sexes
   (D) due primarily to the increase in trade at the port
   (E) a threat to the republican ideals of the Revolution

PROBLEM SET #8

The passage below is followed by questions based on its content. After reading the passage, choose the best answer to each question. Answer all questions on the basis of what is *stated* or *implied* in that passage.

The societies in which shamanism has flourished have been small, relatively self-sufficient social systems which see themselves as coping directly with their natural worlds.
5 Like all human beings, the members of such groups lived in a world of uncertainty. The presence of a person who could maintain contact with the cosmic forces of the universe directly, who could make sense of both the
10 measured order of ordinary times and the catastrophes of drought, earthquake, or flood, was of incalculable value.
    More complex social systems tend to have "institutionalized" specialists who transmit
15 information without explicit recourse to the supernatural. Such societies have priests and prophets, not shamans, at the overt level. But the line between shaman and prophet is tenuous. The prophet usually does not enjoy
20 the legitimacy within his society that is granted the shaman. His is a voice crying in the wilderness, not that of the legitimate curer and philosopher. Despite the differences, the prophet can be seen as a kind of shaman, and
25 thus the study of shamanism illuminates some of the obscurities in religious traditions.

1. The primary purpose of the passage is to

    (A) explain the differences between shamans in small and large societies
    (B) describe the reasons why shamans are esteemed in certain societies
    (C) discuss the roles of shamans as well as prophets in social systems
    (D) compare religious leaders in small social systems to those in complex social systems
    (E) argue that the power of the shaman is derived from the supernatural

2. According to the passage, certain social systems rely on shamans in order to

    (A) empower them through a connection with the divine
    (B) mediate disputes and other conflicts between individuals
    (C) give structure and form to an unstable world full of mysteries
    (D) lead them in religious activities such as prayer and worship
    (E) protect them from hostile neighbors and unpredictable forces such as nature

3. The passage suggests that shamans and prophets differ because

    (A) Shamans are more powerful because they have a mandate from their deity.
    (B) Shamans possess a higher social status, due to their ability to call upon the supernatural.
    (C) Shamans are revered as demigods while prophets are considered mortal.
    (D) Shamans are less likely to be challenged by members of their society.
    (E) Shamans maintain greater authority because they live in isolated social systems.

4. According to the passage, shamans and prophets are similar in which of the following ways?

 I. The size and infrastructure of the societies in which they live resemble one another.
 II. Their roles in society are based, in part, on their ability to explain and provide information.
 III. They are accorded a special standing because of their ability to control nature.

(A) II only
(B) I and II only
(C) I and III only
(D) II and III only
(E) I, II, and III

Problem Set #1: Explanations

1. **B** To find the main idea, all you have to do is read the topic sentence for each paragraph and then the final sentence of the entire passage. Remember, always state the main idea in your own words (i.e., paraphrase) before moving on to the answer choices. So what's the main idea for this passage? You should have come up with something like the following: The Civil War was a result of conflicting political ideologies in the North and South.

   (A) is too general. From the second paragraph, you know that the main idea has to have something to do with the Civil War. (B) is a possibility since it talks about the war. (C), like (A), is too broad because it doesn't mention the war. (D) does talk about the war, which is good, but it doesn't really talk about how the war affected the party system, which is bad. (E) is too specific. Though it does talk about the war, it doesn't take into account the topic sentence for the first paragraph. The best answer is (B).

2. **C** Use "political parties" as your lead word. It takes you to the very beginning of the passage. Remember, paraphrase what you read before you move on to the answer choices. What does the passage say about political parties today? That they purposefully avoid ideology.

   (A) goes a little too far. The passage does say that parties should try to represent "broad coalitions of varying interests," but that doesn't mean that all parties are the same. (B) misrepresents information in the passage. Lines 10–11 ("Such a view implies . . . ") suggest that "the peaceful operation of the political system is the highest social value" in certain circumstances, but you don't know that to be true for political parties today. (C) is a good match for your paraphrase. (D) isn't mentioned at all in the passage. (E) goes a little too far. It's implied that political parties only address problems of little import because they don't want conflict, but you don't know that parties rarely have disputes. The best answer is (C).

3. **E** "Carl Becker," clearly, should be the lead word you use, and you can find the lead word in the middle of the first paragraph. Well, why does the author mention Carl Becker? Paraphrase the answer before you look at the answer choices. The author mentions Carl Becker because he wants to cite someone who supports his main idea: Ideology can be very divisive—after all, it caused the Civil War.

(A) misrepresents information in the passage. The passage does talk about political sociologists, but it doesn't say they disagree with Becker. (B) may be true, but it's not the reason *why* the author mentions Becker. (C) goes too far. Becker thinks ideology is divisive, but he's not saying we should therefore avoid it. (D) is really the point the political sociologists are making, not Becker. (E) is the only answer left, and guess what? It matches your paraphrase. (E) is the best answer.

4. **A** Use "party system . . . Civil War" as your lead word. This should take you to lines 24-28 ("Before the 1850's, the second American . . . "). What do the lines say about the party system? Basically, that it was artificial because it failed to reflect the tension between the North and South. Remember, always paraphrase before looking at the answer choices.

(A) looks as if it's a good match. (B) is the exact opposite of what you're looking for. (C) misrepresents information from the passage. (D) suggests the parties were responsible for conflict. From the passage, you know they wanted to avoid conflict. (E) mentions the Republicans, who are discussed in the passage, but not until much later. The best answer is (A).

5. **D** This question can be answered using the main idea. What's the main idea? That ideology caused the Civil War. If you look at the last sentence of the passage, it confirms the main idea.

(A) talks about slavery, not ideology. (B) talks about political parties, not ideology. (C) talks about slavery again, not ideology. (D) does talk about ideology, so it looks good. (E) doesn't talk about ideology, so it's wrong. The best answer is (D).

6. **D** The lead word is clearly "free labor," which can be found at the beginning of the second paragraph. What does the passage say about free labor? That it was a "justification of ... northern society." To paraphrase: free labor was the ideology that motivated the North.

(A) goes too far. The ideology of free labor was responsible for the Civil War, but it didn't cause the South to leave the Union immediately. (B) is tricky. Free labor did distinguish the North from the South, but the North didn't create the ideology just to make itself different from the South. (C) isn't quite right. The ideology allowed the North to condemn the South overall—not its secession. (D) looks like a good match. (E) goes too far. Free labor represented the interest of the North, period. The ideology was about more than just materialism.

7. **D** For a tone question, anything too extreme must be wrong. (E) is out, as a result, as is (A). So you're left with (B), (C), and (D)—each of which is pretty moderate. So use "Republican" as your lead word to find out how the author feels about the party.

The second paragraph talks about the Republicans, and clearly, the author is pretty neutral in tone. So the best answer is (D).

Problem Set #2: Explanations

1. **C** This specific question has a line reference, so the part of the passage that contains the answer isn't too hard to find. However, don't forget that you need to read about five lines before the line reference, as well as five lines after. Also, remember that once you locate the answer, paraphrase it before looking at the answer choices.

The answer to the question is contained in the last few lines of the passage. It may seem that "objective reality can be discovered," but because "what we know depends on how we came to know it," maybe not. To paraphrase: It looks like the author is mentioning an objective reality because we think there is one but there really isn't.

(A) is a bad answer choice because it mentions something you didn't read at all—a lack of order and structure. (B) misinterprets what you read—it's a combination of what we know and how we know that matters. (C) looks good since it says "not possible." (D) goes a little too far. An objective reality may not exist, but nothing in the passage says *why* we think there is one. (E) is incomplete. Our perception of reality is a combination of what we know and how we know—not just how we know. (C) is the best answer.

2. **B** This is a specific question. Use "what we know" in the question as a lead word. Once you find the lead word, remember to read about five lines above and five lines below. So where do you find "what we know"? At the very beginning of the passage.

Apparently, "What we know is generally considered to be a result of our exploration and understanding of the real world, of the way things really are." To paraphrase: it's our contact with the real world that determines what we know.

(A) is a bad answer choice because it discusses the imagination. Imagination isn't mentioned at all in the passage. (B) is okay—it mentions interaction with the real world. (C) is talking about mental processes, so it can't be right. (D) mentions the physical, but since it also includes the mental, it's wrong. (E) is way out there—education isn't discussed at all in the passage. The best answer is (B).

3. **B** This is really a general question at heart—in other words, to answer this question, you need to focus on the main idea. What's the main idea of the passage? Well, if you read the first few sentences of the passage and then the last sentence, you should come up with something like this: what we know is a sticky process because it depends not only on the outside world but also on our mental activity.

Given the main idea, which answer choice is best? (A) mentions customs and prejudices. From the passage, you really don't know what the author thinks about customs and prejudices. (B) is a possibility. The main idea, remember, talks about what we know and how it's a sticky process. (B) says something along the lines of truth being a sticky thing. (C) is a little tricky. The passage does discuss the outside world and our relation to it, but does it ever suggest that our knowledge is vague and incomplete? No—only that the process of knowing is very complicated. (D) goes a little too far. The author would certainly agree that the mind is complex—mental activity is an important factor in what we know. But use your common sense. Is the mind so complex that we can't determine what's real or not? No. (E) is half good and half bad. The author would probably agree that our perception of reality is sometimes skewed, but do you know anything about whether he thinks we're rational or not? No. The best answer, then, is (B).

Problem Set#3: Explanations

1. *A* This is a main idea question. To find the main idea, all you have to do is read the first two sentences of the first paragraph, the topic sentence for each remaining paragraph, and then the last sentence of the entire passage. Remember to state the main idea in your own words before looking at the answer choices. So what's the main idea? To talk about Forster and how he really wasn't a very "modern" writer.

    (A) talks about Forster and modernity, so it looks okay. (B) is too specific. The passage does compare Forster to these writers, but it's not the main point. (C) is too specific as well. It's a summary of the last paragraph. (D) is off the mark entirely. Finally, (E) is too specific. Revolutions in science and art are mentioned in the first paragraph, but that's about it. The best answer is (A).

2. *D* This is a specific question. Use "Victorianism" as your lead word. Remember, once you find the lead word, read about five lines above and five lines below. So where can you find "Victorianism"? At the end of the first paragraph. What does the passage say about Forster and Victorianism? That Forster stepped away from Victorianism, but not entirely. Don't forget to paraphrase before you go to the answer choices.

    (A) goes too far. Forster did step away from Victorianism, just not completely. (B) goes too far as well. Forster didn't cling to Victorianism's ideals. (C) is too extreme. Forster moved away from Victorianism, but not that completely. (D) looks like a good match for your paraphrase. (E) goes off target. Again, Forster did reject Victorianism, at least to a certain extent. The best answer is (D).

3. *C* This specific question tells you exactly where in the passage to go because of the line references. Remember, though, you need to read a little bit before the line reference as well as a little bit after. Well, why does the author say Forster is atavistic? To paraphrase: because even though he was a modern writer, and not a Victorian one, he was closer to Victorianism in some ways than he was to modernity. Don't forget to paraphrase before looking at the answer choices.

    Eliminate (A) because it discusses individualism, not Forster's tension with modernity. Eliminate (B) because it's a little off.

The author doesn't say Forster was completely unconnected. (C) is okay for now; it suggests that Forster and modernity were somewhat in conflict. (D) is the opposite of what you're looking for. (E) goes too far. Forster didn't belief in Victorianism completely. So the best answer is (C).

4. **D** This is a specific question. Use "modern" and "literary" as the lead word. Remember, once you find the lead word, read about five lines before the lead word and five lines after. So where can you find "modern" combined with "literary"? In the second paragraph. How did most modern writers write? Well, they rejected Victorianism completely. Also, they wrote in an "obscure and idiosyncratic" fashion. Remember, always answer the question in your own words before going on to the answer choices.

(A) is definitely out—don't forget modern writers hated Victorianism. (B) is too extreme. You don't know that modern writers rejected *all* beliefs and ideals. (C) is partly true—modern writers wrote obscurely. But were they ironic? Who knows. (D) is a good paraphrase for "obscure and idiosyncratic." (E) is too extreme. Did modern writers lack *any* structure? The best answer is (D).

5. **D** This is a specific question. Use "Lawrence" as your lead word. He's mentioned twice in the passage, once in the second paragraph and once in the third. From the second paragraph, you know that Lawrence rejected Victorianism and that he wrote in an "obscure and idiosyncratic" fashion. From the third, you know that Lawrence had a "didactic moral content." Now that you've got a paraphrase, go to the answer choices.

(A) is half true. Lawrence probably did condemn the life of the bourgeoisie since he rejected Victorianism. But personal relations? The only thing mentioned in the passage about personal relations has to do with Forster. (B) isn't true at all. Remember, Lawrence writes obscurely. The congenial relationship between reader and writer is a characteristic of Victorianism. (C) is out because nowhere are Joyce and Lawrence compared. (D) is a possibility. Right before the passage talks about Lawrence's "didactic moral content," it says Forster never got critics in a big debate because they thought he lacked moral content. (E) goes a little too far. It's probably true that there are differences between Lawrence and Forster—Forster was a less typical modern writer than Lawrence. But you don't really know anything about the ideas in Lawrence's novels. Therefore, the best answer is (D).

6. **D** This tone question is general, and it's definitely a "gimme." How do you think the author feels? From the main idea alone, you can tell he likes Forster. That means (A), (B), and (C) aren't right. Between (D) and (E), which is better? The less extreme. So (D) is the best answer.

7. **D** This is a weird question. In other words, expect this question to be pretty time-consuming. What do you do for Roman numeral questions? Work with one Roman numeral at a time. For statement I, use "society" and "Forster's writings" as the lead word. That should take you to the last few sentences in the second paragraph. What does the passage say about the characters in Forster's books and society? That they do rebel—although not completely—against a society that inhibits. So statement I is true. Eliminate (B) and (C) since they don't contain statement I.

Moving on to statement II . . . From the main idea, you know that Forster's works are not typical of the modern literary movement. But does that mean he failed to be radical? This statement goes too far. Eliminate (E) because it contains statement II.

Moving on to statement III . . . Use "moral" as a lead word. That takes you to the last paragraph. And it does say that critics don't get heated up over Forster's ideas. So statement III is true—which means the best answer is (D). (A) can't be right because it doesn't contain statement III. (Note that you don't even have to look at statement IV.)

Problem Set #4: Explanations

1. **D** This is a general question. For any general question, focus on the main idea. The main idea of the passage can be found by reading the first two sentences of the first paragraph, the topic sentence of each remaining paragraph, and the last sentence of the entire passage. So what's the main idea? To paraphrase: that the natural selection theory doesn't explain all of evolution. Always state the main idea in your own words before looking at the answer choices.

(A) goes too far. Natural selection isn't perfect at explaining all of evolution, but it's still very powerful according to the passage. (B) is true, but it's not the main point of the passage. (C) is a little off. The passage doesn't say anything about making changes to the theory—just that the theory doesn't cover everything. (D) looks like a good match for your paraphrase. (E) is way off target. The best answer is (D).

2. **C** This is a specific question. Use "natural selection" as your lead word. Once you find the lead word, don't forget to read about five lines before it and five lines after it. So where does the passage talk about "natural selection"? In the first and second paragraphs. The first paragraph defines natural selection; the second paragraph talks about the limitations of natural selection. Therefore, focus on the second paragraph. What does that paragraph say about natural selection? That it doesn't take into account other causes for evolution besides a struggle for reproductive success. Always paraphrase the answer to the question before looking at the answer choices.

(A) discusses isolation, which isn't mentioned anywhere in the lines you read. (B) also discusses something you didn't read. (C) is a good match for your paraphrase. (D) talks about human intervention, which you didn't read. (E) misinterprets what you read. Lower and higher levels are discussed, but not in terms of their having problems with reproducing.

3. **A** For this specific question, use "history" as your lead word. Don't forget, once you find the lead word, read about five lines above the lead word and five lines after it. History is mentioned in the third and fourth paragraphs. Both discuss the problems with history—that there's no way to predict what's going to happen. History is about events randomly coinciding. Therefore, the author probably sees the study of history as being very complex.

(A) is okay for now. It sort of matches the idea of very complex. (B) is too extreme. (C) is also a bit on the extreme side. (D) goes too far. There are problems with the study of history but that doesn't mean the study of history isn't worthwhile. (E) goes too far. The study of history isn't insupportable. The best answer, then, is (A).

4. **C** This specific question has a very easy lead word to find: *"Homo sapiens."* Still, don't forget that you need to read about five lines before the lead word and five lines after. So why does the passage talk about *Homo sapiens*? Look at the fifth paragraph: to give weight to the idea that life comes about through a random coinciding of events. Always paraphrase the answer before looking at the answer choices.

    (A) is mentioned in the paragraph, but it's not the reason why *Homo sapiens* are discussed. (B) focuses on length instead of randomness. (C) talks about randomness, so it should be kept. (D) discusses natural selection, which isn't the point. (E) is a little off. It's not the intricacy of events that matters—it's the randomness. The best answer is (C).

5. **C** This is a specific question. Use "evolutionary theory" as your lead word. Don't forget that once you find the lead word, you need to read about five lines before it and five lines after. So where is "evolutionary theory"? In the last paragraph. Why might we be reluctant to let go of traditional evolutionary theory? Because such an act would be "highly contrary both to conventional deterministic models of Western science and to the deepest social traditions and psychological hopes of Western culture." In other words, letting go of traditional evolutionary theory is a scary prospect because it would mean changing the way we look at the world. Always paraphrase before looking at the answer choices.

    (A) talks about Darwin, so eliminate it. (B) is a little off. Giving up the theory doesn't mean we lose all order and structure. (C) is a good match for your paraphrase. (D) talks about other scientific theories, which isn't the point. (E) talks about history, which is off target. The best answer is (C).

6. **C** This is really a general question. What do we need to do for any general question? Think about the main idea. The main idea of this passage is the following: The natural selection theory is not a complete explanation of evolution. The best answer choice has to go with the flow of the main idea.

    (A) misinterprets information from the passage. If you use "history" as a lead word, that takes you to the third and fourth paragraphs. Those paragraphs say that the study of history can be satisfactory, at least "if evidence be adequate." (B) isn't true. Natural selection is about the struggle for reproductive success—which doesn't take into account random events. The second paragraph says as much when it discusses lower levels of organisms. (C) goes with the flow of the main idea, especially since it conveys the idea of randomness. (D) goes back to history again. We found out from (A) that history can be satisfactory, but what else? That it's hard to predict, not easy. (E) is too extreme. Theories aren't *always* inadequate. So the best answer is (C).

7.   *D*   This is a general question. So focus on the main idea—in other words, the first two sentences of the first paragraph, the topic sentence of each remaining paragraph, and the final sentence of the entire passage. How is the passage organized? Well, natural selection is explained, and then problems with it are noted in a lot of detail. Always paraphrase the answer to a question before looking at the answer choices.

(A) is a bad answer choice because it says natural selection is rejected. The theory isn't rejected, just noted as incomplete. (B) is okay for the first half, but bad for the second half. Conditions are never stated. (C) is okay for the first half, but bad for the second half. Observations that support it aren't made. (D) is a good match for your paraphrase. (E) is okay for the first half, but bad for the second half. The passage does question natural selection but not by applying it to a different field of study. (Don't get thrown by the discussion of history.) The best answer is (D).

Problem Set #5: Explanations

1.   *E*   This is a main- idea question. To find the main idea, all you have to do is read the first two sentences of the first paragraph, the topic sentence of each remaining paragraph, and then the last sentence of the entire passage. Don't forget to state the main idea in your own words before looking at the answer choices. So what's the main idea? How gender differences are preserved or enforced in the workplace.

(A) talks about the reconstruction of gender. Not what you're looking for. (B) discusses nontraditional jobs, not gender differences. (C) mentions pervasiveness, which isn't the point. (D) is a little off because of the word "why." The passage isn't about why we can't ignore gender differences. (E) is the only answer choice remaining, and it's a good match for your paraphrase. The best answer is (E).

2. **B** This is a specific question that tells you exactly where to go to find the answer: the first paragraph. So how is the first paragraph organized? Well, it starts out with a statement about gender differences. Then it makes a definition, and after that, it provides a specific example. Remember, it's important that you answer the question with your own words before looking at the answer choices.

(A) is out because the paragraph doesn't start out with a specific. (B) is okay, as is (C), but (D) isn't because the paragraph doesn't start out with a hypothesis. Finally, (E) is out because there's no criticism made at the beginning of the paragraph.

You're down to (B) and (C). Look at (B). A clarification (or definition) is made, and then specific examples are given. (B) is okay. What about (C)? Specific situations are cited, but there's no generalization at the end. (B) is the best answer.

3. **C** This is a specific question. "Internal stratification" is clearly the lead word, and you can find the lead word at the beginning of the very first paragraph. Don't forget to read about five lines before the lead word as well as five lines after. So what is internal stratification? When men and women have the same job, but in that job, they are given different tasks to perform. Remember, it's always important to paraphrase before looking at the answer choices.

(A) isn't an inference you can make. Women and men have the same jobs is the point. (B) isn't an inference you can make. It might be true, but nothing about internal stratification suggests it. (C) looks good—especially because it agrees with the main idea about gender differences. (D) isn't quite as good as (C). It could be true, but nothing about internal stratification suggests it. (E), finally, is like (B) and (D). It could be true, but nothing about internal stratification suggests it. The best answer is (C).

4. **B** This is a specific question, and the question tells you exactly where to go in the passage: the last paragraph. What's the point of the last paragraph? That gender differences aren't always

"forced on people." In other words, people sometimes enforce gender differences themselves. It's always important to paraphrase the answer to a question before looking at the answer choices.

(A) is the opposite of what you're looking for. It's the internal that's important, not the external. (B) looks like a good match for the paraphrase. (C) is a little off. Male nurses and female marines are nontraditional, but they actually enforce gender differences, too. (D) isn't quite right. The statement is true, but it's not the point of the last paragraph. (E) is way off target. The best answer is (B).

5. **C** This is a weird question. In other words, it's pretty time-consuming. What do you do for questions-in-the-answer-choices questions? Look for a lead word in each answer choice and then see if the question can be answered. A good lead word in (A) might be "dress" or "behave." That takes you to the second paragraph. Is the question answered? No. All you know is that rules are dictated, not how people feel about them. The lead word in (B) is "internal stratification." That takes you to the first paragraph. Is the question answered? No. How widespread internal stratification is is never discussed. A good lead word in (C) is "corporate women." That takes you to the third paragraph. In that paragraph, the author explains how corporate women are more visible and how this makes them more secretive and less independent. So can the question be answered? Yes. A lead word for (D) is "supervisors." That takes you to the fourth paragraph. Is the question answered? No. All you know is that supervisors uphold gender differences, not why. Finally, a lead word for (E) is "male nurses." That takes you to the second paragraph and the last paragraph. Neither one discusses how male nurses cope, so the question is not answered. The best answer is (C).

6. **D** This is a weird question. What do we know about weird questions? That they're very time-consuming. Okay—what should you do for an EXCEPT question? Play the Yes/No game. Start by finding a lead word for each answer choice. The lead word in (A), "words," takes you to the fourth paragraph. Do managers use language to enforce gender differences. Yes. So

put a Y next to (A). The lead word in (B), "dress," takes you to the second paragraph. Do dress codes enforce gender differences? Yes. So put a Y next to (B). The lead word in (C), "internal pressure," takes you to the last paragraph. Does internal stratification enforce gender differences? Yes. Put a Y next to (C). Use "coworkers" in (D) as a lead word. "Coworkers" doesn't take you anywhere in the passage, so put a N next to (D). The lead word in (E), "different duties," takes you to the first paragraph. Do different duties for men and women enforce gender differences? Yes. Put a Y next to (E).

Which answer choice is not like the others? (D). It's the only answer choice with an N next to it. So (D) is the best answer.

7. **A** This is a specific question. To find out what would logically follow the last sentence, read the last one or two sentences of the passage. What do the last two sentences discuss? How male nurses and female marines insist on their masculinity or femininity. So what would logically follow? Something about keeping gender differences intact.

(A) mentions gender differences and their reinforcement, so it looks good. (B) isn't right because the last few sentences don't mention changing the mind-sets of others. (C) goes too far. States of conflict aren't the issue. (D) misrepresents the information in the last paragraph. Internal pressures are discussed, but not as greater than the external. Finally, (E) goes off on a tangent. How to overcome gender differences isn't the point. The best answer is (A).

Problem Set #6: Explanations

1. **B** To find the main idea of a passage, all you have to do is read the first two sentences of the first paragraph, the topic sentence for each remaining paragraph, and then the final sentence of the entire passage. Since this passage is only one paragraph long, you may want to read a little more than just the first two sentences at the beginning.

So what's the point of the passage? It's talking about epidemics caused by meningitis. Don't get caught up in the science. To say the main idea is epidemics and meningitis is fine.

(A) isn't right because there's no mention of epidemics. (B) looks good because it has both epidemic and meningitis. (C) is too specific—it says nothing about meningitis. (D) is a possibility since it talks about outbreak and meningitis. (E) is too specific—it doesn't say anything about epidemics.

You're down to (B) and (D). Which answer choice is better? Well, the first two sentences of the passage talk about the cause of the epidemics, not the problems. Therefore, the best answer is (B).

2. **D** This is a weird question—i.e., it's a very time-consuming question. On an EXCEPT question, what should you do? Play the Yes/No game. Start with answer choice (A). Does the author provide an explanation in the passage? Yes. He suggests what might cause a meningitis epidemic to occur. Put a Y next to (A). Move on to (B). Does the author make a comparison? Yes. He talks about making an analogy to an influenza outbreak. Put a Y next to (B). Go on to (C). Does the author suggest a cause for an effect? Yes. Once again, the author talks about what might cause a meningitis epidemic. Put a Y next to (C). On to (D). Does the author provide a definition? No. Nowhere in the passage is a definition given. Put a N next to (D). Finally, (E). Does the author make an inference? Yes. He says in line 7 the findings suggest ("These findings do suggest . . . "), which means he's making an inference. Put a Y next to (E).

   Which answer choice is not like the others? (D)—it's the only N. Therefore, the best answer is (D).

3. **C** This is a specific question. Use "antigenic shift" as your lead word. It takes you to the end of the paragraph. Don't forget that you should read about five lines above the lead word as well as five lines after. So what does the passage say about antigenic shifts? That they take place when immunity wanes, which allows some clones to escape surveillance and start an epidemic. Make sure you make this paraphrase before moving on to the answer choices.

   Does (A) match your paraphrase? No. Nowhere in the passage does it talk about clones *changing* their surface antigens. What about (B)? No. There's nothing in the passage about shared antigens outnumbering different antigens. (C)? It's a pretty good match. (D)? No. The passage doesn't say clones direct themselves at the weakest elements of the population. (E)? No. There's nothing about sharing a resistance to immunity. The best answer is (C).

Problem Set #7: Explanations

1. **C** To find the answer to this general question, determine what the main idea is. How do you find the main idea? By reading the first two sentences of the first paragraph, the topic sentence of each remaining paragraph, and then the last sentence of the entire passage. What is the main idea? That the evolving economy in New York produced class conflict and gender conflict. Always paraphrase the main idea before looking at the answer choices.

    (A) is too specific. Middle-class women are discussed, but they're not the main point. (B) is too general. It talks about the economy, but not about class and gender. (C) looks like a good match for your paraphrase. (D) is too specific. The cult of domesticity is mentioned in the passage, but it's not the main point. (E) is too specific. It says nothing about the economy. The best answer is (C).

2. **E** This is a specific question that uses a line reference. Don't forget that you should read not just the line reference, but about five lines above the line reference and five lines below. So why does the author say "We know most about the male participants"? As a way to discuss class conflict between men *and* as a way to preface class conflict between women. In other words, we don't know a lot about the female participants but here is what we do know. Always paraphrase the answer to a question before looking at the answer choices.

    (A) isn't quite right. The author isn't *challenging* the studies about men. (B) is a little off. Yes, class conflict is at issue, but debate is not. (C) is bad because the passage never talks about why only men have been looked at. (D) contains a true statement—class conflict did have an impact on industrial development—but that's not the point of the author saying "We know most about the male participants." (E) is the best match for your paraphrase and it is the best answer. This question is a great example of how much of reading comprehension is *not* about finding the best answer. It's about finding the answer that is *least bad*. In other words, get the right answer by eliminating the ones that have to be wrong.

3. *E* This is a specific question. Use "middle-class men" and "working-class men" as your lead word. That takes you to the second paragraph. What does the paragraph say about the similarities between the two groups? That they both believed the welfare of the country depended on them. Don't forget that you must paraphrase the answer to a question before looking at the answer choices.

(A) misinterprets the information in the paragraph. It's suggested that the groups didn't particularly like each other, but you don't know whether they saw each other as obstructions. (B) is true of middle-class men, but not working-class men. (D) mentions something you didn't read about—namely, women. (E) is a good match for your paraphrase. It's the best answer.

4. *A* This is a specific question. Use "home" as your lead word. That should take you to the third paragraph. What does the passage say about women and the home? That "In their consignment to the household as the sole domain of proper female activity, women suffered a constriction of their social engagements; at the same time, they gained power within their families that also vested them with greater moral authority in their own communities." In other words, women lost power by being restricted to the home, but also gained power at the same time. Always paraphrase before looking at the answer choices.

(A) is a great match for your paraphrase. (B) misinterprets what you read. You don't know if taking charge of the home was a challenge to male authority. (C) misinterprets information from the passage. You don't know that women were responsible for reconstructing the duties of parents and the roles of children. It could have been men. (D) is a little tricky. Women did participate in missionary activity, but you don't know they increased that participation after taking charge of the home. (E) is also tricky because women did try to reform the city, but was this a result of taking charge of the home? You don't know. The best answer is (A).

5. **D** This is a specific question. Use "cult of domesticity" as your lead word. That takes you to the fourth paragraph. The very first sentence in that paragraph sums up what the cult of domesticity did. It produced class conflict. Middle-class women went out and tried to get rid of the "perfidies of working-class life" in the name of domesticity. Always paraphrase the answer before looking at the answer choices.

(A) is wrong because women weren't completely confined to the home. They were working in the public eye in their efforts to reform the city. (B) is off because middle-class women cherished the cult of domesticity—not lower-class women. (C) mentions republicanism, which you didn't read in the sentences surrounding the lead word. (D) talks about class conflict, so it looks good. (E) says something you just don't know to be true. The best answer is (D).

6. **E** This is a specific question. Use "middle-class reformers" as your lead word. That should take you to the last paragraph. What do you learn about reformers? That "In confronting the working poor, reformers created and refined their own sense of themselves as social and spiritual superiors capable of remolding the city in their own image." In other words, reformers were trying to make the working class just like them. Always paraphrase the answer to a question before going to the answer choices.

(A) mentions Protestantism, which is discussed in the paragraph, but also mentions converting, which isn't discussed. (B) is almost right, but not quite. You don't know that the reformers were consciously trying to gain power. For all you know, their efforts were a sincere attempt to help. (C) suggests that reformers were actively seeking to end class tensions. That's something you just don't know. (D) contains information that is true—women did do missionary work—but you don't know if reformers *encouraged* women to do so. Finally, (E) is a good match for your paraphrase. It's the best answer.

7. **B** This is a specific question. Use "economy" as your lead word. That takes you to the first paragraph. According to the first paragraph, "The appearance of new social classes was both cause and result of industrial development and commercial expansion."

In other words, class conflict was responsible for and a product of the changing economy. Always paraphrase before you go to the answer choices.

(A) mentions reform, which you didn't read about in the paragraph. (B) is a good match for your paraphrase. (C) says something that's not true. The economy caused gender conflict; it didn't temper gender conflict. (D) says something you don't know for sure to be true. (E) mentions the Revolution, which you didn't read about in the paragraph. The best answer is (B).

Problem Set #8: Explanations

1. *C* To find the main idea, just read the first two sentences of the first paragraph, the topic sentence of each remaining paragraph, and then the final sentence of the entire passage. What's the main idea, then? To talk about shamans and prophets.

    (A) is a little too general. It doesn't mention prophets at all. (B) is discussed in the passage, but it's not the main point. (C) looks good because it talks about both shamans and prophets. (D) is too general. Religious leaders is vague—you want an answer choice that mentions shamans and prophets explicitly. (E) is too specific. Shamans and the supernatural are mentioned in the passage, but that's not the main point. The best answer is (C).

2. *C* This is a specific question. "Shamans" isn't a great lead word since it's mentioned throughout the passage, but that's the best you can do. You could look for "shamans" along with "social systems" to guide you a little bit better. "Shamans" and "social systems" are both mentioned in the first paragraph, so try reading there first. What do societies rely on shamans? Because they "could maintain contact with the cosmic forces of the universe directly . . . make sense of both the measured order of ordinary times and the catastrophes of drought, earthquake, or flood." In other words, shamans are good because they make the world make sense.

    (A) isn't quite right. Empowering isn't the point. (B) talks about mediation, which you just didn't read about. (C) talks about structure and form, so it could match your paraphrase. (D) is never stated outright, so you don't know it to be true. (E) is half good, half bad. Shamans did explain unpredictable forces in nature, but hostile neighbors? You just don't know. The best answer is (C).

3. **D** This is a specific question. Use "shamans" and "prophets" as the lead word. That takes you to the second paragraph. What does the passage say about how they differ? "The prophet usually does not enjoy the legitimacy within his society that is granted the shaman. His is a voice crying in the wilderness, not that of the legitimate curer and philosopher." So the prophet doesn't have quite the standing or the power of the shaman. Always paraphrase the answer to a question before going to the answer choices.

    (A) mentions a mandate from a god. You didn't read that, so it can't be right. (B) is half true. Shamans do have more standing, but is that based upon their communication with the supernatural? You don't know. (C) goes too far. Shamans are respected, clearly, but are they demigods? Who knows. (D) has to be true since shamans have more standing and power than do prophets. (Note the moderate language—"less likely.") Finally, (E) is half true. Shamans do have greater authority—but is it because they live in isolated social systems? You don't know. The best answer is (D).

4. **A** This is a weird question. In other words, it's very time-consuming. How do you deal with Roman numeral questions? By working on one Roman numeral at a time. Focus on statement I first. Use "size" as a lead word. In the first paragraph, the passage says shamans live in small societies. In the second paragraph, the passage says prophets live in more complex societies. Therefore, statement I isn't true. Eliminate (B), (C), and (E) because each contains statement I.

    At this point, only (A) and (D) are left. They both contain statement II, so you know statement II has to be true. All you need to look at, then, is statement III. Statement III talks about controlling nature. This may be true for shamans, but what about prophets? You just don't know. The best answer is (A).

CHAPTER

7

Antonyms

A VOCABULARY TEST

At heart, antonyms are a vocabulary test. The only difference is instead of finding the same meaning of a particular word, you're looking for a word that's opposite in meaning. For example:

INCENSED:

(A) mollified
(B) ecstatic
(C) entertained
(D) peeved
(E) satisfied

As with analogies, we call the word in capitalized letters the stem. The answer choices are, of course, the answer choices.

COVER IT UP

There are basically three groups into which we can divide words that show up on antonyms:

1. Words you know

2. Words you sort of know

3. Words you don't know at all

A word you know is one that you can provide a definition for. A word you sort of know is one that you can use in a sentence. Or maybe you can tell if it's a positive word or a negative word. However, you can't define it. A word you don't know at all is one that you've never heard or seen before.

A WORD YOU KNOW

Let's start with how to tackle a word that you know. The first thing you should do is focus on the word. In other words, don't get distracted by the answer choices . If you have to cover up the answer choices with your hand to make sure you don't look at them, so be it. Now that your attention is on the stem word, make a simple opposite for it. Let's go back to the example above. The stem word is INCENSED. INCENSED means very angry. A simple opposite for INCENSED, then, is *very happy*.

Once you've made a simple opposite for the stem word, you can look at the answer choices. Go through each and every answer choice (as you always do in verbal), and pick the one that's the best match for your simple opposite. As with sentence completions, the best match for your simple opposite doesn't have to be an exact match. In other words, you don't have to look for *very happy* in the answer choices. You just need to look for something very close to it.

(A) mollified
(B) ecstatic
(C) entertained
(D) peeved
(E) satisfied

In this case, the best answer is (B) because *ecstatic* does mean *very happy*. Notice that it's very important to look at all the answer choices because (A) and (E) are attractive, especially if you're working too quickly. Try another one:

DECAY:

(A) adorn
(B) arise
(C) flower
(D) beatify
(E) bedaub

A simple opposite for DECAY is *grow*. Clearly, (A) and (B) don't mean *grow*. (C) looks good. (D) and (E) contain hard words that you may not know. You can't cross them out just because you don't know what *beatify* and *bedaub* mean. However, you can guess (C) over (D) and (E) because you know that (C) definitely works. Most of the time you see an antonym that has an easy word like DECAY, the correct answer will also have an easy word.

QUIZ #1

For each of the following questions, make a simple opposite for the stem word.

1. CALLOUS: TENDER

2. HAPHAZARD: CALCULATE

3. INDOLENCE: PAIN OR ACTIVE

4. AUSTERE: COPIUS

5. ANNUL: VALIDATE

QUIZ #2

For each of the following questions, make a simple opposite for the stem word. Then pick the answer that is the best match.

1. BESTOW: GIVE

   (A) condense
   (B) dispossess *DESPOJAR, DESAHUCIAR*
   (C) contribute
   (D) disregard
   (E) accuse

2. AUTHENTICATE: AUTENTIFICAR

   (A) restore
   (B) misrepresent *TERGIVERSAR*
   (C) disallow *rechazar, ANULAR*
   (D) invalidate
   (E) demolish

3. DECREPIT:

   (A) powerful
   (B) nurturing *CRIAR, EDUCAR*
   (C) just
   (D) impressive
   (E) conspicuous — *LLAMATIVO, NOTORIO*

4. PUNGENT: MORDAZ

   (A) benevolent
   (B) meek *SUAVE, DOCIL*
   (C) bland *INSIPIDO, SOSO, INSULSO*
   (D) harmful
   (E) piercing

5. PINNACLE:

   (A) moderation
   (B) underestimation
   (C) lowest point
   (D) suppression
   (E) unvalued object

A WORD YOU SORT OF KNOW

So far, so good. Things start getting a little trickier, though, when the stem word is one that you only sort of know. If you come across a stem word you sort of know, there are three possible ways to attack it:

1. Opposites for the answer choices

2. Positive/Negative

3. Word Association

OPPOSITES FOR THE ANSWER CHOICES

Since you can't define the stem word exactly—and so can't make a simple opposite for it—try starting with the answer choices instead. Make a simple opposite for each answer choice and then ask yourself if the opposite could be the meaning of the stem word. Let's try this technique with the example we looked at earlier.

INCENSED:

(A) mollified *APLACAR, APACIGUAR*
(B) ecstatic
(C) entertained
(D) peeved *MOLESTAR, IRRITAR*
(E) satisfied

Let's say that you're not sure what INCENSED means. Therefore, take a look at the answer choices.

What's a simple opposite for (A), *mollified*? *Mollified* means appeased, so a good opposite would be along the lines of *provoked* or *irritated*. Does INCENSED mean *provoked* or *irritated*? No. So eliminate (A).

What's a simple opposite for (B), *ecstatic*? Since *ecstatic* means very happy, a good opposite is *very angry*. Does INCENSED mean *very angry*? Yes. (B) looks good, but be sure to check the remaining answer choices.

What's a simple opposite for (C), *entertained*? *Bored*, maybe. Well, does INCENSED mean *bored*? No. Get rid of (C).

What's a simple opposite for (D), *peeved*? *Peeved* means annoyed, so a good opposite would be along the lines of *made happy*. Does INCENSED mean *made happy*? No. Eliminate (D).

What's a simple opposite for (E), *satisfied*? *Unsatisfied* works. Does INCENSED mean *unsatisfied*? No. Throw out (E).

Once again, we've proved that (B) is the best answer.

Let's try another one. For each blank line, write a word that is a good opposite for the answer choice.

UNADULTERATED:

(A) mismanaged _____
(B) consecrated _____
(C) persecuted _____
(D) reprieved _____
(E) defiled MANCHAR, CORROMPER

A good opposite for *mismanaged* is *managed well*. Does UNADULTER-ATED mean *managed well*? No.

A good opposite for *consecrated* is *profaned*. Does UNADULTERATED mean *profaned*? No.

A good opposite for *persecuted* is *treated well*. Does UNADULTERATED mean *treated well*? No.

A good opposite for *reprieved* is *condemned*. Does UNADULTERATED mean *condemned*? No.

A good opposite for *defiled* is *pure*. Does UNADULTERATED mean *pure*? Yes.

The best answer, then, is (D). Notice how important it is to go through each answer choice. Also notice that distracting answer choices are those that mean the same thing as the stem word—not the opposite.

Okay, one more:

SANCTION:

(A) credit _____
(B) disapprove _____
(C) inform _____
(D) elaborate _____
(E) devalue _____

A good opposite for *credit* is *discredit*. Is that what SANCTION means? No.

A good opposite for *disapprove* is *approve*. Is that what SANCTION means? Looks good.

A good opposite for *inform* is—well, is there really a good opposite for *inform*? If an answer choice doesn't have an opposite, then it can't be right. *Inform* doesn't work, then.

Does *elaborate* have a good opposite? Not really.

A good opposite for *devalue* is *value*. Is that what SANCTION means? No. So the best answer is (B). Once again, make sure you check out (A) through (E). And be aggressive—challenge the words in the answer choices. Do they really have opposites or not? You may find that some of them don't.

POSITIVE/NEGATIVE

Making opposites for the answer choices works well when you sort of know the stem word pretty well. There are other times when the stem word you sort of know is one that you just barely sort of know. In this case, try using Positive/Negative. Positive/Negative takes advantage of the fact that certain words have connotations. For example, we all would say the word *intelligent* has a positive connotation while the word *boastful* has a negative one.

Well, if you sort of know that the stem word is positive, then what do you know about the correct answer? It has to be negative. Similarly, if you sort of know that the stem word is negative, then you know the correct answer has to be positive. Finally, if you sort of know that the stem word is either positive or negative, then what else do you know? That any answer choice that is neutral can't be right. Try the following example:

CENSURE:

(A) speak in praise of
(B) increase the value of
(C) shy away from
(D) take without consent
(E) leave in its original state

If you know that CENSURE is a negative word, then you can eliminate any answer choice that is negative as well. (A) is positive, so leave it in. (B) is also positive, so leave it in, too. (C) and (D), however, are both negative, so eliminate them. (E) isn't really positive or negative. Possibly, it's slightly positive, but CENSURE is a very negative word, so it probably isn't right. You're left with (A) and (B). At this point, just guess. You have a 50 percent chance of getting the question right. As it turns out, the best answer is (A). CENSURE means to blame.

As you can see from this example, Positive/Negative won't necessarily get you to the right answer, but it can do some effective POE. And when you only sort of know a word, it can be pretty helpful.

WORD ASSOCIATION

Sometimes you only sort of know a word because you've heard it used in a sentence or a phrase. In other words, you associate that word with something. Take a look at the following example:

> BOYCOTT:
>
> (A) negate
> (B) deflect
> (C) engender
> (D) patronize
> (E) entitle

Probably you've heard the word BOYCOTT used before, as in "to BOYCOTT the Olympics." Well, let's use "BOYCOTT the Olympics" to our advantage. Let's substitute each answer choice for BOYCOTT in the phrase.

Does *"negate* the Olympics" make sense? Not unless you can kill a sporting event.

Does *"deflect* the Olympics" make sense? Definitely not.

Does *"engender* the Olympics" make sense? Not really.

Does *"patronize* the Olympics" make sense? Sure.

Does *"entitle* the Olympics" make sense? Nope.

So the best answer is (D).

Word Association is a great technique to use if you've heard a word used before in a specific way. Also, keep in mind that sometimes Word Association can help you determine whether a word is positive or negative. In other words, you can use Positive/Negative and Word Association in conjunction to do some good POE.

QUIZ #3

For each of the following questions, determine whether the word is positive or negative.

1. PEREMPTORY:

2. CAPTIOUS:

3. ABSTEMIOUS:

4. TORTUOUS:

5. PROPAGATE:

6. VITUPERATE:

7. PROFLIGATE:

8. SPURIOUS:

9. SATURNINE:

10. ALACRITY:

11. DELETERIOUS:

12. OBVIATE:

13. NOISOME:

14. REDOUBTABLE:

15. SEDULOUS:

ANTONYMS **7**

QUIZ #4

For each of the following questions, pretend that you sort of know the stem word. Try to do some POE by making opposites for the answer choices or by using Positive/Negative or Word Association.

1. UNREQUITED: *NO CORRESPONDIDO*

   (A) beneficial
   (B) attractive
   (C) indulgent
   (D) ethical
   (E) reciprocated

2. IMPUGN: *PONER EN DUDA, CUESTIONAR, IMPUGNAR*

   (A) forestall — *PREVENIR, ADELANTAR*
   (B) commend
   (C) extend
   (D) conspire
   (E) attribute

3. CAPITULATE:

   (A) accomplish
   (B) lament
   (C) endorse *ENDORSAR, APROBAR*
   (D) stand fast *MANTENERSE EN PIE, EMPECINARSE*
   (E) demand

4. NIGGARDLY: *TACAÑO*

   (A) vexing
   (B) potent
   (C) magnanimous
   (D) accommodating
   (E) prudish *GAZMOÑO, REMILGADO*

5. SALIENT: *SALIENTE, NOTABLE*

   (A) inconspicuous
   (B) disdainful *DESDEÑOSO, DE DESDÉN*
   (C) attentive
   (D) empty
   (E) informative

6. ABDICATE:

   (A) flourish
   (B) subdue
   (C) struggle
   (D) disperse
   (E) appropriate

7. HALCYON: *→ FELIZ*

   (A) arousing
   (B) explicit
   (C) insinuating
   (D) disquieted *INQUIETAR*
   (E) bemoaning *LAMENTAR*

8. HACKNEYED: *TRILLADO, GASTADO*

   (A) ornamental *DECORATIVO*
   (B) uncertain
   (C) faithful
   (D) unprecedented
   (E) winning

9. ABEYANCE: *ESTAR en DESUSO*

   (A) restoration of activity
   (B) acquiescence to authority
   (C) toleration of depravity
   (D) insistence on decorum
   (E) preservation of honor

10. ABERRATION:

   (A) idleness
   (B) clarification
   (C) allusion
   (D) refinement
   (E) conformity

11. PHLEGMATIC: *IMPASIBLE, FLEMÁTICO*

   (A) contrary
   (B) unsettled
   (C) informed
   (D) duplicated
   (E) lively

12. PROBITY: *HONRADEZ, INTEGRIDAD*

   (A) yield *RENDIR, PRODUCIR*
   (B) indecency
   (C) cowardice
   (D) expediency
   (E) renown

13. PERFUNCTORY: SUPERFICIAL, SOMERO

    (A) uncommitted
    (B) compelling
    (C) thorough
    (D) arbitrary
    (E) fostering

14. PRODIGAL:

    (A) besmirched MANCHAR, MANCILLAR
    (B) virtuous
    (C) pompous
    (D) unaffected
    (E) economical

15. VOLUBLE:

    (A) untalkative
    (B) fleeting MOMENTÁNEO
    (C) unqualified
    (D) suave
    (E) emphatic

A WORD YOU DON'T KNOW AT ALL

A word you don't know at all is one that you hate. If you ever come across a stem word that you've never seen before, don't waste your time. Be aggressive and guess. Then move on. The worst thing you can do is agonize over which answer choice is best when you haven't any clue what the stem word means.

To guide you in guessing, here're some last resorts:

1. Eliminate answer choices that contain words without opposites.

2. Pick an answer choice that is extreme—that is, very positive or very negative.

Probably the most effective POE tool is the first one: Eliminate words that don't have opposites. Always start off here, and then once you've done all the POE you can, just guess—pick the most extreme.

QUIZ #5

On the following questions, pretend that you don't know the stem word at all. Use your guessing techniques to eliminate bad answer choices. Then be aggressive and guess—pick the answer choice that is the most extreme.

1. CANARD:

   (A) an improper gesture
   (B) a concealed object
   (C) a defined position
   (D) a true story
   (E) a casual lie

2. INFRANGIBLE:

   (A) breakable
   (B) mixable
   (C) aggressive
   (D) transitory
   (E) violating

3. CAVIL:

   (A) patronize
   (B) denounce
   (C) approve
   (D) consummate
   (E) fabricate

4. MACERATE:

   (A) concur
   (B) reflect
   (C) harden
   (D) officiate
   (E) liquefy

5. FRIABLE:

   (A) tactile
   (B) durable
   (C) wavering
   (D) conventional
   (E) disheveled

SECONDARY MEANINGS

Before we wrap up antonyms, a quick note. Often, ETS tests the secondary meanings of words. For example, look at the following antonym:

RAIL:

(A) consolidate
(B) extol
(C) substantiate
(D) encourage
(E) emote

Is ETS talking about a RAIL that you can sit on? No. It's talking about the verb RAIL. You can tell ETS wants the verb definition of RAIL by looking at the answer choices. They're all verbs. What part of speech the answer choices are in can help you determine if ETS is using a secondary meaning.

QUIZ #4

The following words have both primary definitions and secondary definitions. Provide the two meanings for each word.

1. novel

2. table

3. color

4. plastic

5. convention

6. individual

7. industry

8. secrete

9. gauge

10. marshal

IN SUMMARY

Antonyms, once again, are largely a vocabulary test. Either you know the words or you don't. Still, there are some techniques to help you eliminate wrong answer choices. What's most important is that you take enough time to get an antonym right when it's a word you know or sort of know—and that you be aggressive and guess when it's a word you don't know at all. So be honest with yourself while working on antonyms. What kind of word is it: one you know, sort of know, or have never seen in your life?

When you know the stem word . . .

1. Make a simple opposite for the stem word. Then pick the answer choice that best matches your opposite. Watch out for answer choices that have the same meaning as the stem, and make sure to go through all of the choices.

When you sort of know the stem word . . .

1. Make opposites for the answer choices and see which opposite has the same meaning as the stem word. Remember, if a word doesn't have an opposite, it can't be right.

2. Use Positive/Negative or Word Association.

When you don't know the stem word at all . . .

1. Eliminate words with no opposites.

2. Pick the answer choice that is the most extreme.

QUIZ #1: ANSWERS

1.   sensitive

2.   not random; ordered

3.   working hard; diligence

4.   not strict

5.   reinstate

QUIZ #2: ANSWERS

1.   B Simple opposite: *take away*

2.   D Simple opposite: *prove false*

3.   A Simple opposite: *strong*

4.   C Simple opposite: *flavorless*

5.   C Simple opposite: *bottom*

QUIZ #3: ANSWERS

1.   –

2.   –

3.   +

4.   –

5.   +

6.   –

7.   –

8.   –

9.   –

10.   +

11. –

12. –

13. –

14. +

15. +

QUIZ #4: ANSWERS

1. *E* Try Word Association. Have you heard of the phrase
"UNREQUITED love"? Use this phrase with each answer choice.
Does *beneficial* love make sense? Not really. *Attractive* love? Not
great. *Indulgent* love? Not great. *Ethical* love? No. *Reciprocated*
love? Yes. The best answer is (E).

2. *B* Try Positive/Negative. IMPUGN is a negative word, so its
opposite has to be positive. (A) is negative, so cross it out. (B) is
positive, so leave it in. (C) is neither positive nor negative, so
cross it out. (D) is negative, so cross it out. (E) could be either
positive or negative, so it's probably not a good choice. The best
answer is (B).

3. *D* Try Positive/Negative. CAPITULATE is a negative word, so its
opposite has to be positive. (A) is positive, so leave it in. (B) is
negative, so cross it out. (C) is positive, as is (D), so leave both
in. (E) is negative, so cross it out. Now try making opposites for
each answer choice. A simple opposite for (A) is *fail.* Is that
what CAPITULATE means? Not quite. A simple opposite for
(C) is *not support*. Is that what CAPITULATE means? No. A
simple opposite for (D) is *give in*. Is that what CAPITULATE
means? Yes. The best answer is (D).

4. *C* Try Positive/Negative. NIGGARDLY is a negative word, so its
opposite has to be positive. (A) is negative, so cross it out. (B),
(C), and (D) are all positive, so leave them in. (E) is negative, so
cross it out. Now try Word Association. Have you heard of the
phrase "NIGGARDLY sum of money"? Use that phrase with
each remaining answer choice. Does *potent* sum of money make
sense? Not really. Does *magnanimous* sum of money make

sense? Sort of. Does *accommodating* sum of money make sense? No. The best answer is (C).

5. **A** Try Positive/Negative. SALIENT is a positive word, so its opposite must be negative. (A) is negative, so keep it. (B) is negative, too, so leave it in. (C) is positive, so cross it out. (D) is negative, so it's okay. (E) is positive, so cross it out. Now use Word Association. Have you heard of the phrase "Go over the SALIENT points"? Test that phrase on the remaining answer choices. Does *inconspicuous* points make sense? Sort of. What about *disdainful* points? No. *Empty* points? Maybe. At this point, you have two answer choices left—(A) and (D). If that's all you know about SALIENT, then just guess. You have a 50 percent chance of getting the question right. The best answer is (A).

6. **E** Try Word Association. Have you heard of the phrase "ABDICATE the throne"? Does *flourish* the throne make sense? No. Does *subdue* the throne? Maybe. Does *struggle* the throne? No. Does *disperse* the throne? No. Does *appropriate* the throne. Yes. Between (B) and (E), which makes more sense? (E). It's the best answer.

7. **D** Try Positive/Negative. HALCYON is a positive word, so its opposite must be negative. (A) is positive, so cross it out. (B) could be either positive or negative, so it's probably not right. (C), (D), and (E) are all negative, so leave them in. If you don't know anything else about HALCYON, then just guess—you have a one-in-three chance of getting the question right. The best answer is (D).

8. **D** Try making simple opposites for the answer choices. A simple opposite for (A) is *plain*. Does HACKNEYED mean *plain*? No. A simple opposite for (B) is *certain*. Does HACKNEYED mean *certain*? No. A simple opposite for (C) is *unfaithful*. Does HACKNEYED mean *unfaithful*? No. A simple opposite for (D) is *done before*. Does HACKNEYED mean *done before*? Sort of. A simple opposite for (E) is *unattractive*. Does HACKNEYED mean *unattractive*? No. The best answer is (D).

9. **A** Try making simple opposites for the answer choices. A simple opposite for (A) is *cessation of activity*. Is that what ABEYANCE means? (Think of the phrase "held in ABEYANCE.") Maybe. A simple opposite for (B) is *challenge to authority*. Is that what ABEYANCE means? No. A simple opposite for (C) is *refusing to tolerate depravity*. Is that what ABEYANCE means? No. A simple opposite for (D) is *disregard of decorum*. Is that what ABEYANCE means? No. A simple opposite for (E) is *wasting away of honor*. Is that what ABEYANCE means? No. The best answer is (A).

10. **E** Try making simple opposites for the answer choices. A simple opposite for (A) is *activity*. Is that what ABERRATION means? No. A simple opposite for (B) is *confusion*. Is that what ABERRATION means? No. There's not a strong opposite for (C), so it can't be the right answer. A simple opposite for (D) is *vulgarity*. Is that what ABERRATION means? No. A simple opposite for (E) is *deviancy*. Is that what ABERRATION means? Yes. The best answer is (E).

11. **B** Try Positive/Negative. PHLEGMATIC is a positive word, so its opposite must be negative. (A) and (B) are negative, so leave both in. (C) is positive, so cross it out. (D) could be slightly negative, so leave it in. (E) is positive, so cross it out. If that's all you know about PHLEGMATIC, then just guess. You have a one-in-three chance of getting the question right. The best answer is (B).

12. **B** Try Positive/Negative. PROBITY is a positive word, so its opposite must be negative. (A) is neither positive nor negative, so it can't be right. (B) is negative, so leave it in. (C) is negative, so leave it in. (D) is positive, as is (E), so cross them out. Now make simple opposites for each answer choice. A simple opposite for (B) is *decency*. Is that what PROBITY means? Yes. A simple opposite for (C) is *bravery*. Is that what PROBITY means? No. The best answer is (B).

13. **C** Try Word Association. Have you heard of the phrase "PERFUNCTORY kiss"? Use that phrase on the answer choices. Does *uncommitted* kiss make sense? Maybe. Does *compelling* kiss make sense? Yes. Does *thorough* kiss make sense? Yes. Does

arbitrary kiss make sense? Not really. Does *fostering* kiss make sense? No. If that's all you know about PERFUNCTORY, then just guess. You have a one-in-three chance of getting the question right. The best answer is (C).

14. *E* Try Word Association. Have you heard of "the PRODIGAL son" in the Bible? If you have, that tells you PRODIGAL has a negative meaning. Its opposite, then, must be positive. (A) is negative, so cross it out. (B) is positive, so keep it. (C) is negative, so cross it out. (D) and (E) are positive, so keep them. If that's all you know about PRODIGAL, then just guess. You have a pretty good chance of getting the question right. The best answer is (E).

15. *A* Try Positive/Negative. VOLUBLE is a negative word, so its opposite must be positive. (A) is positive, so keep it. (B) is negative, so eliminate it. (C) can be either positive or negative, depending on context, so keep it. (D) is positive, so keep it. (E) is positive, so keep it. Now what? You weren't able to do any POE. Try making opposites for the answer choices. A simple opposite for (A) is *talkative*. Is that what VOLUBLE means? Yes. Still, check out the remaining answer choices. A simple opposite for (B) is *permanent*. Is that what VOLUBLE means? No. A simple opposite for (C) is *qualified*. Is that what VOLUBLE means? No. A simple opposite for (D) is *clumsy*. Is that what VOLUBLE means? No. A simple opposite for (E) is *indecisive*. Is that what VOLUBLE means? No. The best answer is (A).

QUIZ #5: ANSWERS

1. *D* Who cares? If you don't know what the stem word means at all, just make sure each answer choice does have an opposite, then guess. Don't waste time!

2. *A* Who cares? If you don't know what the stem word means at all, just make sure each answer choice does have an opposite, then guess. Don't waste time!

3. *C* Who cares? If you don't know what the stem word means at all, just make sure each answer choice does have an opposite, then guess. Don't waste time!

4. *C* Who cares? If you don't know what the stem word means at all, just make sure each answer choice does have an opposite, then guess. Don't waste time!

5. *B* Who cares? If you don't know what the stem word means at all, just make sure each answer choice does have an opposite, then guess. Don't waste time!

QUIZ #6: ANSWERS

1.   noun: prose narrative

        adjective: new; strange

2.   noun: a piece of furniture

        verb: to put aside for an indefinite amount of time

3.   noun: tint; hue

        verb: exaggerate

4.   noun: synthetic material

        adjective: capable of being molded

5.   noun: meeting; assembly

        noun: custom

6.   noun: single member or person

        adjective: separate

7.   noun: manufacturing activity

        noun: diligence

8.   verb: emit

        verb: hide; conceal

9.   noun: instrument for measuring

        verb: estimate; judge

10.   noun: high official

        verb: arrange in order

PROBLEM SET #1

Directions: Each question below consists of a word printed in capital letters, followed by five lettered words or phrases. Choose the lettered word or phrase that is most nearly <u>opposite</u> in meaning to the word in capital letters.

28. VARIEGATED:

   (A) uniform
   (B) unprecedented
   (C) infrequent
   (D) incomprehensible
   (E) presumable

29. SOLICITOUS:

   (A) belittling
   (B) ardent
   (C) indicative
   (D) inattentive
   (E) aspiring

30. CONFORMITY:

   (A) fluctuation
   (B) diminution
   (C) inflexibility
   (D) differentiation
   (E) disparity

31. BLASPHEME:

   (A) anticipate
   (B) reprimand
   (C) mollify
   (D) revere
   (E) revel

32. PIQUANT:

   (A) effervescent
   (B) insipid
   (C) obsolete
   (D) hoary
   (E) irksome

33. GERMANE:

   (A) irrepressible
   (B) circuitous
   (C) sumptuous
   (D) avaricious
   (E) extraneous

34. EFFRONTERY:

   (A) effacement
   (B) chasteness
   (C) audacity
   (D) malaise
   (E) banter

35. FACTITIOUS:

   (A) objective
   (B) erroneous
   (C) genuine
   (D) problematic
   (E) partial

36. VAGARIOUS:

   (A) predictable
   (B) stringent
   (C) widespread
   (D) affluent
   (E) sociable

37. VIM:

   (A) commotion
   (B) despondency
   (C) discord
   (D) lethargy
   (E) potency

38. CABAL:

   (A) well-disciplined unit
   (B) revered society
   (C) public organization
   (D) legal party
   (E) united front

PROBLEM SET #2

<u>Directions</u>: Each question below consists of a word printed in capital letters, followed by five lettered words or phrases. Choose the lettered word or phrase that is most nearly *opposite* in meaning to the word in capital letters.

28. COMMENSURATE:

   (A) unimpressive
   (B) inconclusive
   (C) insignificant
   (D) uneven
   (E) inconvenient

29. REVILE:

   (A) welcome
   (B) spurn
   (C) compliment
   (D) utilize
   (E) demean

30. EXHUME:

   (A) investigate
   (B) return
   (C) air out
   (D) bury
   (E) grieve over

31. TACIT:

   (A) reluctant
   (B) unabashed
   (C) dour
   (D) flirtatious
   (E) spoken

32. REALIZE:

   (A) disclose
   (B) thwart
   (C) misrepresent
   (D) collapse
   (E) coerce

33. FLOTSAM:

   (A) valuable object
   (B) cherished memento
   (C) unusual antique
   (D) common item
   (E) creative endeavor

34. INCIPIENCY:

   (A) dispersion
   (B) detachment
   (C) extrusion
   (D) cessation
   (E) misrepresentation

35. QUOTIDIAN:

   (A) arousing
   (B) holy
   (C) manic
   (D) exceptional
   (E) methodical

36. JADED:

   (A) humorous
   (B) original
   (C) jovial
   (D) blessed
   (E) enlivened

37. VACUITY:

   (A) spaciousness
   (B) repleteness
   (C) fruition
   (D) rotundity
   (E) maturity

38. NUBILE:

   (A) emaciated
   (B) not marriageable
   (C) inactive
   (D) lacking in taste
   (E) awkward

PROBLEM SET #3

Directions: Each question below consists of a word printed in capital letters, followed by five lettered words or phrases. Choose the lettered word or phrase that is most nearly *opposite* in meaning to the word in capital letters.

28. WILLFUL:

    (A) yielding
    (B) pleasant
    (C) calculated
    (D) rational
    (E) indirect

29. DORMANCY:

    (A) sluggishness
    (B) adaptability
    (C) boldness
    (D) consciousness
    (E) enthusiasm

30. ACUITY:

    (A) callousness
    (B) full of criticism
    (C) arrogance
    (D) shortsightedness
    (E) lack of insight

31. PROMULGATE:

    (A) diminish
    (B) revise
    (C) dismiss
    (D) truncate
    (E) revoke

32. EMASCULATE:

    (A) invigorate
    (B) incite
    (C) scour
    (D) purge
    (E) appropriate

33. ROUT:

    (A) uneasy stalemate
    (B) desperate act
    (C) unconditional surrender
    (D) joyous union
    (E) organized attack

34. SPECULATIVE:

    (A) destitute
    (B) confirmed
    (C) concrete
    (D) magnanimous
    (E) governable

35. DILATORY:

    (A) retracting
    (B) closed up
    (C) overextended
    (D) speeding up
    (E) cutting

36. NUGATORY:

    (A) having many consequences
    (B) possessing great worth
    (C) tending toward simplicity
    (D) free from guilt
    (E) deserving of blame

37. TYRO:

    (A) a philanthropist
    (B) an expert
    (C) a lackey
    (D) a miser
    (E) a prodigy

38. HAUTEUR:

    (A) adulation
    (B) gravity
    (C) humbleness
    (D) amicability
    (E) frivolity

PROBLEM SET #4

28. DISTEND:

    (A) restrict
    (B) limit
    (C) wrinkle
    (D) contract
    (E) reject

29. ARTLESS:

    (A) immodest
    (B) deceptive
    (C) demonstrative
    (D) common
    (E) delightful

30. PROCRASTINATE:

    (A) respond remorsefully
    (B) work rapidly
    (C) reject entirely
    (D) address immediately
    (E) complete fully

31. AFFABLE:

    (A) penitent
    (B) stubborn
    (C) retiring
    (D) languishing
    (E) disconsolate

32. INFINITESIMAL:

    (A) brief
    (B) eternal
    (C) powerful
    (D) huge
    (E) limited

33. DUCTILE:

    (A) infirm
    (B) imperceptible
    (C) unmalleable
    (D) climactic
    (E) perilous

34. APTNESS:

    (A) inexperience
    (B) timeliness
    (C) disinclination
    (D) unsuitability
    (E) virtuosity

35. CALLOW:

    (A) full-fledged
    (B) worn- out
    (C) somber
    (D) reflective
    (E) unproblematic

36. IGNOMINY:

    (A) honorable conduct
    (B) faithful adherence
    (C) careful exposition
    (D) vague suggestion
    (E) vigorous action

37. CELERITY:

    (A) dishonesty
    (B) cheerfulness
    (C) vividness
    (D) slowness
    (E) infamy

38. ABJURATION:

    (A) impotence
    (B) odiousness
    (C) fickleness
    (D) affirmation
    (E) vitality

PROBLEM SET #5

28. ARREST:

   (A) indulge
   (B) replace
   (C) speed up
   (D) go forth
   (E) initiate

29. DISCOUNT:

   (A) throw into confusion
   (B) simplify for convenience
   (C) declare with emphasis
   (D) gather one's composure
   (E) maintain as important

30. STANCH:

   (A) distill
   (B) commingle
   (C) make impure
   (D) increase the flow of
   (E) diminish in value

31. BEATIFY:

   (A) canonize
   (B) condemn
   (C) purge
   (D) pillage
   (E) debilitate

32. COMELY:

   (A) boorish
   (B) generous
   (C) unattractive
   (D) moderate
   (E) petty

33. IMPORTUNATE:

   (A) unimpressive
   (B) argumentative
   (C) not well-schooled
   (D) not urgent
   (E) vindicated

34. SANGUINE:

   (A) pallid
   (B) extenuated
   (C) impalpable
   (D) openness
   (E) protuberant

35. CATHOLIC:

   (A) irreligious
   (B) obstinate
   (C) close-minded
   (D) brazen
   (E) disreputable

36. SECRETE:

   (A) disclose
   (B) emit
   (C) enclose
   (D) attract
   (E) filter

37. CONDIGN:

   (A) undeserved
   (B) permissible
   (C) legitimate
   (D) disfavored
   (E) endorsed

38. SOPHISTIC:

   (A) sound
   (B) opportune
   (C) possible
   (D) coherent
   (E) merciful

PROBLEM SET #1: EXPLANATIONS

28. **A** If you know what the stem word means, make a simple opposite for it. VARIEGATED means varied, so a simple opposite might be something like *unvaried*. Does (A) mean *unvaried*? Yes. Does (B)? No. Does (C)? No. Does (D)? No. Does (E)? No. The best answer is (A).

29. **D** If you're not sure what the stem word means, you can do one of three things: (1) make simple opposites for the answer choices, (2) try Positive/Negative, or (3) try Word Association. Go with Positive/Negative. SOLICITOUS is a positive word, so its opposite must be negative. (A) is negative, so leave it in. (B) is positive, so eliminate it. (C) doesn't really have an opposite, so it can't be right. (D) is negative, so leave it in. (E) is positive, so cross it out.

You're left with (A) and (D). Try making a simple opposite for each answer choice. A simple opposite for *belittling* is *praising*. Does SOLICITOUS mean *praising*? No. A simple opposite for *inattentive* is *attentive*. Does SOLICITOUS mean *attentive*? Yes. (D) is the best answer.

30. **E** When you know the stem word, make a simple opposite for it. CONFORMITY means agreement, so a simple opposite for it might be *disagreement*. Does (A) mean *disagreement*? No. Does (B)? No. Does (C)? Not really. Does (D)? Not quite. Does (E)? Yes. Looking at every answer choice is important because (D) is a close second.

31. **D** If you're not sure what the stem word means, you can do one of three things: (1) make simple opposites for the answer choices, (2) try Positive/Negative, or (3) try Word Association. Go with Positive/Negative. BLASPHEME is a negative word, so its opposite must be positive. (A) is sort of positive, so leave it in. (B) is negative, so cross it out. (C) is positive, so leave it in. (D) is positive, as is (E), so leave both in.

Now what? Try making simple opposites for the answer choices. *Anticipate* in (A) means give advance thought to. A simple opposite, then, might be *put off*. Does BLASPHEME mean *put off*? No. *Mollify* in (C) means pacify, so a simple opposite might be *incite*? Does BLASPHEME mean *incite*? No. *Revere* in (D) means honor. A simple opposite, then, might be *dishonor*. Does BLASPHEME mean *dishonor*? Yes—but don't forget (E). *Revel* in (E) means take pleasure in, so a simple opposite might be *displease*. Does BLASPHEME mean *displease*? No. The best answer is (D).

Note that you can also approach this question by using Word Association. You might have heard a form of BLASPHEME before (*blasphemous* or *blasphemy*) used in a religious way—e.g., to commit *blasphemy*.

32. *B* If you're not sure what the stem word means, you can do one of three things: (1) make simple opposites for the answer choices, (2) try Positive/Negative, or (3) try Word Association. Go with Word Association. Have you heard PIQUANT used before to describe food? If so, use this knowledge to your advantage. Is it possible to have *effervescent* food? *Effervescent* means bubbly, so (A) isn't likely. Is it possible to have *insipid* food? Sure—*insipid* means tasteless. Leave (B) in. Is it possible to have *obsolete* food? No—food can go bad, but it can't be outdated. Eliminate (C). Is it possible to have *hoary* food? If you don't know what *hoary* means, you can't cross (D) out. Is it possible to have *irksome* food? Probably not. Cross out (E).

The remaining answer choices are (B) and (D). Go with what works. (B) is the best answer.

33. *E* If you're not sure what the stem word means, you can do one of three things: (1) make simple opposites for the answer choices, (2) try Positive/Negative, or (3) try Word Association. Go with Positive/Negative. GERMANE is a positive word, so its opposite must be negative. (A) is negative, so leave it in. (B) is somewhat negative, so leave it in, too. (C) is positive, so eliminate it. Don't cross out (D) if you don't know what *avaricious* means. (E) is negative, so leave it in.

Now what? Try making simple opposites for the answer choices. A simple opposite for (A) is *repressible*. Does GERMANE mean *repressible*? No. A simple opposite for (B) is *straightforward* or *direct*. Is that what GERMANE means? No. (D) you have to skip if you don't know what *avaricious* means. A simple opposite for (E) is *relevant*. Does GERMANE mean relevant? Yes. Between an answer choice that contains a word you don't know and an answer choice that works, go with the one that works. (E) is the best answer.

34. **A** If you're not sure what the stem word means, you can do one of three things: (1) make simple opposites for the answer choices, (2) try Positive/Negative, or (3) try Word Association. Go with Positive/Negative. Since EFFRONTERY is a negative word, its opposite has to be positive. (A) and (B) are both positive, so leave them in. (C) and (D), though, are both negative, so eliminate them. (E) is positive, so it's okay.

Now what? Try making opposites for the answer choices. A simple opposite for (A) is *boldness*. Is that what EFFRONTERY means? Yes. Still, check the remaining answer choices. A simple opposite for (B) is *impurity* or *indecency*. Does that match EFFRONTERY? No. A simple opposite for (E) is *serious talk*. Is that what EFFRONTERY means? No. The best answer is (A).

35. **C** When you don't know the stem word at all, don't waste time. Look at the answer choices and see if you can eliminate any that don't have opposites. Then guess —pick the answer choice that is the most extreme. For this question, each of the answer choices does have an opposite. So guess. The most extreme answer choices are (B) and (C). The best answer, as it turns out, is (C). FACTITIOUS means false.

36. **A** If you're not sure what the stem word means, you can do one of three things: (1) make simple opposites for the answer choices, (2) try Positive/Negative, or (3) try Word Association. Go with Word Association. You've probably seen a form of VAGARIOUS before: *vagary*. The phrase you might have heard using *vagary* is "*vagaries* of fortune." From the phrase, you can divine that VAGARY is a negative word. Therefore, its opposite is positive. (A) is positive, so leave it in. (B) is negative, so cross it out. (C) is slightly positive, so leave it in. (D) and (E) are both positive so leave them in, too.

Go back to the phrase "*vagaries* of fortune." Try using the phrase with the answer choices. Does *predictable* fortune make sense? Sure. Does *widespread* fortune make sense? Not really. Does *affluent* fortune make sense? Yes. Does a *sociable* fortune make sense? No.

You're down to (A) and (D). In other words, you've got a 50 percent chance of getting this question right, so just guess. The best answer is actually (A).

37. **D** If you're not sure what the stem word means, you can do one of three things: (1) make simple opposites for the answer choices, (2) try Positive/Negative, or (3) try Word Association. Go with Word Association. Have you ever heard of the phrase "VIM and vigor"? This should tell you that VIM is a positive word. Its opposite, then, must be negative. (A), (B), (C), and (D) are all negative, so they could be right. (E) is positive, so it can't work. Cross it out. What does the phrase "VIM and vigor" indicate about VIM? Sounds like it means something to do with energy. The opposite of energy is *lack of energy*, so *lethargy* in (D) is the best answer.

38. **C** When you have no idea what the stem word means, don't waste time. Look at the answer choices and see if you can eliminate any that don't have opposites. Then guess—pick the answer choice that is the most extreme. For this question, each of the answer choices does have an opposite. So guess. The most extreme answer choice is (B). As it turns out, however, the best answer is (C). A CABAL is a secret group, usually one engaged in intrigue.

PROBLEM SET #2: EXPLANATIONS

28. **D** When you know the stem word, make a simple opposite for it. COMMENSURATE means equal, so a simple opposite is *unequal*. Does (A) mean *unequal*? Not quite. (B)? No. (C)? Not quite. (D)? Yes. (E)? No. The best answer is (D).

29. **C** When you know the stem word, make a simple opposite. REVILE means *abuse*, so a simple opposite might be *treat well*. Does (A) match? Not really. Does (B)? No. (C)? Sure. (D)? No. (E)? No. The best answer is (C).

30. **D** EXHUME is probably a word you sort of know. If you can't provide a definition for EXHUME, then you have one of three options: (1) make simple opposites for the answer choices, (2) try Positive/Negative, or (3) try Word Association. Go with Word Association. Have you heard of the phrase "EXHUME a dead body"? Use that phrase with the answer choices. In (A): *investigate* a dead body? Maybe. In (B): *return* a dead body?

No. In (C): *air out* a dead body? Not likely. In (D): *bury* a dead body. Sure. In (E): *grieve over* a dead body? Yes.

You're left with (A), (D), and (E). What now? Make simple opposites for the answer choices. A simple opposite for (A) might be *ignore*. Is that what EXHUME means? No. A simple opposite for (D) is *unearth*. Is that what EXHUME means? Yes. A simple opposite for (E) is *celebrate*. Is that what EXHUME means? No. The best answer is (D).

31. *E* When you sort of know the stem word, you have one of three options: (1) make simple opposites for the answer choices, (2) try Positive/Negative, or (3) try Word Association. Go with Word Association. Have you heard of the phrase "TACIT approval"? Use that phrase with the answer choices. In (A): *reluctant* approval? Maybe. In (B): *unabashed* approval? Maybe. In (C): *dour* approval? No. In (D): *flirtatious* approval? No. In (E): *spoken* approval? Maybe.

You're left with (A), (B), and (E). Try making simple opposites for the answer choices. A simple opposite for (A) is *eager*. Does TACIT mean *eager*? No. A simple opposite for (B) is *embarrassed*. Is that what TACIT means? No. A simple opposite for (E) is *silent*. Is that what TACIT means? Close. (E) is the best answer.

32. *B* REALIZE isn't too hard a word, but be careful—REALIZE is often used to mean understand. But just because it's used that way doesn't mean that understand is the definition of REALIZE. What does REALIZE actually mean? Pretty much what it sounds like—make real. In other words, REALIZE means *accomplish*. A simple opposite for REALIZE, then, is *not accomplish*. Does (A) give you that? No. What about (B)? Sort of. (C)? No. (D)? No. (E)? Definitely not. The best answer is (B).

33. *A* FLOTSAM is the type of word that you either know or you don't know at all. Unless you sail a lot, you probably don't know the word. Since you don't know the word, you basically have to guess. But before you guess, look at the answer choices and see if you can eliminate any because the word it contains doesn't have an opposite. (B) doesn't really have a strong opposite, nor does (C).

You're left with (A), (D), and (E). At this point guess—choose the one that is the most extreme. (D) isn't very extreme, nor is (E). A good guess, therefore, is (A). And it is the best answer. FLOTSAM is debris, usually the floating wreckage of a ship.

34. *D* When you know the stem word, make a simple opposite for it. If something is *incipient* (a form of INCIPIENCY), it's about to happen. So a simple opposite for INCIPIENCY is *something not happening*. Does that match (A)? No. (B) doesn't work either. (C) isn't a good match, but (D) is okay. Finally, (E) doesn't work. Therefore, the best answer is (D).

35. *D* When you don't know the stem word at all, just guess. Don't waste a lot of time on a question like this. However, do try to do some POE. Are there any answer choices you can eliminate that don't have opposites? No. Each answer choice could have an opposite. Therefore, guess—pick the answer choice that is the most extreme. (A) is pretty extreme, as are (B), (C), and (D). So pick—it doesn't really matter which one. Just be aggressive and don't waste time. As it turns out, the best answer is (D) because QUOTIDIAN means common or ordinary.

   This question is a great example of why it's a good idea to improve your vocabulary. Antonyms are basically a vocabulary test: if you know the stem word, an antonym is easy; if you don't, good luck.

36. *E* JADED is a word that you probably sort of know. You can't provide a definition of it, but you do know that it's negative. The right answer, then, must be positive. Unfortunately, (A), (B), (C), (D), and (E) are all positive, so you can't do any POE.

   What now? Try making simple opposites for the answer choices. A simple opposite for (A) is *not funny*. Is that what JADED means? No. A simple opposite for (B) is *unoriginal*. Is that what JADED means? No. A good opposite for (C) is *very sad*. Is that what JADED means? No. A good opposite for (D) is *condemned*. Is that what JADED means? No. A good opposite for (E) is *tired*. Is that what JADED means? Yes. The best answer is (E).

37. *B* You may not have seen VACUITY before, but you probably have seen a form of it: *vacuous*. Don't let the noun form of *vacuous* throw you. You know that *vacuous* means empty, so a good

opposite for VACUITY is *fullness*. (A) doesn't quite work. (B) does, however. (C) doesn't quite fit, and (D) definitely doesn't. Finally, (E) isn't a good match. The best answer, then, is (B).

This question is easy to miss if you work too quickly. (A) and (C) are both attractive if you don't take the time. Remember, accuracy is more important than speed.

38. **B** Even though you've probably heard the word NUBILE before, make sure you *don't* treat it as a word you know. Can you provide a solid definition for NUBILE? If you can't, then it's a word that you only sort of know. For a word you sort of know, you can (1) make opposites for the answer choices, (2) use Positive/Negative, or (3) use Word Association. Go with Word Association. Have you heard the phrase "NUBILE young woman" before? If so, then you associate the word NUBILE with attractiveness. A good opposite for the stem word, then, is *unattractiveness*. Does (A) work? Not really. *Emaciated* means overly thin. What about (B)? It could work. (C)? No. (D)? No. (E)? Maybe.

You're left with (B) and (E). Since you have a 50 percent chance of getting this question right, just guess. The best answer is actually (B). Though you might associate NUBILE with attractiveness, it actually means marriageable.

PROBLEM SET #3: EXPLANATIONS

28. **A** When you know the stem word, make a simple opposite for it. WILLFUL means stubborn, so a simple opposite might be *docile*. Does (A) match *docile*? Yes. Still, check the remaining answer choices just in case. (B) doesn't match, so eliminate it. (C) doesn't work, nor does (D), so cross them both out. Finally, (E) doesn't match, so the best answer is (A).

29. **D** When you know the stem word, make a simple opposite for it. DORMANCY is a state of sleep, so a simple opposite might be a *state of awakeness*. (A) is a synonym of DORMANCY—not an antonym—so cross it out. (B) doesn't match, nor does (C), so eliminate both. (D) looks pretty good, but check out (E) just in case. (E) isn't quite right, so the best answer is (D).

30. *E* You may think you don't know the word ACUITY, but you probably do. ACUITY is just a form of *acute*. What does *acute* mean? Perceptive. So a simple opposite for ACUITY is *no perception*. Does (A) match *no perception*? No. Does (B)? No. (C)? No. (D) isn't quite right, so check out (E). (E) is a good match—therefore, it's the best answer.

31. *E* PROMULGATE is one of those words that you hear used all the time, but you don't know the definition for. Since PROMULGATE is a word you only sort of know, you can't make an opposite for it. Instead, you have one of three ways to attack this question: (1) make simple opposites for the answer choices, (2) use Positive/Negative, or (3) use Word Association. Go with simple opposites for the answer choices. A simple opposite for (A) is *increase*. Does PROMULGATE mean *increase*? No. A simple opposite for (B) is *leave alone*. Does PROMULGATE mean *leave alone*? No. A simple opposite for (C) is *pay attention to*. Is that what PROMULGATE means? No. A simple opposite for (D) is *lengthen*. Is that what PROMULGATE means? No. A simple opposite for (E) is *put forth*. Is that what PROMULGATE means? It's the closest out of the five choices. (E) is the best answer.

32. *A* You've probably heard the word EMASCULATE used before, but you might not know its definition. If that's the case, don't make a simple opposite for EMASCULATE. Instead, you can (1) make simple opposites for the answer choices, (2) use Positive/ Negative, or (3) use Word Association. Go with Positive/ Negative. EMASCULATE is a negative word, so its opposite must be positive. (A) is positive, so it's okay. (B) and (C) are negative, so eliminate them. (D) could be either positive or negative, depending on context. Leave it in for now. (E) is positive, so leave it in, too.

Now what? Try Word Association. You've probably heard of men being EMASCULATED in the sense that they somehow lose power. So EMASCULATE means something like take power away. A simple opposite, then, might be *give power*. Does (A) match? It could. Does (D)? No. What about (E)? No. The best answer is (A).

33. **E** If you only sort of know the stem word, you can do one of three things: (1) make simple opposites for the answer choices, (2) use Positive/Negative, or (3) use Word Association. Try Word Association. You might have heard ROUT used before in sports when one team completely defeats another—as in "it was a ROUT." ROUT, then, has something to do with being defeated, so a simple opposite might be something like *victory*. (A) isn't a good match, nor is (B) or (C). (D) is a bit too much. (E) isn't a perfect match, but it's the best one. The best answer is (E).

34. **C** SPECULATIVE is another one of those words which you've probably heard a lot, but you can't give a definition for. Since that's the case you can (1) make simple opposites for the answer choices, (2) use Positive/Negative, or (3) use Word Association. Try Positive/Negative. SPECULATIVE is slightly negative, so its opposite has to be slightly positive. (A) is negative, so eliminate it. (B) is positive, so leave it in. (C) is also positive, so it's okay. Finally, (D) and (E) are positive, so leave them in.

    What now? How about Word Association. Have you heard of the phrase "SPECULATIVE thought"? Try applying this phrase to the answer choices. Does a *confirmed* thought make sense? It could. Does a *concrete* thought make sense? Yes. Does a *magnanimous* thought make sense. Maybe. Does a *governable* thought make sense? Not really.

    You're left with (B), (C), and (D). At this point, just guess. (D) probably isn't a good pick—*magnanimous* thought is okay, but it's not great. So choose either (B) or (C). You have a 50 percent chance of getting the question right. As it turns out, the best answer is (C). SPECULATIVE means *theoretical*.

35. **D** If you don't know DILATORY at all, don't waste time on this question. Try to POE by eliminating answer choices without opposites, and then guess—pick the answer choice that is most extreme. Each answer choice for this question does have an opposite, so you can't do any POE. Pick, then, the most extreme. (C), (D), and (E) are the most extreme, so choose one of them. As it turns out, the best answer is (D). DILATORY means delaying.

    This question is a good example of why you should improve your vocabulary. If you do know what DILATORY means, it doesn't take very long to do the question and get it right. If you don't know what DILATORY means, then you're pretty much stuck. What's important is that you don't spend too much time on any antonym if you don't know the word at all.

36. *B* NUGATORY is a word that you might sort of know. Since it's a word that you only sort of know, you can (1) make simple opposites for the answer choices, (2) use Positive/Negative, or (3) use Word Association. Try Positive/Negative. NUGATORY is a negative word, so its opposite must be positive. (A) and (E) are both negative, so eliminate them.

You're left with (B), (C), and (D). Each answer choice has an opposite, so you can't do any more POE. Therefore, guess—pick the choice that is the most extreme. That would probably be (B)—and (B) is the best answer.

37. *B* TYRO is probably a word you sort of know. Therefore, you have three options: (1) make simple opposites for the answer choices, (2) use Positive/Negative, or (3) use Word Association. Try Positive/Negative. TYRO is a negative word, so its opposite must be positive. (C) and (D) are both negative, so cross them out.

If you don't know anything else about TYRO, then you just have to guess. But before you do that, try to do some POE. Are there any answer choices left that don't really have opposites? (E) possibly. A *prodigy* is a young person who is very talented. So you're left with (A) and (B). Pick the choice that is the most extreme. (B) is more extreme than (A), and guess what? It's the best answer.

38. *C* Most likely, HAUTEUR is a word you sort of know. Therefore, you have three options: (1) make simple opposites for the answer choices, (2) use Positive/Negative, or (3) use Word Association. Try Positive/Negative. HAUTEUR is negative, so its opposite must be positive. (B) is slightly negative, so eliminate it. (E) is slightly negative, too, so cross it out.

You're left with (A), (C), and (D). You can't do any more POE because each of the answer choices has an opposite. Therefore, just pick the answer choice that is the most extreme. (A) is the most extreme, so it's a good guess. As it turns out, though, the best answer is (C). HAUTEUR means arrogance.

Even though you missed this question, don't despair. You had only a very slight knowledge of HAUTEUR, and yet you were able to get the question down to three choices. A one-in-three chance of getting a question right isn't bad. In fact, it's quite good.

PROBLEM SET #4: EXPLANATIONS

28. **D** When you know the stem word, make a simple opposite for it. DISTEND means swell out, so a simple opposite might be *shrink*. Does (A) match *shrink*? Not quite. What about (B)? No. (C)? Not quite. (D)? Yes. (E)? No. The best answer is (D).

29. **B** When you know the stem word, make a simple opposite for it. ARTLESS means something along the lines of natural, so a simple opposite might be *unnatural*. Does (A) match *unnatural*? No. What about (B)? Possibly. What about (C)? No. (D)? Not quite. (E)? No. The best answer is (B).

30. **D** When you know the stem word, make a simple opposite for it. PROCRASTINATE means to put off, so a simple opposite might be *do right away*. Is (A) a good match? No. What about (B)? Not quite. (C)? No. (D)? Looks good, but still, check out (E). (E) isn't quite right, so the best answer is (D). This question is easy— as long as you don't work too quickly and look at all the answer choices.

31. **C** If you're not entirely sure what AFFABLE means, then you have three options: (1) make simple opposites for the answer choices, (2) use Positive/Negative, or (3) use Word Association. Start off with Positive/Negative. AFFABLE is a positive word, so its opposite must be negative. (A) is positive, so eliminate it. (B) through (E) are all negative, so leave them in.

Now try making simple opposites for the answer choices. A simple opposite for (B) might be *yielding*. Is that what AFFABLE means? No. A simple opposite for (C) might be *outgoing*. Is that what AFFABLE means? Sort of. A simple opposite for (D) might be *active*. Is that what AFFABLE means? No. A simple opposite for (E) might be *happy*. Is that what AFFABLE means? Not quite. The best answer is (C).

32. **D** If you're not sure what INFINITESIMAL means, then you have three options: (1) make simple opposites for the answer choices, (2) use Positive/Negative, and (3) use Word Association. Start off with Positive/Negative. INFINITESIMAL is a slightly negative word, so its opposite must be positive. (A) is negative, so cross it out. (B) through (D) are all positive, so leave them in. (E) is negative, so eliminate it.

Now what? If Positive/Negative is the extent of your knowledge of INFINITESIMAL, then don't waste time. Each of the remaining answer choices has an opposite, so you can't do any POE. So just guess—pick the answer choice that is the most extreme. In this case, (B) or (D) are the most extreme possibilities. The best answer is actually (D) because INFINITESIMAL means very, very small.

33. **C** If you aren't entirely sure what DUCTILE means, then you have three options: (1) make simple opposites for the answer choices, (2) use Positive/Negative, or (3) use Word Association. Start off with Positive/Negative. DUCTILE is a slightly positive word, so its opposite must be negative. (A), (B), and (C) are all negative, so leave them in. (D) is positive, so cross it out. (E) is negative, so keep it.

Now what? If you don't know anything else about DUCTILE, then don't waste time. See if you can eliminate any answer choice because it doesn't have an opposite; then, just guess. For this question, each answer choice remaining does have an opposite, so you can't do any POE. So guess—pick the answer choice that is the most extreme. (E) is the most extreme, so it's a good guess. However, the best answer is actually (C) because DUCTILE means flexible or able to be shaped.

34. **D** You probably know a form of APTNESS: *apt*. Use this knowledge to your advantage. If something is *apt*, then it's appropriate. A simple opposite for APTNESS, then, is *inappropriateness*. (A) isn't a good match, nor is (B). (C) doesn't work, but (D) looks good. Finally, (E) isn't quite what you're looking for. The best answer is (D).

35. **A** If you aren't sure what CALLOW means, then you have three options: (1) make simple opposites for the answer choices, (2) use Positive/Negative, or (3) use Word Association. Try Word

Association. Have you ever heard of the phrase "CALLOW youth"? Apply this phrase to each answer choice. Does *full-fledged* youth make sense? It could. What about *worn-out* youth? Not quite. *Somber* youth? Maybe. *Reflective* youth? Again, maybe. *Unproblematic* youth? Sure.

So you're left with (A), (C), (D), and (E). Try making simple opposites for each answer choice. A simple opposite for (A) might be immature. Is that what CALLOW means? Yes. Still, check out the remaining answer choices. A simple opposite for (C) might be *happy*. Is that what CALLOW means? No. A simple opposite for (D) might be *headstrong*. Is that what CALLOW means? No. A simple opposite for (E) might be *problematic*. Is that what CALLOW means? No. The best answer is (A).

36. **A** If you aren't sure what IGNOMINY means, then you have three options: (1) make simple opposites for the answer choices, (2) use Positive/Negative, or (3) use Word Association. Start off with Positive/Negative. IGNOMINY is a negative word, so its opposite must be positive. Each answer choice is positive, except (D), so get rid of (D). Now what? If Positive/Negative is the limit of what you know about IGNOMINY, then don't waste time. Make sure that each remaining answer choice does have an opposite; then just guess. In this case, the remaining answer choices do have opposites, so you can't do any more POE. So guess. Pick the answer choice that is the most extreme. (A) and (B) are both pretty extreme, so either one is a good guess. As it turns out, the best answer is (A). IGNOMINY means disgrace.

37. **D** If you aren't sure what CELERITY means, then you have three options: (1) make simple opposites for the answer choices, (2) use Positive/Negative, and (3) use Word Association. Start off with Positive/Negative. CELERITY is a positive word, so its opposite must be negative. (A) is negative, so keep it. (B) and (C) are positive, so eliminate them. (D) is negative, so it's okay, as is (E).

At this point, if you don't know anything else about CELERITY, check the remaining answer choices to ensure each has an opposite. Then, just guess. For this question, each answer choice left does have an opposite, so guess. Pick the one that is the most extreme. (A), (D), and (E) are all pretty extreme, so any one is a good guess. As it turns out, the best answer is (D). CELERITY means speediness.

38. *D* If you aren't sure what ABJURATION means, then you have three options: (1) make simple opposites for the answer choices, (2) use Positive/Negative, and (3) use Word Association. Start off with Positive/Negative. ABJURATION is a negative word, so its opposite has to be positive. Eliminate (A), (B), and (C) because each is negative.

You're left with (D) and (E). (D) and (E) each has an opposite, so you can't do any more POE. Therefore, just guess—you have a 50 percent chance of getting the question right. Pick the answer choice that is more extreme. Either (D) or (E) is a good guess because each is pretty extreme. As it turns out, the best answer is (D). ABJURATION means renunciation.

PROBLEM SET #5: EXPLANATIONS

28. *E* When you know the stem word, make a simple opposite for it. ARREST means stop, so a simple opposite might be *start*. Does (A) mean *start*? No. Does (B)? No. Does (C)? Not quite. Does (D)? No. Does (E)? Yes. The best answer is (E).

29. *E* When you know the stem word, make a simple opposite for it. DISCOUNT means to disregard, so a simple opposite might be *regard well*. Does (A) match? No. What about (B)? No. (C)? Not quite. (D)? No. (E)? Yes. The best answer is (E).

30. *D* If you're not quite sure what STANCH means, then you have three options: (1) make simple opposites for the answer choices, (2) use Positive/Negative, or (3) use Word Association. Try Word Association. Have you heard of the phrase "STANCH the flow of blood"? Use that phrase on the answer choices. Does *distill* the flow of blood make sense? No. Does *commingle* the flow of blood make sense? Not quite. Does *make impure* the flow of blood make sense? Maybe. Does *increase the flow of* blood make sense? Yes. Does *diminish in value* the flow of blood make sense? No. Between (C) and (D), which makes more sense? Definitely (D). The best answer is (D).

31. **B** If you don't know for sure what BEATIFY means, then you have three options: (1) make simple opposites for the answer choices, (2) use Positive/Negative, or (3) use Word Association. Try Positive/Negative. BEATIFY is a positive word, so its opposite has to be negative. (A) is positive, so cross it out. (B) is negative, so leave it in. (C) is slightly positive, so cross it out. (D) is negative, so leave it in. (E) is negative, so leave it in.

    You're left with (B), (D), and (E). Try making simple opposites for the answer choices. A simple opposite for (B) is *bless*. Is that what BEATIFY means? Yes. Still, check out (D) and (E). It's hard to come up with a good opposite for *pillage* in (D), which means plunder. Therefore, (D) probably isn't right. A simple opposite for (E) is *strengthen*. Is that what BEATIFY means? No. Therefore, the best answer is (B).

32. **C** If you don't know for sure what COMELY means, then you have three options: (1) make simple opposites for the answer choices, (2) use Positive/Negative, or (3) use Word Association. Try Positive/Negative. COMELY is a positive word, so its opposite must be negative. (B) and (D) are both positive, so eliminate them. (A), (C), and (E) are all negative, so keep them.

    At this point, if you don't know anything else about COMELY, just guess. If you pick the answer choice that is most extreme, you might pick (A) or (C). As it turns out, (C) is the best answer. COMELY means having a pleasing appearance.

33. **D** If you don't know for sure what IMPORTUNATE means, then you have three options: (1) make simple opposites for the answer choices, (2) use Positive/Negative, or (3) use Word Association. Try Positive/Negative. IMPORTUNATE is a negative word, so its opposite must be positive. (A), (B), and (C) are all negative, so cross them out. (D) is positive, as is (E), so leave them in.

    You're left with (D) and (E). What now? Try making simple opposites for the answer choices. A simple opposite for (D) is *urgent*. Is that what IMPORTUNATE means? Yes—still, check (E). A simple opposite for (E) is *blamed*. Is that what IMPORTUNATE means? No. The best answer is (D).

34. **A** If you don't know for sure what SANGUINE means, then you have three options: (1) make simple opposites for the answer choices, (2) use Positive/Negative, or (3) use Word Association. Try Word Association. You might have heard SANGUINE used before as a color—red. Therefore, the opposite of SANGUINE should have something to do with color. *Pallid* in (A) means pale, so leave it in. (B) doesn't have anything to do with color, so cross it out. (C) doesn't either, nor does (D) or (E), so cross them all out. The best answer is (A).

35. **C** If you don't know for sure what CATHOLIC means, then you have three options: (1) make simple opposites for the answer choices, (2) use Positive/Negative, or (3) use Word Association. Try Positive/Negative. CATHOLIC is a positive word, so its opposite must be negative. Unfortunately, (A) through (E) are all negative, so you can't do any POE.

    What now? If you really don't have any idea what CATHOLIC means, then just guess. Don't waste time—pick the one that is the most extreme. As it turns out, the best answer is (C) because CATHOLIC means liberal or universal.

36. **A** When you know the stem word, make a simple opposite. SECRETE means give off, so a simple opposite might be *suck in*. Do any of the answer choices match? No. Does this mean there is no right answer? No—it means that it's the secondary definition of SECRETE that's being tested.

    What's the secondary definition of SECRETE? If you don't know, then don't waste time. Just guess—pick the answer choice that is the most extreme. But if you know the secondary definition, then this question is easy. SECRETE means to conceal (as in to make secret), so a simple opposite might be *reveal*. Does (A) match *reveal*? Yes. What about (B)? No. (C)? No. (D)? No. (E)? No. The best answer is (A).

37. **A** CONDIGN, most likely, is a word you just don't know at all. If that's the case, don't waste time. Make sure each answer choice has an opposite and then guess—pick the one that is the most extreme. As it turns out, the best answer is (A). CONDIGN means deserved or appropriate.

38. **A** If you don't know for sure what SOPHISTIC means, then you have three options: (1) make simple opposites for the answer choices, (2) use Positive/Negative, or (3) use Word Association. Try Positive/Negative. SOPHISTIC is a negative word, so its opposite must be positive. Unfortunately, (A) through (E) are all positive, so you can't do any POE.

What now? How about Word Association? Have you heard of the phrase "SOPHISTIC reasoning" before? Try using that phrase on the answer choices. Does *sound* reasoning make sense? Yes. Does *opportune* reasoning? Not really. Does *possible* reasoning? Sure. Does *coherent* reasoning? Yes. Does *merciful* reasoning? Not really.

You're left with (A), (C), and (D). If you don't know anything else about SOPHISTIC, then don't waste time. Make sure the remaining answer choices have opposites and then pick the one that is the most extreme. As it turns out, the best answer is (A). SOPHISTIC means false or faulty.

CHAPTER

8

Vocabulary

WORDS, WORDS, WORDS

Some people hate nothing more than memorizing new words. Well, in the land of ETS, tough luck for them. The most surefire way of getting a quick boost in verbal points on the GRE is to improve your vocabulary. We've given you a lot of techniques to use for the verbal questions, and they're very powerful—but they're even more powerful when you combine them with a good vocabulary. It's as simple as that. Remember, sentence completions, analogies, and antonyms test, in large part, your knowledge of words.

THE HIT PARADE

The first step to improving your vocabulary is to learn the Hit Parade. In total, there are 305 words on this list, so start studying them as soon as possible. Expanding your knowledge of words is a long-term process—you can't do it in a day. The sooner you start, the better off you are.

As we've mentioned before, the Hit Parade is a list of the words that are most frequently tested on the GRE. We've compiled this list by gathering every single printed GRE available and putting all of the verbal sections into our computer. The computer runs a program developed by our research teams in New York City, and then spits out the Hit Parade. Pretty straightforward.

BEYOND THE HIT PARADE

For those of you who are aggressive and want more than the Hit Parade, do we have more words? Yes. Not in this book, unfortunately, but easily accessible. If you want even more words, we recommend that you purchase The Princeton Review's *Word Smart I* and *Word Smart II*. Each is a small book that provides you with an alphabetical list of words commonly used on standardized tests. It also contains quizzes and drills to test your knowledge of the words in the book.

ANYTHING ELSE?

What else? Well, if you want to be very strict, carry a dictionary and some flash cards with you everywhere you go. Any time you run across a word you don't know very well (or don't know at all), write it down on a flash card and look it up. It doesn't matter where you see the words — they could be in this book, in a practice GRE, in a magazine you subscribe to, in a book you're reading. You just want to get in the habit of gathering words you're unfamiliar with.

HOW TO STUDY

Well, what's the best way to learn new words? Quite truthfully, it's going to vary from person to person. There's no one method that's proven to be perfect in every way. Of course, we have ideas on what are good ways to study, but before we get to that, let's break down all words in the English language into three groups.

1. Words that you know

2. Words that you sort of know

3. Words that you don't know at all

If you've read the chapter on antonyms already, then this probably sounds familiar. What's a word that you know? One that you're comfortable with, familiar with. Most importantly, one that you can provide a definition for. What's a word that you sort of know? It's one that you can't define exactly, but you know whether it's positive or negative, or maybe you can use it in a sentence. A word that you don't know at all is, of course, a word that you've never seen. (Or maybe you've seen it; you just have no idea what it means.)

MORE ON HOW TO STUDY

Okay, now that we've structured the mass of words out there, how should you study them? Our favorite is flash cards. That means you stick the word on one side and then the definition on the other.

But don't stop there. Flash cards that have only definitions usually aren't too helpful because they're so boring. Don't make the process of learning new words so rote and dry—because if the flash cards are boring, then you probably won't learn the words very well. So spruce up your flash cards. Besides writing the definition of the word . . .

1. Put down what part of speech the word is. Sometimes a word can have more than one part of speech: for example, *acclaim*. It can be both a noun and a verb.

2. Write a sentence that uses the word. Don't just write any sentence. In that sentence, try to give some context that tells you what the word means if you didn't have the definition handy.

3. Write a mnemonic. Mnemonic is a fancy way of saying "memory device." For example, you can associate the word with a phrase that you know. If you wanted to remember the word *dock*, you might think of the phrase "*dock* your pay." Or tag a word to a person or thing. Maybe you know someone who fakes being sick to avoid work. That person is a *malinger*. Or make a word play. To help you remember the word *egregious*, think of it as "egg" and "Regis." Well, Regis Philbin is a bad egg—he's conspicuously bad. And that's what *egregious* means.

The whole point is to do things to help you learn words. You should memorize definitions as well, of course, but if you have a sentence or a mnemonic for a word, you'll find that the word sticks in your brain that much better.

Okay, without further ado . . . the Hit Parade.

GRE HIT PARADE

Word	Part of Speech	Definition

Group 1

aberrant	adjective	deviating from the norm
alacrity	noun	eager and enthusiastic willingness
anomaly	noun	deviation from the normal order, form or rule; abnormality
approbation	noun	an expression of approval or praise
assuage	verb	to ease or lessen; to appease or pacify
audacious	adjective	daring and fearless; recklessly bold
capricious	adjective	inclined to change one's mind impulsively; erratic; unpredictable
censure	verb	to criticize severely; to officially rebuke
chicanery	noun	trickery or subterfuge
connoisseur	noun	an informed and astute judge in matters of taste; expert
discordant	adjective	conflicting; dissonant or harsh in sound
disparate	adjective	fundamentally distinct or dissimilar
eloquent	adjective	well-spoken; expressive; articulate
enervate	verb	to weaken; to reduce in vitality
ennui	noun	dissatisfaction and restlessness resulting from boredom or apathy
equivocate	verb	to use ambiguous language with a deceptive intent

Word	Part of Speech	Definition
exculpate	verb	exonerate; to clear of blame
exigent	adjective	urgent; pressing; requiring immediate action or attention
filibuster	noun	intentional obstruction, esp. using prolonged speechmaking to delay legislative action
ingenuous	adjective	artless; frank and candid; lacking in sophistication
inured	adjective	accustomed to accepting something undesirable
irascible	adjective	easily angered; prone to temperamental outbursts
laud	verb	to praise highly
magnanimity	noun	the quality of being generously noble in mind and heart, esp. in forgiving
martial	adjective	associated with war and the armed forces
mundane	adjective	of the world; typical of or concerned with the ordinary
nascent	adjective	coming into being; in early developmental stages
nebulous	adjective	vague; cloudy; lacking clearly defined form
neologism	noun	a new word, expression, or usage; the creation or use of new words or senses
noxious	adjective	harmful; injurious
obtuse	adjective	lacking sharpness of intellect; not clear or precise in thought or expression
obviate	verb	to anticipate and make unnecessary
onerous	adjective	troubling; burdensome
parody	noun	a humorous imitation intended for ridicule or comic effect, esp. in literature and art
perennial	adjective	recurrent through the year or many years; happening repeatedly
perfunctory	adjective	cursory; done without care or interest
prattle	verb	to babble meaninglessly; to talk in an empty and idle manner
prescience	noun	foreknowledge of events; knowing of events prior to their occurring

Handwritten annotations: filibuster → OBSTRUCCIONISTA; ingenuous → ESTAN ACOSTUMBRADO O' HABITUADO A ALGO; laud → LOAR; noxious → NOCIVO; onerous → ONEROSO (PESADO, molesto / que resulta costoso); perfunctory → SUPERFICIAL, SOMERO; prattle → PARLOTEO, COTORREO; prescience → CLARIVIDENCIA

Word	Part of Speech	Definition
prevaricate	*verb* ~~(to please (deseo de ayudar))~~	to deliberately avoid the truth; to mislead
refute	*verb*	to disprove; to successfully argue against
relegate	*verb*	to forcibly assign, esp. to a lower, place or position
solicitous *—ATENTO*	*adjective*	concerned and attentive; eager
sporadic	*adjective*	occurring only occasionally, or in scattered instances
static	*adjective*	not moving, active or in motion; at rest
stupefy	*verb*	to stun, baffle or amaze
tortuous	*adjective*	winding; twisting; excessively complicated
truculent	*adjective*	fierce and cruel; eager to fight
voracious	*adjective*	having an insatiable appetite for an activity or pursuit; ravenous
waver *—OSCILAR,* ~~IS THAT A VERB?~~	*verb*	to move to and fro; sway; to be unsettled in opinion

Group 2

→ fugarse

The robers absconded To their hideout

abscond *(WITH FUNDS) → HUIR*	*verb*	to depart clandestinely; to steal off and hide
ameliorate *→ mejorar*	*verb*	to make better or more tolerable
arduous	*adjective*	strenuous, taxing, requiring significant effort
ascetic	*noun*	one who practices rigid self-denial, esp as an act of religious devotion
austere *(prueba irrefutable)*	*adjective*	without adornment; bare; severely simple; ascetic
axiom *→ AXIOMA — AXIOMATICO, EVIDENTE*	*noun*	a universally recognized principle
axiomatic	*adjective*	taken as a given; possessing self-evident truth
bucolic	*adjective*	rustic and pastoral; characteristic of rural areas and their inhabitants
canonical	*adjective*	following or in agreement with canonical requirements
contentious *→ CONFLICTIVO, MUY DISCUTIDO*	*adjective* *→ PENDENCIERO*	argumentative; quarrelsome; causing controversy or disagreement

The matter was very contentious with the audience.
At the meeting the vicepresidente probes himselfe to be a contentious person when debate was opened.

Word	Part of Speech	Definition
convoluted	*adjective*	complex or complicated
culpable	*adjective*	deserving blame
disabuse	*verb*	to undeceive; to set right
eclectic	*adjective*	composed of elements drawn from various sources
effrontery	*noun*	extreme boldness; presumptuousness.
ephemeral	*adjective*	brief; fleeting
erudite	*adjective*	very learned; scholarly
eulogy	*noun*	a speech honoring the dead
extemporaneous	*adjective*	improvised; done without preparation
facetious	*adjective*	playful; humorous
fulminate	*verb*	to loudly attack or denounce
hyperbole	*noun*	an exaggerated statement, often used as a figure of speech
lucid	*adjective*	clear; easily understood
oscillation	*noun*	the act or state of swinging back and forth with a steady, uninterrupted rhythm
paean of praise	*noun*	a song or hymn of praise and thanksgiving
penurious	*adjective*	penny-pinching; excessively thrifty; ungenerous
perfidy	*noun*	intentional breach of faith; treachery
pernicious	*adjective*	extremely harmful; potentially causing death
perspicacious	*adjective*	acutely perceptive; having keen discernment
pious	*adjective*	extremely reverent or devout; showing strong religious devotion
precipitate	*adjective*	acting with excessive haste or impulse
precipitate	*verb*	to cause or happen before anticipated or required
precursor	*noun*	~~acting with excessive haste or impulse~~
predilection	*noun*	a disposition in favor of something; preference
prolific	*adjective*	producing large volumes or amounts; productive
qualms	*noun*	misgivings; reservations; causes for hesitancy

Handwritten annotations:

(ARGUMENT) ENREVESADO

ENTROLLADO, ENROSCADO

YOUR THEORY IS SO CONVOLUTED THAT I CAN'T HARDLY UNDERSTAND IT.

DESENGAÑAR

DESCARO

IMPROVISADO

OCURRENTE, INGENIOSO, OCURRENTE

HIPERBOLA (exageración)

Himno de alegría, alabanzas

tacañería — económico, frugal, ahorrativo

miserable, pobrísimo

PERFIDIA (Deslealtad, Traición o falta de fidelidad)

PIO

PRECIPITADO, APRESURADO

PRECURSOR

DUDAS — RECELOS, DUDAS

ESCRUPULO (he had no qualms about throwing them on the street)

Word	Part of Speech	Definition
quiescence → INACTIVIDAD	noun	stillness; motionlessness; quality of being at rest
recant → RETRACTARSE, DESDECIR	verb	to retract, esp. a previously held belief
redoubtable → TEMIBLE	adjective	awe-inspiring; worthy of honor
reticent	adjective	quiet; reserved; reluctant to express thoughts and feelings
satire	noun	a literary work that ridicules or criticizes a human vice through humor or derision → MOFA, BURLA
sordid	adjective	characterized by filth, grime, or squalor; foul → MISERIA, VILEZA ↳ to live in squalor
squalid → miserable, vil	adjective	sordid; wretched and dirty as from neglect
squander → DESPILFARRAR, DERROCHAR	verb	to waste by spending or using irresponsibly
stoic	adjective	indifferent to or unaffected by pleasure or pain; steadfast
stymie → bloquear a alguien	verb	to block; thwart
supplant	verb	to take the place of; supersede
synthesis	noun	the combination of parts to make a whole
torpid → ALETARGADO	adjective	lethargic; sluggish; dormant
torque	noun	a force that causes rotation
ubiquitous → UBICUO OMNIPRESENTE	adjective	existing everywhere at the same time; constantly encountered; widespread
veracity	noun	truthfulness; honesty
vilify → VILIPENDIAR	verb	to defame; to characterize harshly
virulent	adjective	extremely harmful or poisonous; bitterly hostile or antagonistic

→ WHEN THE BAD WEATHER ABATES WILL GO LOOK FOR THE CANOE

Group 3

→ AMAINAR, → ELOGIO, PREMIO, GALARDÓN (HE WILL BE GIVEN AN ACCOLADE FOR HIS GOOD GRADES)

Word	Part of Speech	Definition
abate	verb	to lessen in intensity or degree
accolade	noun	an expression of praise
adulation	noun	excessive praise; intense adoration
aesthetic	adjective	dealing with, appreciative of, or responsive to art or the beautiful
avarice	noun	greed, esp for wealth
burgeon → FLORECER, RETOÑAR, PROSPERAR	verb	to grow rapidly or flourish

Word	Part of Speech	Definition
cacophony	noun	harsh, jarring, discordant sound; dissonance
canon	noun	an established set of principles or code of laws, often religious in nature
castigation	noun	severe criticism or punishment
catalyst	noun	a substance that accelerates the rate of a chemical reaction without itself changing
catalyst	noun	a person or thing that causes change
caustic	adjective	burning or stinging; causing corrosion
chary	adjective	wary; cautious; sparing
cogent	adjective	appealing forcibly to the mind or reason; convincing
complaisance	noun	the willingness to comply with the wishes of others
contrite	adjective	regretful; penitent; seeking forgiveness
dearth	noun	smallness of quantity or number; scarcity; a lack
demur	verb	to question or oppose
didactic	adjective	intended to teach or instruct
discretion	noun	cautious reserve in speech; ability to make responsible decisions
disinterested	adjective	indifferent; free from self-interest
dogmatic	adjective	stubbornly opinionated
ebullience	adjective	the quality of lively or enthusiastic expression of thoughts and feelings
elegy	noun	a mournful poem, esp. one lamenting the dead
emollient	adjective	soothing, esp. to the skin; making less harsh; mollifying
empirical	adjective	based on observation or experiment
enigmatic	adjective	mysterious; obscure; difficult to understand
esoteric	adjective	intended for or understood by a small, specific group
exonerate	verb	to remove blame
fallacy	noun	an invalid or incorrect notion; a mistaken belief

Handwritten annotations:
- YOU HAVE TO BE CHARY WHEN IT COMES TO SPENDING MONEY
- CAUTELOSO
- (PARQUEDAD)
- CONVINCENTE, CONTUNDENTE
- COMPLACENCIA
- CONTRITO, ARREPENTIDO
- ESCASEZ (comida, recursos), CARENCIAS (de ideas)
- OBJETAR, PONER REPAROS (without demur → sin poner reparos)
- elegía
- emoliente (que sirve para ablandar)
- EMPÍRICO (de la experiencia)
- falacia

Word	Part of Speech	Definition
furtive	*adjective*	marked by stealth; covert; surreptitious
gregarious	*adjective*	sociable; outgoing; enjoying the company of other people
harangue	*verb*	to deliver a pompous speech or tirade
heretical	*adjective*	violating accepted dogma or convention
impecunious	*adjective*	lacking funds; without money
incipient	*adjective*	beginning to come into being or to become apparent
inert	*adjective*	unmoving; lethargic; sluggish
innocuous	*adjective*	harmless; causing no damage
intransigent	*adjective*	refusing to compromise
inveigle	*verb*	to obtain by deception or flattery
morose	*adjective*	sad; sullen; melancholy
odious	*adjective*	evoking intense aversion or dislike
opaque	*adjective*	impenetrable by light; not reflecting light
peruse	*verb*	to examine with great care
preen	*verb*	to dress up; to primp; to groom oneself with elaborate care
prodigious	*adjective*	abundant in size, force, or extent; extraordinary
putrefy	*verb*	to rot; to decay and give off a foul odor
quaff	*verb*	to drink deeply
sanction	*noun*	authoritative permission or approval; a penalty intended to enforce compliance
urbane	*adjective*	sophisticated; refined; elegant
viscous	*adjective*	thick; sticky

Group 4

acerbic	*adjective*	having a sour or bitter taste or character
amalgamate	*verb*	to combine several elements into a whole
amenable	*adjective*	agreeable; responsive to suggestion
bolster	*verb*	to provide support or reinforcement
bombast	*noun*	self-important or pompous writing or speech
bombastic	*adjective*	pompous; grandiloquent

Word	Part of Speech	Definition
credulous	adjective	tending to believe too readily; gullible
diatribe	noun	a harsh denunciation
fawn	verb	to flatter or praise excessively
fervent	adjective	greatly emotional or zealous
flout	verb	to demonstrate contempt for, as in a rule or convention
fortuitous	adjective	happening by fortunate accident or chance
garrulous	adjective	pointlessly talkative, taking too much
germane	adjective	relevant to the subject at hand; appropriate in subject matter
glib	adjective	marked by ease or informality; nonchalant; lacking in depth; superficial
halcyon	adjective	calm and peaceful
hubris	noun	arrogant presumption or pride
idolatrous	adjective	given to intense or excessive devotion to something
imminent	adjective	about to happen; impending
imperturbable	adjective	marked by extreme calm, impassivity and steadiness
impetuous	adjective	hastily or rashly energetic; impulsive and vehement
implacable	adjective	not capable of being appeased or significantly changed
indifferent	adjective	having no interest or concern; showing no bias or prejudice
intrepid	adjective	steadfast and courageous
laconic	adjective	using few words; terse
malleable	adjective	capable of being shaped or formed; tractable; pliable
maverick	noun	an independent individual who does not go along with a group or party
mendacity	noun	the condition of being untruthful; dishonesty
mercurial	adjective	characterized by rapid and unpredictable change in mood
meticulous	adjective	characterized by extreme care and precision; attentive to detail

Word	Part of Speech	Definition
mollify	*verb*	to calm or soothe; to reduce in emotional intensity
obdurate	*adjective*	unyielding; hardhearted; intractable
obfuscate	*verb*	to deliberately obscure; to make confusing
obsequious	*adjective*	exhibiting a fawning attentiveness
obstinate	*adjective*	stubborn; hardheaded; uncompromising
opprobrium	*noun*	disgrace; contempt; scorn
ostentatious	*adjective*	characterized by or given to pretentiousness.
pedantic	*adjective*	the parading of learning; excessive attention to minutiae and formal rules
pervade	*verb*	to permeate throughout
pervasive	*adjective*	having the tendency to permeate or spread throughout
phlegmatic	*adjective*	calm; sluggish; unemotional
pirate	*verb*	to illegally use or reproduce
plethora	*noun*	an overabundance; a surplus
polemical	*adjective*	controversial; argumentative
pragmatic	*adjective*	practical rather than idealistic
rancorous	*adjective*	characterized by bitter, long-lasting resentment
rhetoric	*noun*	the art or study of effective use of language for communication and persuasion
salubrious	*adjective*	promoting health or well-being
sedulous	*adjective*	diligent; persistent; hard-working
solvent	*adjective*	able to meet financial obligations; able to dissolve another substance
soporific	*adjective*	causing drowsiness; tending to induce sleep

Group 5

Word	Part of Speech	Definition
aggrandize	*verb*	to increase in intensity, power, or prestige
alchemy	*noun*	a medieval science aimed as the transmutation of metals, esp. base metals into gold

Word	Part of Speech	Definition
anachronism	noun	something or someone out of place in terms of historical or chronological context
astringent	adjective	having a tightening effect on living tissue; harsh; severe
contiguous	adjective	sharing a border; touching; adjacent
convention	noun	a generally agreed-upon practice or attitude
cynicism	noun	an attitude or quality of belief that all people are motivated by selfishness
decorum	noun	polite or appropriate conduct or behavior
derision	noun	scorn, ridicule, contemptuous treatment
desiccate	verb	to dry out or dehydrate; to make dry or dull
dilettante	noun	one with an amateurish or superficial interest in the arts or a branch of knowledge
disparage	verb	to slight or belittle
divulge	verb	to disclose something secret
immutable	adjective	not capable of change
inimical	adjective	damaging; harmful; injurious
intractable	adjective	not easily managed or directed; stubborn, obstinate
neophyte	noun	a recent convert; a beginner; novice
presumptuous	adjective	overstepping due bounds (as of propriety or courtesy); taking liberties
pristine	adjective	pure; uncorrupted; clean
probity	adjective	adherence to highest principles; uprightness
proclivity	noun	a natural predisposition or inclination
profligate	adjective	excessively wasteful; recklessly extravagant
propensity	noun	a natural inclination or tendency, penchant
prosaic	adjective	dull; unimaginative
pungent	adjective	characterized by a strong, sharp smell or taste

Handwritten annotations:
- ASTRINGENTE (que contrae los tejidos)
- ADUSTO, AUSTERO
- Mofa, burla {this was greeted with hoots of derision → "ESTO FUE RECIBIDO CON UNA GRAN MOFA"}
- DESPRECIO, MENOSPRECIO
- DESECAR
- DILETANTE (Que cultiva un arte o un campo del saber como aficionado y no como un profesional)
- DESPRECIAR, MENOSPRECIAR
- DESAIRAR A, HACER UN DESAIRE
- MENOSPRECIAR, QUITAR IMPORTANCIA
- HOSTIL, ADVERSO
- PROBIDAD
- LIBERTINO, DISOLUTO
- DESPILFARRADOR, DERROCHADOR
- PROSAICO (Que resulta vulgar o sin interés)
- SABOR → ACRE
- COMENTARIO → MORDAZ

Word	Part of Speech	Definition
quixotic	*adjective*	foolishly impractical; marked by lofty romantic ideals
quotidian	*adjective*	occurring or recurring daily; commonplace
rarefy	*verb*	to make or become thin, less dense; to refine
recondite	*adjective*	hidden; concealed; difficult to understand; obscure
refulgent	*adjective*	radiant; shiny; brilliant
renege	*verb*	to fail to honor a commitment; to go back on a promise
shard	*noun*	a piece of broken pottery or glass
sparse	*adjective*	thin; not dense; arranged at widely spaced intervals
spendthrift	*noun*	one who spends money wastefully
subtle	*adjective*	not obvious; elusive; difficult to discern
tacit	*adjective*	implied; not explicitly stated
terse	*adjective*	brief and concise in wording
tout	*verb*	to publicly praise or promote
trenchant	*adjective*	sharply perceptive; keen; penetrating
unfeigned	*adjective*	genuine; not false or hypocritical
untenable	*adjective*	indefensible; not viable; uninhabitable
vacillate	*verb*	to waver indecisively between one course of action or opinion and another; waver
variegated	*adjective*	multicolored; characterized by a variety of patches of different color
vexation	*noun*	annoyance; irritation
vigilant	*adjective*	alertly watchful
vituperate	*verb*	to use harsh condemnatory language; to abuse or censure severely or abusively; berate
volatile	*adjective*	readily changing to a vapor; changeable; fickle; explosive

(handwritten annotations:)
rarefy — ENRIQUECER
recondite — REFULGENTE
renege — FALTAR A SU PALABRA
shard — CASCO, FRAGMENTO de arcilla
sparse — ESCASO
spendthrift — DERROCHADOR
tout — OFRECER, PREGONAR
trenchant — MORDAZ
unfeigned — NO FINGIDO, VERDADERO
untenable — INSOSTENIBLE
variegated — MULTICOLOR, ABIGARRADO
vituperate — VITUPERAR (llenar de injurias); berate → REGAÑAR
volatile — fickle → INCONSTANTE, VOLUBLE

Word	Part of Speech	Definition
GROUP 6		
acumen	*noun*	quick, keen, or accurate knowledge or insight
adulterate	*verb*	to reduce purity by combining with inferior ingredients
archaic	*adjective*	outdated; associated with an earlier, perhaps more primitive, time
aver	*verb*	to state as a fact; to confirm or support
dissemble	*verb*	to disguise or conceal; to mislead
eccentric	*adjective*	departing from norms or conventions
endemic	*adjective*	characteristic of or often found in a particular locality, region, or people.
evanescent	*adjective*	tending to disappear like vapor; vanishing
exacerbate	*verb*	to make worse or more severe
grandiloquence	*noun*	pompous speech or expression
hackneyed	*adjective*	rendered trite or commonplace by frequent usage
hedonism	*noun*	devotion to pleasurable pursuits, esp. to the pleasures of the senses
hegemony	*noun*	the consistent dominance of one state or ideology over others
iconoclast	*noun*	one who attacks or undermines traditional conventions or institutions
impassive	*adjective*	revealing no emotion
impunity	*noun*	immunity from punishment or penalty
inchoate	*adjective*	in an initial stage; not fully formed
infelicitous	*adjective*	unfortunate; inappropriate
insipid	*adjective*	without taste or flavor; lacking in spirit; bland
loquacious	*adjective*	extremely talkative
luminous	*adjective*	characterized by brightness and the emission of light
malevolent	*adjective*	having or showing often vicious ill will, spite, or hatred

Handwritten annotations:
- acumen → perspicacia, tino
- aver → AFIRMAR, ASEGURAR
- dissemble → OCULTAR, DISIMULAR
- hackneyed → TRILLADO, GASTADO,
- iconoclast: ICONOCLASTA (Que rechaza el culto a las imagenes sagradas) (Que no respeta las normas o los valores admitidos por la tradición)

Word	Part of Speech	Definition
misanthrope	noun	one who hates all other humans
mitigate	verb	to make or become less severe or intense; to moderate
occlude →ocluir	verb	to obstruct or block
pedagogy	noun	the art or profession of training, teaching, or instructing
penury	noun	poverty; destitution
pine languidecer, consumirse	verb	to yearn intensely; to languish; to lose vigor
pith meollo	noun	the essential or central part
pithy conciso	adjective	precise and brief
placate	verb	to appease; to calm by making concessions
platitude tópico	noun	a superficial remark, esp. one offered as meaningful
plummet caer en picado	verb	to plunge or drop straight down
prodigal ‹ despilfarrador	adjective	recklessly wasteful; extravagant; profuse; lavish
profuse	adjective	given or coming forth abundantly; extravagant
proliferate	verb	to grow or increase swiftly and abundantly
queries preguntas	noun	questions; inquiries; doubts in the mind; reservations.
querulous ‹ quejumbroso	adjective	prone to complaining or grumbling; quarrelsome
recalcitrant	adjective	obstinately defiant of authority; difficult to manage
repudiate	verb	to refuse to have anything to do with; disown
rescind	verb	to invalidate; to repeal; to retract
reverent	adjective	marked by, feeling, or expressing a feeling of profound awe and respect
specious ‹ especioso (Aparente, engañoso)	adjective	seeming true, but actually being fallacious; misleadingly attractive

Word	Part of Speech	Definition
spurious *— falso, espurio*	adjective	lacking authenticity or validity; false; counterfeit
subpoena	noun	a court order requiring appearance and/or testimony
succinct	adjective	brief; concise
superfluous	adjective	exceeding what is sufficient or necessary
surfeit *— hartar saciar*	verb	excess; overindulgence
tenacity	noun	the quality of adherence or persistence to something valued
tenuous	adjective	having little substance or strength; flimsy; weak
tirade *— diatriba*	noun	a long and extremely critical speech; a harsh denunciation
transient *Transitorio*	adjective	fleeting; passing quickly; brief
zealous *entusiasta*	adjective	fervent; ardent; impassioned

AUTHOR BIO

Yung-Ye Wu has worked at The Princeton Review since 1993. She began as an instructor and later worked in research and development as the director of high school, graduate, and international courses.

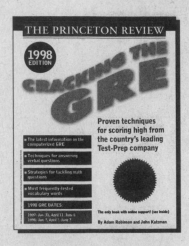